l

Lee's Dispatches

From the portrait by Wm. E. Marshall

LEE'S DISPATCHES

Unpublished Letters of
General Robert E. Lee, C.S.A.

to

Jefferson Davis and the War Department of
The Confederate States of America

1862-65

From the Private Collection of
Wymberley Jones de Renne, *of Wormsloe, Georgia*

Edited with an Introduction and Notes by
DOUGLAS SOUTHALL FREEMAN

NEW EDITION

With Additional Dispatches and Foreword by
GRADY McWHINEY

LOUISIANA STATE UNIVERSITY PRESS
Baton Rouge and London

Louisiana Paperback Edition, 1994
03 02 01 00 99 98 97 96 95 94   5 4 3 2 1

Library of Congress Catalog Card No. 57-14522

The paper in this book meets the guidelines for permanence and durability of the
Committee on Production Guidelines for Book Longevity of the Council on
Library Resources. (∞)

FOREWORD

IRONICALLY, Robert E. Lee is a symbol of American unity. When great Americans are mentioned, he is never omitted. His Americanism, like his military genius, is beyond challenge. Yet, essentially, Lee was a Virginian; a gentleman of the Old South; and the hero of a rebellion against the United States. That the South would canonize him—that Southern streets, parks, public buildings, towns and even a university bear his name—is understandable. What is unique is that no other nineteenth-century Southerner is so well known or is so universally admired. It is indicative of Marse Robert's national popularity that his name is still used with considerable commercial success (a facet of fame the reticent and reserved Lee, who lived quietly after the war on a college president's salary, would not have approved). Economically reconstructed Southern proprietors constantly dupe their fellow countrymen as well as Yankee tourists into sleeping in Robert E. Lee motels, eating at Lee restaurants, or buying bourbon from Lee bars and liquor stores, despite the fact that Lee's wartime sleeping quarters were usually quite humble, his table exceedingly modest, and his liquids rarely more potent than buttermilk.

Why has the reputation of the great Virginian en-

dured? Not just because of his military genius, his
unfailing devotion to duty, or because he represents
American motherhood's ideal of filial virtue. More
than these, Lee, like Abraham Lincoln, is a genuine folk hero. He is not the railsplitter turned
philosopher-humanitarian, but the other side of the
coin—the rebel-conservative, like Washington, so
characteristically American. Scion of a distinguished family who was compelled by lack of wealth
to pursue the martial life, Lee is the warrior-aristo-
crat, kind to his slaves, democratically low-church
Anglican; the perfect paterfamilias who took inno-
cent pleasure in having his children tickle his feet;
the beloved chieftain of butternut-clad fighters for
the lost cause. Gallant, courageous, upright, he is
the American Galahad—the untarnished knight,
handsomely whiskered like a prophet of old, dressed
in immaculate Confederate gray, sitting Traveler
with dignity and patient determination. Indeed, he
is a father symbol. Had his side been victorious
he could have hardly refused the Presidency. In
losing, however, he won not only the devotion of
successive generations south of the Potomac but the
love and esteem all Americans traditionally bestow
upon noble figures of high tragedy.

If part of his enduring popularity rests upon his
magnificent failure, part of it also rests upon a diligent set of writers. Over fifty biographers have
praised, criticized or tried to explain Robert E. Lee.
Every aspect of his life has been examined by ardent
investigators who have followed him all the way
from Texas to Heaven and have revealed their find-

ings under such intimate titles as: *The Face of Lee,*
The Heart of Lee, The Shadow of Lee, and even *The*
Soul of Lee. One writer dubbed his life of the great
rebel *Robert E. Lee, Unionist.*

Confronted with so many volumes, varying in
emphasis and interpretation, how is one to obtain
an understanding of Lee? A sensible course might
be to read the best biography. Fortunately, the
choice is an easy one—the late Douglas Southall
Freeman's *R. E. Lee.* A distinguished historian of
the Civil War period calls it "The greatest military
biography ever written by or about an American."

Freeman's brilliant four-volume study certainly
reveals a great deal about Lee. But to truly understand a man, and Lee is no exception, the earnest
student must go beyond the best biographer's account. To satisfy himself and do justice to his own
intellect he must, in a small way, do his own research. He must see the words and sentences that
Lee wrote; feel the strains of war and death, the
hard march, the trying wait. He must see the war
unfold as it does in Lee's own words before he can
understand Lee.

By providing access to Lee's writing, Freeman
has again vastly aided the student. For nearly half
a century his admirable edition of *Lee's Dispatches*
has been not only the best one-volume collection of
Lee's wartime missives but a splendid example of
Dr. Freeman's careful research, prodigious knowledge of the war, and his impressive ability to clearly
set Lee's words in their proper perspective. Long
out of print and unavailable, *Lee's Dispatches* has

become a classic in Civil War libraries. Since a new edition seemed called for, the editors of G. P. Putnam's Sons have done Civil War enthusiasts a real service in reissuing this volume. Not a word of the original edition has been changed.

Eleven dispatches which were not available when the original edition was published are included in the Appendix. Although revealing nothing revisionistic about Lee, these new dispatches do further illuminate certain aspects of his character by indicating his feelings about various individuals and events.

Dispatch No. 205, for example, is additional proof that even after Lee took command of the Army of Northern Virginia he was still consulted on problems in other departments. The same dispatch also shows that early in the war Lee realized that troops extended along a railroad could not protect it as well as those concentrated at strategic points.

Lee's attitude toward farmers faced with enemy raids is evidenced in Dispatch No. 207. Constantly worried about how to feed his army, Lee wrote: "The best way for the citizens of the Northern Neck [of Virginia] to save their cattle[,] grain[,} bacon &c from these marauding parties is to send them across the Rapp[ahannoc]ᵏ and sell them to the Confederate government." Civilians, Lee thought, should aid the army by giving the enemy "a wholesome fear of coming into the country."

The difficulties of obtaining capable officers in 1864 is revealed in Dispatches No. 208 and No. 211. Although Generals Joseph B. Kershaw and George

H. Steuart are singled out for praise, Lee sadly reported: "What our officers most lack is the pains & labour of incubating discipline. . . . Many officers have too many selfish views to promote . . . to undertake the task of instructing & disciplining their Commands."

General Lee's realism is displayed in his opinions on how Europeans viewed the war (Dispatch No. 210)—"Our safety depends upon ourselves alone," was his conclusion—and in his estimate of the prospects of peace in March 1865 (Dispatch No. 213). Proposing to meet Grant, Lee hoped "that some good may result, but I must Confess that I am not sanguine. My belief is that he will Consent to no terms, unless Coupled with the Condition of our return to the Union. Whether this will be acceptable to our people yet awhile I Can not say—"

Dispatch No. 214 shows that the use of Negro troops as a last resort to prevent defeat was enthusiastically endorsed by Lee.

The end of the struggle is clearly seen in Dispatch No. 215. "The Enemy is so strong," Lee wrote as he prepared to evacuate Petersburg, "that they will . . . Close us in between the James & Appomattox Rivers—If we remain—"

A number of friends, old and new, have generously helped prepare this book for publication. For invaluable aid in countless ways, I am deeply indebted to Professor David Donald of Columbia University, who read and criticized the Foreword. Professor Ari Hoogenboom of Texas Western College also read the Foreword and offered valuable suggestions and encouragement. Professor Allen W. Moger and Mr. Henry E. Coleman, Jr. of Washington and Lee University and Miss Mattie Russell of Duke University graciously allowed me to use and publish Lee dispatches housed in those two great institutions. Miss Lois Dwight Cole, Editor, G. P. Putnam's Sons, has been uniformly cooperative and helpful.

To the library staffs of Millsaps College and the University of California at Berkeley, I am also obligated.

My wife, Sue McWhiney, traveled and searched for new dispatches with me; with skill she photocopied letters, read critically and sympathetically my efforts, and remained patient throughout.

GRADY McWHINEY

August 7, 1957

INTRODUCTION

THE passage of years and the death of his comrades-in-arms have increased rather than diminished the fame of General Robert E. Lee as a military commander. Detractors and panegyrists alike are dead. The careless overstatements of partisans have given place to the cool analysis of impartial investigators; rigid comparisons of his strategy and tactics with those of other great captains have assured him a place higher than if somewhat different from that assigned him by his contemporaries.

The publication and study of the *Official Records* of the Union and Confederate Armies have unquestionably been the chief reasons for this more general recognition of Lee's military genius. Prior to the appearance of the Records, his fame rested on the unreliable testimony of such foreign critics as the Comte de Paris and upon the more friendly, though scarcely more accurate statements of lieutenants who wrote largely from memory and inevitably fell into errors more or less serious. But with the completion of the Records, Lee's campaigns have been scrutinized in the calm light of indisputable evidence. Documents unknown have been located, reports and correspondence that his early biographers scarcely thought to exist have been given to the world.

And while it cannot be said that the Records have ever been exhausted or even adequately handled by any critic of Lee's military actions, they have at least fixed his fame and have given to recent *critiques*—Alexander's for instance—a perspective and a precision lacking in earlier works.

It is a pleasure for a Southern student to be able to make this statement of the worth of the Records in establishing the lasting reputation of one who is, in every sense, the popular idol of many million Southerners. It is an equal pleasure to attest the high standard of accuracy set by this monumental publication. The Records have, of course, been condemned by many writers as the embodiment of everything unscholarly and unscientific in historical documents and they undoubtedly suffer from a rigid arrangement that separates, sometimes by volumes, related papers of interest and importance. The Records suffer also from an index which is the despair of beginners. But with all these faults, and others that might be named, the Records are surprisingly accurate and surpassingly complete. A comparison of the reprints of General Lee's reports in the Records with the letter-book copies from which the printed text was prepared, shows good judgment in selection and the most painstaking care in transcription. Where letters of importance were omitted, their content was misleading or obscure; where errors are made, they are generally to be attributed to originals that are often lacking in clearness. Further comparison of the Records with the letter-book of President Jefferson Davis and with miscellaneous papers of the Southern Historical Society confirm the editor's belief in the general accuracy of the Records.

This much has been said in behalf of this great store-house of war history not only because it is praise well merited but because the contents and the omissions of the Records explain the reasons for the publication of this volume of correspondence. In the nature of things, the compilers of the Records could not hope to collect all documents relating to the most active military officer of the Confederate army. There are many breaks and omissions in the published correspondence of General Lee,— some of them consequential, some of them trifling.[1] In the case of a less renowned officer, or one whose campaigns were not so critically studied in the military schools of the world, the omission of a few hundred telegrams or letters would not be important. But in the case of General Lee, whose every written line was a lesson in war, the world wants all the correspondence of himself and of his secretaries.

It is for this reason, among others, that this collection of General Lee's unpublished correspondence with President Jefferson Davis and with the War Department of the Confederate States is presented to the public. Some of the letters broaden our view of Lee's strategy and throw significant light on dis-

---

[1] In this connection the casual reader must be cautioned against one classification in the *Official Records* with which every student has been forced to contend—the arbitrary distinction between "reports" and "correspondence." One may search in vain through the correspondence for a desired letter—only to find it placed with the reports. On the other hand, many minor reports are treated as correspondence and are placed in different volumes from hundreds of similar dispatches.

puted movements; the whole, in the editor's judgment, deserves publication as it complements, fills out and, at the same time, epitomizes the many dispatches and reports scattered through the bulky volumes of the Records.

To our present information of General Lee's plans and campaigns these dispatches make new additions in the following respects:

1. They show that when plans were under consideration for the defence of Richmond in 1862, it was proposed to strengthen the army of General Jackson in the Valley of Virginia, to wage a vigorous offensive campaign against the North and, if need be, to abandon the Confederate capital. While the significance of the letter disclosing these facts is explained at some length in the notes (see *infra*, No. 2), its importance will at once be apparent to those who have believed that the adopted strategy of the campaign from Mechanicsville to Harrison's Landing was the only course proposed in Confederate councils. The new dispatch printed in this collection must at least be accepted as proof that the plan ultimately adopted was an alternative maturely considered. Doubtful and obscure references would indicate that General Whiting may have been the author of the bold proposal to strengthen Jackson while Lee held McClellan from Richmond.[1]

2. This correspondence shows that the Second Manassas campaign was undertaken by General Lee as a defensive measure, the purpose of which

---

[1] See the biographical sketch of Whiting in *Confederate Military History* (cited throughout as C. M. H.), 4, 352 ff.

was to throw back the Federals beyond the Rappahannock line and to open the way for more important
offensive operations. But as the latter were contingent upon reinforcements and supplies which were
not forthcoming, the plan, whatever may have been its
details, was not carried out in its fulness. Lee's lucid
statement of his purposes in Dispatch No. 29 will
repay careful study by those interested in his strategy.

3. The dispatch in this collection on the Gettysburg campaign (No. 60) may with good reason be
regarded as the most definite statement yet made
of the Confederate commander's calm view of the
unfortunate march into Pennsylvania. General Lee
did not avail himself of privileged confidential correspondence to place on others the blame that
undoubtedly was theirs but, with his habitual magna-
nimity, chose to assume the responsibility as on the
battlefield. Incidentally, this dispatch would seem
to contradict some of General Longstreet's conclusions as to Lee's alleged admissions of error regarding
his movements at Gettysburg. These points are
more fully discussed in the notes.

4. This correspondence dates back the conscious
acceptance of defensive tactics on the part of General
Lee to the time when he renewed his Rapidan line
after the return from Pennsylvania. At that early
date, it would appear from his correspondence, he
realized that his only hope lay in meeting the Federals
on the ground he chose within the territory which the
Rapidan made his natural frontier, once the Potomac
was crossed. The reference on this point is brief
but direct (No. 61).

5. This correspondence is peculiarly rich in its contribution to the campaign from the Rapidan to the James and shows Lee's strategy from a somewhat different angle. Indeed, if historians have erred in giving him too great credit for his crossing of the James, they have failed to give General Grant credit for the mystifying tactics he pursued from Spottsylvania Court-House to Cold Harbor. This correspondence shows that the real direction of the "left flank" movement was, for some time, concealed from the Confederate commander. Lee knew, of course, after the first uncertainty in March, 1864 (Dispatch No. 80), that Grant's objective was Richmond, but more than once he was in doubt whether Grant would continue his pressure on the Confederate right or move along the line of the Richmond, Fredericksburg and Potomac Railroad. With this doubt in his mind defensive tactics which high critics have declared faultless seem all the more remarkable. Lee's whole plan of campaign during this period, based on the hope of reinforcements, is more adequately outlined in this correspondence than in the *Official Records* or in any of Lee's biographies.

6. The movement of Grant's army across the James River, June 14, 1864, is here presented in a manner much more creditable to both the Confederate and the Northern commanders than in current versions and known documents. To the editor this movement has always seemed one of the most misunderstood as well as one of the most important in the history of the war in Virginia. Studying every movement of the enemy and accustomed by long

campaigning to expect the use of large bodies of troops where he was least able to resist them, General Lee must have realized for days before it occurred that the crossing of the James and the investment of Richmond from the south were at least as probable as the continuance of such frontal assaults from the north and northeast as those at Cold Harbor. Lee must, indeed, have regarded the adoption of such a course as more than probable and for several reasons. Richmond was more strongly fortified on the north than on the south side of the James; the country above the river was more broken and included that stretch of the Chickahominy which had been a death-trap to McClellan in 1862; communications *via* the James were much easier and much less liable to interruption than the lines from Fredericksburg or from West Point; Grant's superior force made it expedient that he draw out Lee's army on a long line such as was offered on the south side of the James rather than to permit his antagonist to continue those inner line tactics which cost the lives of so many thousand Federals from the Rapidan to Cold Harbor. The communications which might be cut from the south were vital to the Confederates. All of this, though here argued *a priori*, must have been so obvious in 1864 that it is scarcely creditable to General Lee's known ability to deny that it was taken into account by him. The letters now made public settle the question beyond doubt and show that while Lee was not certain when Grant would cross the James and could not, in consequence, strip the northern defences until he was sure his opponent had moved, he fully expected what happened. The credit due General Grant for the brilliancy with which he executed this move is not lessened by the fact that it was foreseen. Rather it would seem that Grant deserves more praise for his ability to throw his advance corps across the river and to pause only on the outskirts of Petersburg, when it is understood that General Lee, anticipating such a course, could not hazard his own position in the face of Federal cavalry or move troops in time to check it. Viewed in this light, then, the new dispatches of June 14–16 may be said to exculpate General Lee from blame for inactivity while increasing the reputation of General Grant for a brilliant transfer of base.

7.   These dispatches present the situation in the winter of 1864 and in the spring of 1865 much more lucidly than do the scattered reports and the brief correspondence in the *Official Records*. They show, in particular, how Lee's whole plan of holding Richmond was dependent upon troops that were not sent him and on supplies which were frequently cut off. Again and again during the dark winter of 1864–65, he pleaded with the Confederate authorities in Richmond to improve the transportation, even the circuitous route *via* the Piedmont and Richmond and Danville railroads, in order that he might keep his men from starvation. More than once he turned from watching his aggressive opponent to explain how soap was needed for the army, how the Piedmont Railroad might be put in proper condition, how the conscription service might be improved and how detailed men might be brought back to the

ranks. One cannot read these dispatches without feeling regret that a genius so great should have been forced to devote itself to matters of administration which should be the first care of the bureau heads. Step by step, in these dispatches, the conditions that made the evacuation of the Richmond line a necessity are candidly explained by General Lee. The whole forms a most interesting chapter.

Not to mention other items of almost equal interest, it is hoped that this correspondence, by its conciseness and common tenor, will give the student a new and inspiring view of General Lee as a great commander. Certain conclusions will, we believe, be forced upon the reader who studies the dispatches which General Lee day by day forwarded the head of the Confederate government. Through them runs the same spirit, the same courage, the same consideration for the sensibilities of others. Whether telling of the first victory won or of the last line abandoned, they show the fixed mind and the intrepid fidelity of one whom neither adversity nor success could shake.

They show, for example, that relations between General Lee and President Davis never reached that degree of restraint that rendered frank confidence and full co-operation impossible. Some writers, with little knowledge of General Lee or in forgetfulness of his character, have intimated the contrary, and among surviving officers of the Army of Northern Virginia there has long been the tradition that relations between their commander and the President more than once were on the verge of rupture. Some have dated their alleged misunderstanding as far back as Fredericksburg, some pretend to trace it from the Pennsylvania campaign, others think it began in the summer of 1864. In none of these new letters—where such feeling would appear, if ever— and in none of the correspondence heretofore published, is there the least evidence of such strained relations as have been suggested. Possible misunderstandings there may have been; a serious break there was not and could not have been between two men, both of them patriots, both fully conscious of the dire results of friction. It is true that from 1863 to the end of this correspondence that friendship, one may almost say love, which marks earlier letters is less emphasized; but if this was due to any other cause than the pressure of public burdens, that cause does not appear. No man other than a dissembling hypocrite—and of that not even his many enemies accused Mr. Davis—could have written such a letter as that in which the President urged on General Lee the chief command of the army in 1865; no man could have replied as did General Lee to one in whom he did not have full confidence. As it is not probable that new correspondence of importance between General Lee and Mr. Davis is now in existence unpublished, it may safely be concluded that until the end there was full co-operation and absolute frankness between them, unbroken even by the officious though patriotic and well-meant activity of General Bragg in 1864.

Again, these letters make it plain that in his relations with his subordinates, General Lee was slow to blame and ready to applaud but did not hesitate frankly to state his opinions when properly required to do so, and would not, in any circumstances, recommend men whom he deemed unworthy, incapable or inexperienced. This is a side of the great commander which could easily be sketched from general knowledge of his character, but a side regarding which, as all students know, little specific information is to be had. General Lee was most unwilling after the war to discuss the demerits of his lieutenants and, as in the case of General Jubal A. Early in 1864–65, saved their feelings where possible. But from this correspondence which, as we shall presently show, it seems probable Mr. Davis kept separate from his general files, General Lee will appear as frankness itself in expressing his opinion of a man whose appointment to a post might be disastrous to the cause of the Confederacy. It is with no small regret that these judgments of General Lee's subordinates, even when expressed by himself, have been included in this collection. Written as they were of patriotic men who did their honest best, and written, too, by the one man whose opinion of military worth has been regarded as absolutely final in the South, some of these criticisms must strike deep even now. But as reflecting the character of a man who put duty above friendship, these letters have seemed to us an essential part of the correspondence. General Lee's uncertainty as to the merits of General John B. Hood as successor to General Joseph E. Johnston (*infra*, Nos. 158 and 159) is typical of the letters that illustrate that side of his character. The criticism is kindly in tone and sympathetic in spirit but it makes it plain that General Lee regarded the valorous Texan as a doubtful choice for the command of a great army. This message was not sent on General Lee's own motion but in response to the President's insistent request, nay, order, for an opinion. We may fancy with what regret General Lee wrote his criticism of one whose valor he had himself rewarded, one whose service none was more willing than he to attest. Yet we cannot but regret that Mr. Davis acted on his own opinion of General Hood rather than on the judgment of one who knew Hood and had only his country and his conscience to serve by speaking frankly from his knowledge.

Equally pointed is General Lee's unwillingness to recommend the promotion of his chief-of-artillery, Brigadier-General W. N. Pendleton. By every tie, the commander was bound to his courageous cannoneer. Pendleton came from Lexington and was a friend of that hero whom Lee held as first among his corps commanders; he was a minister of that church of which General Lee was a devout member; he had shown his courage on every field since as captain of a battery he told his soldiers at First Manassas (so the story goes) to "give 'em hell, boys,—and God have mercy on their souls." But because he could not see that General Pendleton had shown his capacity for a higher position, General Lee was unwilling to recommend his promotion on other grounds. It was the same spirit that made him refuse to take his youngest son from the ranks or to recommend the elevation of his other sons or of his nephew,—the same spirit, differently expressed, that made him select and promote the corps commanders who carried out his plans. For if Lee would not raise men whose ability he questioned, he never hesitated and seldom erred in giving new stars to his worthy lieutenants.

To continue our general analysis of this correspondence, it shows that at no time during the war did General Lee predict the speedy triumph of Confederate arms or even the ultimate success of the South, and that from 1864 the tone of his correspondence while never pessimistic, fully anticipated the final outcome. Strangely enough, in the various biographies of General Lee, little is said of his views as to the issue of the war. His opinions, whatever they were, he seems to have kept to himself and he never permitted himself, in communications with Mr. Davis, to indulge in predictions of independence achieved. In some of his addresses to the army one reads, as is to be expected, inspiring appeals for valor that cannot be defeated, and in some of his letters to Mr. Davis, notably in those preceding the invasion of Maryland in 1862, there are hopeful references to European recognition. But these apart, his expressions are always guarded and his forecasts are never roseate. Whether this meant that he merely refrained from arousing hopes that might be shattered or whether he really believed the struggle hopeless cannot be determined in the light of present information. If the former were the case, his attitude was a credit to his judgment, if the latter, an added proof of his unfailing courage. In either event it must be remembered that he had lived in the North and West, was familiar with the resources of those who opposed him, knew the temper of the Federals and was for these reasons, if for no others, less liable to hasty and over-enthusiastic conclusions than some of his less informed or more provincial colleagues. Few men could have appreciated more fully than he the enormous task confronting the Southern armies; few had minds better equipped to analyze that task.

In these letters will be found frequent expressions of cautious forebodings and of frank warning. It will be noted that General Lee never discredited the valor of his army or voiced the fear that in even encounter his men could ever be worsted. His apprehensions were always in other directions,—could his men be reinforced and fed that they might fight? Lesser fears there were,—that needed ammunition might not be forthcoming, that the army mounts might not be supported, that desertions might weaken him and that recruits might not be sent forward. But these were all subordinate to the daily dread of starvation in the ranks, of losses that could not be made good. It will be noted that the plainest of his early forecasts as to the defeat of his army is in a complaint that supplies are not at hand (No. 135). As the campaign of that year progressed and as his army was more and more impoverished, the tenor of his correspondence is never carping or critical but it is at no time cheerful. Clearly and unshadowed he saw Appomattox from Petersburg.

Altogether apart from their value to the historian of the war, it is hoped that these letters will be of even greater interest to the general reader in exemplifying the character of one who bore success with humility and failure with fortitude. The careful student of General Lee's career may, of course, get the same picture of the man from the hundreds of letters scattered through the ponderous volumes of the *Official Records;* but the hasty reader, it is hoped, will see the same man as fully and as adequately from the letters printed in this volume,—letters that begin immediately after he assumed command of the Army of Northern Virginia and end only when communications with Mr. Davis were being severed just before the evacuation of Richmond. One may look over the General's shoulder, so to speak, and see him in these pages as he writes with his own hand to Mr. Davis of the great struggles of his career; one may know something from these reports of the soul that gave God the glory for the Seven Days' Fight; one may see with what confidence in his Maker and his men he wrote of Second Manassas, of Sharpsburg, of Fredericksburg and of Chancellorsville; one may appreciate the courage that accepted the responsibility for Gettysburg and marched with spirit unafraid from the victorious trenches of Cold Harbor to the blood-stained works of Petersburg; one may bid farewell to him as he makes ready for the last journey to Appomattox and one may end the letters with the belief that Lee the soldier was great but that Lee the man and Christian was greater by far.

The thirty-four months covered by this correspondence subjected the character of Lee to every test by which the heart of man may be tried. The substitute commander of a shattered army, the new hope of a heart-stirred nation, the unbeaten leader of an unvanquished host, the parent bereft of a beloved daughter, the anxious father of a captured, wounded, son, the trustee of a confiscated estate, the idol of the South, the one captain whose nod would have made him dictator, the general of the best army America had ever seen, the trusted head of dwindling regiments and the last hope of an overthrown people, —all these was General Lee from June 2, 1862, to April 1, 1865, the period covered by this correspondence.   During these brief months, he attained and rounded a cycle that occupied Napoleon from Arcola to Waterloo and he tasted much of the sweet and most of the bitter that fell to Frederick the Great during his long years of warfare.   And from it Lee emerged aged and worn, already in the shadow of the grave, but a stronger, nobler man than when he consecrated his sword to the service of Virginia and assumed command of her little army.   His St. Helena at Lexington was more glorious than his Austerlitz at Chancellorsville.

Familiar as are the incidents of General Lee's campaign to all who will read this volume, and well-known as are the movements he chronicles in his letters, it would be superfluous, if not indeed presumptuous to review here the activities of which he writes to Mr. Davis.   The tale of every battle has been told and every march has been made by such an army of historians and biographers that reiteration is worse than tiresome.   But the editor may perhaps be pardoned if he attempts in a few brief paragraphs to interpret those campaigns not in their military bearing and not in their value as important lessons in the art of war but rather in their relation to General Lee's character. We read of a Lincoln softened by the reports of heroism and of sacrifice: may we not learn of a Lee raised to greater heights of nobility by the same things?   This aspect of his career has been too much neglected, too much taken for granted. Writers have found him so splendid a figure when he assumed command that they have not thought that his knighthood could be further exalted by the hardships, the struggles and the anguish of the war. His biographers, in a word, have viewed General Lee as a finished, rounded man before the war began. Yet as one looks at the pictures of Lee taken from the time of the Harper's Ferry raid to his return to Richmond in 1865, one can see the outward evidences of an inward change. Noble he was; nobler he became. The sufferings he endured were worth all they cost him in the example they gave the South of fortitude in disaster and courage in defeat.

General Lee first appears in this correspondence as the untried and untrusted commander of an exhausted army.   The first year of the war had not sustained the promise he gave when first called to lead the armies of Virginia.   Fortune had not favored him, opportunity had not come to him.   The Western Virginia campaign through no fault of his own had brought no glory and no important results; his skilful plans for the defence of Charleston had not yet paid him tribute by baffling the besieger; his services as military adviser to the President were not of a character to make him a popular figure. Johnston had shown his mettle; Beauregard had captured Sumter and had fought at Manassas; the man whom President Davis appointed to succeed the former had the record of neither. The newspapers criticised the selection and the subordinate officers, with that freedom of expression and of thought so characteristic of the Southern armies, murmured against the coming of this "staff" officer.

Nor was the army of which he took command of a spirit calculated to encourage its new head. It had kept McClellan from capturing Richmond by the battle of Seven Pines but it had been able to do nothing more. Camped amid marshes and swamps during a most unfavorable season, those commands which had not been riddled by bullets had been shattered by disease. The men were poorly equipped, many of them were almost untrained; few of them had learned the importance of rigid discipline or had forgotten their traditions of personal independence. The line-officers, chosen in large measure by the men and appointed by the governors of the States, were in many instances grossly incompetent. A new general of small repute in command of a badly organized, broken army, driven to the very walls of its capital by an enemy stronger in numbers and admirably supplied,—the situation could scarcely have seemed worse. But in this crisis neither General Lee's acts nor his letters bespeak the least uneasiness or lack of confidence. One finds in him none of the bluster of Burnside, none of the petulant anxiety of McClellan. If he knew himself unwelcome and not trusted, he displayed no evidence of resentment and assumed no airs of superiority. Very quietly he took command, very vigorously he exercised it. While waiting for reinforcements and while discussing with President Davis the wisdom of an invasion of the North by General Jackson, Lee went busily to work reorganizing the men at his disposal. And when it had been decided to bring General Jackson from the Valley of Virginia and to begin an offensive campaign, all his energies were devoted to the immediate strengthening of his command.

It has long been demonstrated that General Lee was as daring as any leader of his age and the old view of contemporary critics that he appeared best on the defensive has been disproved by a more careful study of his counterstrokes. But it has never been made sufficiently plain that his aggressive qualities were exhibited during his first great campaign as strikingly as at Second Manassas or at Chancellorsville. Not less the preliminaries than the details of the Seven Days' Fight showed him willing to hazard everything in calm reliance upon the ability of his men to execute his plans. A cautious commander would not have dared to change his organization with the enemy in his front: Lee proceeded with the utmost assurance to put new line-officers in command and to give the army a discipline it had never known before. He sent regiments through Richmond with bands playing, he extended his line to the very limit. He was as confident as though he had been preparing for a siege behind

impregnable works.   Then, when Jackson had taken
position on Lee's left and McClellan at length began
to stir, Lee sprang at his opponent's throat with
every regiment he had.   In but little more than a
week the enveloping chain of blue had been shattered
and the broken links were lying not on the Chickahominy but on the James.   With the support he
might reasonably have expected from lieutenants
who never failed him afterwards, Lee might have
kept McClellan from reaching Malvern Hill and
certainly from holding it.   As it was, the quiet "staff"
officer had amazed his subordinates and had caught
the eye of the world by a campaign which had not
been equalled since Napoleon was in his prime.   A
relieved nation breathed freely again and heaped
praise and honors upon the commander who had
been viewed with coldness if not with suspicion a
brief month before.

At the end of May a poor third in popular esteem
to Johnston and to Beauregard, at the end of June
hailed as a hero,—one can imagine what the effect
would have been on a man less stable than Lee.
Napoleon would have made it—as at the end of the
Italian campaign—the occasion for a political up-
heaval, raising him to the first place in power as in
repute; Marlborough would have based upon the
victory new and unreasoning demands for preferment.   Lesser men, the Wallensteins and Popes of
history, would have been exalted by it beyond the
hope of restored usefulness in later campaigns.   Lee
gave the glory to God and devoted his energies not
to the enjoyment of a triumph or to a quest for

distinction, but to the study of his problems and the improvement of his forces. In his correspondence with the Confederate executive, in the dispatches printed here and in those hasty, tender missives to his loved ones, there is not an exultant echo of the ego and scarcely a personal reference to his victories.

Second Manassas tried him in much the same way, with the added factor of a lieutenant whose splendid obedience to orders—if not, indeed, whose brilliant suggestion of a daring movement,—turned a doubtful field into a famous victory. Lee's subordinates must at once have seen, as the public speedily saw, that Jackson's dash to Manassas was the secret of the crushing defeat administered Pope. There was speculation then, as there has been ever since, as to whether Jackson or Lee proposed that amazing flank advance which left the army exposed to possible destruction. But if he knew of this speculation, General Lee neither showed nor felt the slightest jealousy of his powerful "right arm." His reports do full credit to Jackson and his relations with that wonderful captain of men were merely strengthened by this shining example of successful co-operation. Only between Nelson and Collingwood was there ever closer personal friendship than between these two men whose stars might have battled for first place in the Southern sky. And if it seem trivial to dwell on the noble comradeship between Lee and Jackson, this utter elimination of self, let the reader but scan a single page of that never-ending controversy among Federal commanders and find in the contrast one potent reason for the strength of the Army of Northern Virginia.

The next great campaign was, with the possible exception of Gettysburg, the severest test upon the character of Lee. He did not assume the offensive and march into Maryland in obedience to orders he received from the President. He proposed the Antietam campaign himself, regarded the time as favorable and assumed the responsibility that was involved in this effort at demonstrating to neutral Maryland and to skeptical Europe the aggressive power of Southern arms. Even remembering that he neither contemplated nor planned more than an impressive demonstration, it is easy to imagine the effect upon a man of less heroic proportions. Richmond was no longer in danger. The Federals' main army had been driven back across the Potomac. The gray regiments were to march into "the enemy's country"—the very words inspired the army to a frenzy of patriotism. But assuming the offensive did not unbalance the quiet commander who had met McClellan and routed him in a week and had then sent the boastful Pope galloping back to his fortifications. Lee cautioned Mr. Davis not to expect too much, addressed the people of Maryland with tact and spirit and restraining by the most peremptory orders the appetite of soldiers who yearned for the flesh-pots of a country that had never seen a battle. Only when orders were captured and he found himself almost trapped did he show the spirit of the soldier to whom defeat is second only to death. They say he embraced that hotspur Hill when the latter threw his avenging divisions where the battle waxed hardest; and when he met his corps commanders in the road the night after the battle and refused to accept their advice to retire—how graphically Stephen D. Lee told the story—he was not less daring and insistent than at Second Manassas or at Chancellorsville. But in his letters and reports there is the same imperturbable composure, no bitterness at the outcome, no censures on subordinates, only regret that so many had fallen and that so much work remained for those who survived.

Fredericksburg, his next campaign, was the picture-book battle of the war. Meissonier or Édouard Detaille would have gloried in its gray dawn, its assaults, its repulses, its carnage. Lee had laid his trap as the shrewd hunter prepares for the wary game. He did not know Burnside as he knew McClellan but he put before that ambitious commander a bait he could not resist. To cross the river, to take the town and then to move against fortifications that seemed neither strong nor well-manned appeared easy—from the other side of the Rappahannock. Lee waited for his prey with deliberation he seldom showed—the deliberation of Cold Harbor—and when all was ready he sprang the trap. He knew how the steel would bite, he knew how strong was the spring and that day, it is safe to say, Lee the conqueror was more nearly dominant than at any other time. Officers who galloped behind him through the frost of that December morning remember how incisively he gave his orders, how for once he showed himself nettled at the mistake of a staff-officer and

how Napoleon-like he seemed when he inquired the
name of a young, death-dealing artillerist and promoted him at once.   It was, too, at Fredericksburg
that he gave utterance to the only phrase ever known
to have escaped his lips in exultation over victory.
He was standing on the hill that still bears his name
and was watching through his field-glasses the fine
Federal regiments break themselves against his line.
His plan was succeeding; the invaders of his native
State were being driven back.   "It is well war is so
terrible," he said, "or we would grow too fond of it."
In the one sentence is the character of the man!

The correspondence printed in this volume is
barren of reference to Fredericksburg—the victory
was so prompt and so decisive that confidential
communications were unnecessary—but the *Official
Records* are crowded with his formal dispatches and
reports.   In all of these there is the same calm man-
liness and the same humble gratitude.   Victories
such as no American had achieved in a year had only
sobered him and prostrated him the more before
his God.   Indeed, if one turns from public to private
correspondence and reads his heart in those tender
letters he wrote home that winter, one sees Lee more
on his knees than in his saddle.

He entered upon the year 1863 with a series of
victories unbroken from the time he had taken command in front of Richmond and with an army the
morale of which had never been so high.   He ended
the year with the greatest opportunity of his career
lost through the blunders and worse of his subordinates—ended it with his own hope dwindling and

the spirit of his nation already ebbing. It was in every sense the most critical year of his military life —less disastrous than 1864, less fraught with irretrievable defeat than 1865 but more important than either in that it made both years inevitable. If war and adversity could change the heart of a man, the stormy days of 1863 would have broken his calm.

Chancellorsville was the first important engagement of that year and was in line with what had gone before. It cost him Jackson—more valuable than any victory could have been—but it added to his fame. There was about that fight in the wilderness something sinister and demoralizing to his enemies, something fascinating even to-day (September, 1914) when armies greater than those Lee ever dreamed of commanding are battling for the future of a continent. To the Federals Chancellorsville meant more than the defeats of 1861 or 1862. They had not been too hopeful of the raw regiments they had sent during the early days of the war to battle with men trained to the saddle and raised with a musket in their hands. But by 1863, the Federals had hoped that lessons learned in blood would be remembered in bravery and that their troops would withstand the assaults of the Southern host. Instead, when they had clashed in the pines and underbrush and had drawn back for breath, the thunders broke at twilight and fresh troops, sprung as it seemed, from the ground, assailed them in flank and rear. No wonder Washington became discouraged when the reports stated that the first intimation the Federals had of Jackson's approach was the wild scamper across the quiet

camp of the rabbits driven from their shelters by
the silent Confederates! Congressmen and editors
began to ask if naught could stop the "rebel" whose
armies grew stronger with every battle.

When plans for the invasion of Pennsylvania began,
Lee's command was at its highest efficiency. Depleted ranks had been filled with enthusiastic recruits;
deficiencies in arms and equipment had been supplied by capture and by the untiring effort of men
like Gorgas; soldiers who had never tasted defeat
scorned their enemies and believed themselves invincible when led by Lee. As rumor grew credible with
preparations and as the hope of another forward
movement settled into conviction, Lee's army was
jubilant. The invasion of Maryland had been but
practice,—real work was to come now. There was
to be an end of the wearying watch on the Rapidan;
they were to fight beyond the Potomac, to invade
Pennsylvania, to capture the great cities of the East.
"I reckon," wrote one humble private, as he told
his wife that the advance had begun, "I reckon
there will be the old scampering amongst" the Federals "when our main army gets amongst them."
Every soldier "reckoned" on the same "scampering"
and had not the least doubt of the outcome.

In General Lee's correspondence during those
high days of hope there is to be observed no change
in his usual calm, unless it be that it shows a fuller
confidence than ever in the judgment and discretion
of his subordinates. He approached the fatal field
of Gettysburg just as he went into his earlier campaigns, without fear and without bravado. Willing

to trust the valor of his men and the courage of their leaders, he nevertheless realized that the issue was in the hands of the God of battles.

When the fire died away and Pickett's survivors staggered back over the bodies of their slain comrades, the whole world had changed for Lee and for the South. The first defeat had come,—for to him failure to win was always to lose,—the army that had believed itself invincible had been wrecked. If ever there had been a time in history when a defeated craven would have availed himself of others' errors to escape his own responsibility, it was at Gettysburg. Yet Lee met Pickett with the frank acceptance of blame. If, again, there had ever been a campaign when merited reprimand of culpable lieutenants would have absolved the commander-in-chief, it was at Gettysburg. Yet Lee refused to criticise others and bravely bore the brunt.

One may study all of General Lee's letters and reports of the Gettysburg campaign—including the important new item printed in this volume—and will find neither a whine nor a complaint. And his proposal to resign his command was founded not on pique but on patriotism: he honestly though mistakenly believed that the loss of prestige which he fancied he had suffered at Gettysburg would make another commander more useful and more influential than himself. To the credit of Jefferson Davis' judgment let it be said that he apparently never considered the removal of Lee or the willing acceptance of his resignation. Lee after Gettysburg was still Lee. Despite his generous acceptance of the responsibility for what happened at Gettysburg, General Lee doubtless knew the sentiment of the nation. It is in this light that the letter printed in this collection and bearing directly on this subject is of such prime importance. It is not confession and avoidance to his chief. It is not even a hint that while others are to blame, politics makes it better for him to be the victim. It is rather a deliberate acceptance, without carping or innuendo, of a course he believes to be right and politic only because right!

The months from the battle of Gettysburg to the opening of the campaign of 1864 were unmarked by great battles in Virginia but were rendered burdensome by those vexing problems of military routine upon which the maintenance of a field-force depends. Both armies were exhausted by the titanic struggle in Pennsylvania and needed time to recuperate before they could grapple again. Their commanders accordingly devoted themselves to reorganization, recruiting, re-enlisting and to strengthening their ordnance. The Federals, however, escaped the burden that almost crushed General Lee. They had but to call for supplies: the farms of the West and the manufactories of the East could furnish them in almost unlimited quantities. They had but to ask for more men: Congress was quick to devise bounties that would attract the alien where the native stood back. Lee pleaded both for men and for their subsistence: neither was forthcoming. Already the conscription laws "robbed the cradle and the grave" in the homely parlance of the South; and as for supplies, not all the tricks of the Treasury nor all the wiles of the tax collectors could procure them. One has but to read the insistent, the almost feverish appeals of General Lee for men and provisions to realize that he knew the struggle was hopeless without them.

There came with the campaign of 1864 in Virginia —Grant's "left-flank" movement—a few more opportunities for Lee to display his generalship. He met the new Federal chieftain with all his force in Spottsylvania, he hurled him staggering from the bayonet-guarded line at Cold Harbor and he struck with his wonted skill at the Crater. But the star of his military fortune was declining. Even he could not win victories and overcome losses unless recruits and supplies were to be had. The Confederate commissary had collapsed—utterly collapsed —the most fruitful granaries of the South were being captured one after another, the few who came to take the muskets of the many that fell were either boys from their school-books or poltroons from their discovered hiding-places.

A man moulded in proportions less noble would have abused his inefficient colleagues and superiors or would have thrown up his commission in dudgeon. Lee did neither. He warned Mr. Davis, as his duty demanded, that he could not be responsible for the outcome unless his troops were reinforced and fed; but he accepted hardship as his fate and shared the starvation of his men. And when he might have resigned his post and been justified in the eyes of the people, he accepted in meekness and determination the high command Congress and the President con-

ferred upon him.   Never did his manhood shine
more brightly than in the dark days of 1864–65.

The end came.   Through the mud of a torrential
April he rode at the head of his veterans across the
red-clay hills about the Appomattox and to the quiet
county-seat of that name.   He told his lieutenants
that he would rather have died a hundred deaths
than to have surrendered, but when no alternative
offered, he went to the McLean house, pleaded consideration for the men who made up his army and
then went back to write his last report to the President of his dying country.   It was a confession of
defeat—the bitterest words a soldier can write—but
through it breathed the same high spirit that marked
his terse account of Mechanicsville.   And of the
same spirit is his last address to his army, that final
injunction of a departing Arthur.

Men who saw him that first day of June, 1862,
when he galloped across the field of Seven Pines
with President Davis and a brilliant staff, say that
Lee seemed then the very incarnation of knighthood.
Some of the same men, viewing him as he rode back
to Richmond, mud-spattered and travel-worn, say
he looked even nobler then than when his splendid
career was nearing its noon.   He had led one of the
finest armies in history; he had checkmated the
moves of the most worthy foemen his enemy could
bring against him; he had fought with his back to
his capital; he had carried his banners into hostile
States.   Yet he went to Richmond and thence to
Lexington a worthier leader than when he was the
head of an undefeated host.

There remains but to say a few words of the sources and authorities used in preparing this collection and of the history of the letters and telegrams themselves.

The *Official Records* have, of course, been employed throughout not merely as a check-list but as a constant cross-reference guide for the better understanding of the subjects discussed by General Lee.[1] The *Southern Historical Society Papers*, especially the early volumes and the admirable Index, prepared for the State Library of Virginia by Mrs. Kate Pleasants Minor, have proved most useful. The *Atlas* which was printed as a supplement to the *Official Records* has been invaluable. Without this *Atlas* at one's elbow, intelligent study of the movements of the various campaigns is hopeless.

Of primary authorities, the editor may commend to the reader a few of the many hundred as especially important for the study of Lee. The biographies of Long, Cooke, Taylor, McCabe and Fitz Lee are all important; but none is as valuable, from one point of view at least, as the splendid *Recollections and Letters of General Robert E. Lee*, by his son, Captain R. E. Lee, C. S. A. Crowded with the personal letters of the great commander and written from a knowledge which no other biographer could possess, this little volume gives a picture of General Lee infinitely more graphic and more appealing than any yet painted. The *Recollections* should be studied by every general reader who wishes to see with what

---

[1] The *Official Records* are cited as O. R., with the volume, part and page in order, thus: O. R., 25, 2, 621. The reference is always to *Series* 1, unless otherwise stated.

delicacy a great man could write of his own achievements and with what tact and modesty a great man's
son could speak of his father.

Among the many books written by General Lee's
lieutenants and subordinate officers, the most valuable in the editor's judgment, and certainly the one
most frequently used in annotating these letters, is
Brigadier-General E. P. Alexander's *Military Memoirs of a Confederate*. General Alexander wrote as
an old man, with memory a trifle dimmed by the lapse
of time and with some pet theories that could not
be shaken; but what he lacks in these respects he
more than compensated by the careful use of the
Official Records and by a clarity most notable. Few
Southern writers, if, indeed any, have been able as
concisely and as distinctly to describe a campaign or
a battlefield. To beginners, in particular, his book
is most heartily to be recommended.

It is probably unnecessary to commend among
secondary authorities, or to own one's debt to Colonel
G. F. R. Henderson's *Stonewall Jackson, a Military
Biography*. Where the careers of Lee and Jackson
run together, this book is and will doubtless remain
the one best account of their campaigns, and this
apart from the fact that as a literary biography it is
a masterpiece. The South will always regret that
this fine officer in the King's service did not live to
write a biography of Lee worthy to rank with his
Jackson. Had he done so, the greatest need of
Southern history would have been supplied.

The Battles and Leaders of the Civil War, Mr.
Davis' well-known volumes, the familiar biography

of the President by his wife, Johnston's *Narrative*, Alexander H. Stephens' works on the war, McClellan's *Own Story* and Grant's great narrative, written in a spirit of candor and uncolored frankness, are, of course, necessary at all times for their direct or collateral bearing on Lee's campaigns. Jones' *Rebel War Clerk's Diary*, so frequently cited by Mr. Rhodes, is also valuable, despite the writer's provoking fondness for gossip and his inaccuracy in small details.

Of the history of the dispatches in this collection, neither their owner nor the editor has been able to gather anything of consequence. Most of the letters and many of the telegrams are in the autograph of General Lee, some are in the familiar handwriting of Charles Marshall, Walter H. Taylor and others of his staff, some are merely copies made at the receiving telegraph office or transcribed at the War Department for the use of President Davis. They are written on papers of all sorts, from the fine, thin, blue English paper which General Lee seemed to prefer to the coarse "Confederate gray" made in the South during the war. Many of the telegrams are on the printed forms of the telegraph company. The letters are contained in one substantial volume of post-bellum binding, the telegrams in another similar volume. In this form they were purchased of a well-known Southern writer by their present owner, Mr. W. J. De Renne of Wormsloe, Chatham Co., Georgia, an historian and collector to whose patient and discriminating labor the South owes a debt not yet fully appreciated. How these letters came into the possession of the gentleman from whom Mr. De Renne bought them cannot be ascertained at this time; how they happened to be collected can only be surmised from internal evidence.   The editor thinks it certain, however, that these letters and telegrams were from a file kept for his own reference by President Davis himself.   This seems reasonable because: (1) most of the letters, and practically all those of importance, were addressed directly to Mr. Davis and show no evidence of having passed through the hands of other persons, (2) those addressed to the War Department are represented in this collection by copies rather than by originals and are generally marked "for the information of the President," (3) letters sent by Mr. Davis to other executive officers for their use bear endorsements indicating their return to Mr. Davis.

This view is sustained by an analysis of those items of this collection which examinations show to be already in print.   Those which appear in the De Renne collection as copies from the War Department are usually found in the *Official Records*, transcribed from the originals captured after the evacuation of Richmond.   Those sent directly to Mr. Davis—and privately kept by him, if this theory be correct—are seldom found in the *Official Records*. Where such items do appear, comparisons with General Lee's letter-book, made by the editor, have shown that the printed copies came from that source. Letters which were written by General Lee and regarded as too confidential for even his private letter-book do not appear in the *Official Records* or in any other printed collection. This would hardly occur with such regularity had not the originals, sent by General Lee to the President, been carefully and privately preserved by the latter. On the other hand, had they been in Mr. Davis' possession at the time the Records were compiled or when his work on the war was written, they would certainly have been used.

Taking all these facts into consideration, the editor believes that the De Renne papers were kept as a private file by Mr. Davis, were carried or sent South when Richmond fell and were probably lost on the journey along with other papers since recovered.

None of the letters or telegrams located by the editor or his assistants in any printed work appears in this collection, unless it be that the printed copies have escaped the most diligent search that could be made. This process of exclusion has disposed of two-thirds of the De Renne collection but it has perhaps increased the value of the items now presented. All dispatches printed in this volume, it might be well to add, follow the precise spelling, punctuation and arrangement of the originals

The editor, finally, cannot forbear a word of thanks to the friends who have assisted in what has certainly been a labor of love. The owner of the dispatches, Mr. W. J. De Renne, who arranged for their appearance in print, has been generous in overlooking delays and enthusiastic in his encouragement at every stage of the work. The editor could but hope that the future of Southern history were in the keeping of men like Mr. De Renne who combine means for publication with reverent regard for historical accuracy. Captain W. Gordon McCabe, chosen custodian of the papers of General Lee, has given the editor free access to them and has aided with many suggestions, based on an unexcelled, critical knowledge of the war. To Dr. H. J. Eckenrode of the State Library of Virginia, and to the other officials of that splendid collection, notably to Dr. H. R. McIlwaine, Mr. E. G. Swem and Mrs. Kate Pleasants Minor, the editor is under lasting obligations. Miss Susie B. Harrison, House Regent of the Confederate Museum of Richmond has also given generously of her time. With such friends and helpers, even the dullest details of an editorial task are pleasant.

D. S. F.

RICHMOND, 1914.

CONTENTS

xlvii

Contents

Contents

Contents

Contents lvii

Contents

Contents

Contents

Contents

Contents

Contents

Contents

Contents lxvii

No. 168.
October 7, 1864.
PAGE

Federal activities on the Rapidan 300

No. 169.
October 19, 1864.
Further operations in East Tennessee . . . 301

No. 170.
October 25, 1864.
Mr. Stewart's mysterious project—Lee's non-approval . 302

No. 171.
November 2, 1864.
General Law's grievances—Grant's strength—Southern
need of men 304

No. 172.
December 13, 1864.
The Hicksford raid 306

No. 173.
December 14, 1864.
No meat for the army—Meat at Wilmington . . 307

No. 174.
December 17, 1864.
The Federal raid on the Virginia and Tennessee . . 309

No. 175.
December 22, 1864.
Bragg without supplies at Wilmington—Official red tape 310

No. 176.
December 25, 1864.
Operations on the Roanoke 311

No. 177.
January 8, 1865.
The defence of Charleston and of Carolina . . 312

Contents

Contents

Contents

Lee's Dispatches

Lee's Dispatches

No. 1.

NEAR RICHMOND
3 June, '62[1]

Mʳ PRESIDENT

I am extremely grateful for your kind offer of your fine horse & feel most sensibly the consideration & thoughtfulness that prompted it. But I really do not require one at this time & would infinitely prefer your retaining him & allow me to enjoy the sense of your kindness & to call for him when I am in want.

---

[1] This letter was written on the second day after General Lee assumed command of the army defending Richmond. When General Joseph E. Johnston was wounded on the afternoon of May 31, 1862, Major-General Gustavus W. Smith, as second in command, took charge of field operations and directed the movements of the army until he was informed, on June 1, at 2 P.M., that General Lee had been appointed (Smith's report, O. R., 13, 1, 992). In General Lee's personal orders from the President, delivered the same day occurs this passage: " [It] is necessary to interfere temporarily with the duties to which you were assigned in connection with the general service, but only so far as to make you available for command in the field of a particular army" (Davis to Lee, O. R., 13, 3, 568). In taking the field the same afternoon (Alexander, *Military Memoirs*, 89), General Lee faced a situation which was very trying in at least two respects.

My gray has calmed down amazingly,[2] gave me a very pleasant ride all day yesterday & I enjoyed

---

He did not possess the confidence of the army nor was the immediate outlook favorable. His previous service in the Confederate army had been limited to a single campaign in Western Virginia, to coast-defence work at Charleston and to duty as military adviser to the President. His qualities were, accordingly, practically unknown to many of his officers; he was accounted a "staff officer" and, as Longstreet points out, "officers of the line are not apt to look to the staff in choosing leaders of soldiers, either in tactics or strategy" (*From Manassas*, etc., 112). Many of his division commanders received with "misgivings" the President's choice (Longstreet, *loc. cit.*) and young Alexander doubted that Lee possessed "audacity" (*op. cit.*, 110–11). The army, moreover, was embarrassed by the engagements of May 30–June 1; the weather was unspeakably depressing and stubbornly wet. Worse still, a Federal army of almost 100,000 men was thrown in an arc around the Confederate capital, with its outposts within six miles of the city. McClellan's forces rested on Beaver Dam Creek, extended in a southeasterly direction to the Chickahominy, crossed that stream at New Bridge and ran toward the South as far as White Oak Swamp. By sheer good fortune, McClellan had been able to throw sufficient troops across the river to meet the first Confederate attack and had managed to keep bridges over the swollen stream, across which he could send more men. The battle of Seven Pines, fought on three successive days by three different Confederate commanders, was a draw at best and its close, when General Lee reached the field, left the opposing armies in relatively the same positions they had occupied.

[2] "My gray" was Traveller, best beloved of Lee's chargers. Traveller had been bought in Western Virginia from the Broun family in the winter of 1861. He was an iron gray "with black points—mane and tail very dark—sixteen hands high and five years old" (Lee, *Recollections*, 82) and was renowned

his gaits much.   My other horses[3] are improving
& will soon I hope be ready for service.   So I really
with my present riding would not know what to do
with more.   They would not have sufficient exercise
& be uncomfortable to me & themselves.

With a full sense & appreciation of your kindness
& great gratitude for your friendship, I must again
beg to be allowed to ask you to keep the horse in
your service.[4]

With sentiments of profound respect & esteem

I am your obliged & humble servt

R. E. LEE

His Exc[p] President DAVIS

No. 2.

Confidential

H[p]-QRS: NEAR RICHMOND
5 June, '62

His Exc[y]

President DAVIS

After much reflection I think if it was possible
to reinforce Jackson strongly, it would change the

---

for his powers of endurance.   If not properly exercised, he
easily became restless, but in normal times, was "quiet and
sensible" and "afraid of nothing" (Lee, *loc. cit.*).   General
Lee was very fond of the horse and wrote in a feeling manner
of the animal's faithful service.   It should be added, however,
that R. E. Lee, Jr., trying the horse in 1862, gained a most
unfavorable opinion of the gaits of his father's pet.

[3] General Lee's other mounts were Grace Darling, Richmond, Brown Roan, Ajax and Lucy Long.   Two of these
died under hard work and two others had to be put aside.

[4] It was characteristic of General Lee never to accept a
favor he could not promptly return.

character of the War.   This can only be done by the
troops in Georgia, S. C. & N. C.   Jackson could in
that event cross Maryland into Penn[1]— It would
call all the enemy from our Southern Coast & liberate
those states—If these states will give up their troops
I think it can be done.[2]   McClellan will make this

[1] This is the only reference the editor has found to a movement the possibilities of which were obvious.   "Stonewall"
Jackson was at this time in the Valley of Virginia and, on
this very day, reached the town of Harrisonburg in the course
of his memorable campaign.   The battles of Port Republic
and Cross Keys (June 8, 1862) were but three days' distant.
Lee had, it must be remembered, no assurance that their
outcome would be so overwhelming a victory for Southern
arms and he was, of course, basing his theory on nothing more
than the known character and dash of Jackson.   Lee's approval of the plan here proposed at least demonstrates that
he had already settled upon two things,—that an offensive
campaign must be waged to draw the enemy from the South
and that he would finish the Peninsula campaign without
reinforcements from those quarters.   It will be noted, also,
that General Lee's words do not make it plain whether the
plan proposed was of his own devising or was suggested by
President Davis or some one else.   Related correspondence
in the *Official Records* throws no light on this question, with
the exception of one word in a letter from Lee to G. W.
Randolph, Secretary of War. In this (O. R., 11, 3, 575) he
refers to the "troops from Georgia *you* propose" sending
Jackson.   It seems not improbable that "you" is here used
in a particular sense and would not have been so employed
had the sending of troops to Jackson been suggested by Lee
himself.   This, however, is but surmise.   The Records are
silent and contain no further discussion of a plan which was
daring if not altogether practicable.

[2] Aside from the movement against New Orleans and the
activities around Sumter, it will be recalled that at this time

a battle of Posts.[3] He will take position from position, under cover of his heavy guns, & we cannot get at him without storming his works, which with our new troops is extremely hazardous. You witnessed the experiment Saturday.[4] It will require 100,000 men to resist the regular siege of Richmond, which perhaps would only prolong not save it—I am preparing a line that I can hold with part of our forces in front, while with the rest I will endeavour to make a diversion to bring McClellan out. He sticks under his batteries & is working day & night[5]— He is obliged to adhere to the R. R. unless he can reach James river to provision his Army. I am endeavouring to block his progress on the R. R.[6]

there were no important movements on foot east of the Mississippi River, except in Tennessee.

[3] Immediately after the battle of Seven Pines, McClellan realized that an advance movement during the next few days would be extremely hazardous, and accordingly put all his available forces to work entrenching his position. These, he explains, "protected them [his men] while the bridges were being built, gave security to the trains, liberated a larger fighting force, and offered a safe retreat in the event of disaster" (McClellan's *Own Story*, 385). General Lee's prediction that McClellan would make the Peninsula Campaign "a battle of posts" was amply verified by the result.

[4] May 31, the date of Seven Pines.

[5] *Cf.* McClellan to Stanton, June 3, 1862: "Hard at work upon the bridges, removing wounded, &c." (O. R., *loc. cit.*, 212). June 7 (same to same): "I am pushing forward the bridges . . . , and the men are working night and day, up to their waists in water, to complete them" (McClellan, *op. cit.*, 387).

[6] The York River railroad, connecting Richmond with

& have written up to see if I can get made an iron
battery on trucks with a heavy gun, to sweep the
country in our front.[7]   The enemy cannot move his
heavy guns except on the R. R.   You have seen nothing like the roads on the Chick—y bottom.[8]   Our
people are opposed to work.   Our troops officers
community & press.   All ridicule & resist it.   It is
the very means by which McClellan has & is advancing.   Why should we leave to him the whole advantage of labour.   Combined with valour fortitude
& boldness, of which we have our fair proportion, it
should lead us to success.   What carried the Roman
soldiers into all Countries, but this happy combination.   The evidences of their labour last to this day.
There is nothing so military as labour, & nothing
so important to an army as to save the lives of its
soldiers—

I enclose a letter I have rec^d from Genl D. H. Hill,
for your own perusal.[9]   Please return it to me.   I

West Point, located on deep water at the confluence of the
Mattaponi and Pamunkey rivers.

[7] *Cf.* Lee to J. Gorgas, Chief of Ordnance, June 5, 1862
(O. R., *loc. cit.*, 574).   Lee wanted "an iron-plated battery,
mounting a heavy gun, on trucks, the whole covered with
iron, to move along the York River Railroad."   He believed
such a battery would be of "immense advantage."

[8] The bottoms along the Chickahominy, normally heavy
and difficult of access, were at this time almost impassable,
owing to the unusual floods and rain.   Two days later Mc-
Clellan (*op. cit.*, 387) describes them as flooded "to the depth
of three or four feet."

[9] Not found.   Apparently a complaint of inefficiency among
his subordinates.

had taken means to arrest stragglers—I hope he is mistaken about his Brigadiers—I fear not in Rains' case.[10]   Of Featherston[11] I know nothing.   I thought you ought to know it.   Our position requires you should know everything & you must excuse my troubling you.[12]   The firing in our front has ceased.

---

[10] Gabriel J. Rains of North Carolina (1803–1881). Rains was a West Point graduate who saw considerable service in the "old army." He was originally commissioned as colonel of Infantry in Confederate service, but was promoted brigadier-general in September, 1861, assuming command of a brigade under Magruder at Yorktown. He later led a division in the same army, composed of Rains' and Featherston's brigades and the "troops at Gloucester Point." At Seven Pines he commanded his brigade, the 6th and 23rd Georgia and 13th and 26th Alabama. He was much interested in torpedo construction (O. R., *loc. cit.*, 509 ff.) and on June 18, 1862 (S. O., A. N. Va., No. 140, XII., O. R., *loc. cit.*, 608) was assigned to command of the submarine defences of the James and Appomattox. For a sketch of Rains, see *Confederate Military History*, 4, 339 (cited *infra* as C. M. H.). Rains was criticised for his failure to advance a second time after a successful movement on the enemy's left at Seven Pines. But Hill refers to him as "that gallant and meritorious officer" (Report on Seven Pines, O. R., *loc. cit.*, 1, 944).

[11] Winfield Scott Featherston (1821–1891) was a politician before the war and, in May, 1861, was made colonel of the 17th Mississippi regiment. He was commissioned brigadier-general, March 4, 1862, and commanded a brigade at Seven Pines composed of the 27th and 28th Georgia, the 4th North Carolina and the 49th Virginia Infantry. He was later transferred to the Western army (C. M. H., 7, 251–51).

[12] This remark is not without its significance. Lee desired to co-operate fully with Davis and to prevent such action as had given color to the report that Johnston had not com-

I believe it was the enemys shell practice. Col.
Long[13] . . . . . went down early this mor^g to
keep me advised, but as I hear nothing from them
I assume it is unimportant

Very respy & truly

R. E. LEE

No. 3.

H^D-QRS: 7 June, '62

Mr PRESIDENT

I had the honor to receive on my return to my
quarters last ev^g your very kind letter of the 6^1—In
reference to Genl. R. H. Anderson & your conception
of his qualifications I enclose a note from Genl.
Longstreet. I know little of Genl. A. personally
except as Capt: of Dragoons. He was a favourite
in his Regt: & was considered a good officer. I am
told he is now under a pledge of abstinence, which I
hope will protect him from the vice he fell into.[2]

municated his plans fully to the President (Alexander, *op.
cit.*, 92–93).

[13] A. L. Long, later Brigadier-General, military secretary
and biographer to General Lee. The other name is illegible.

[1] Not found.

[2] Longstreet's letter not found. Richard Henry Anderson,
here referred to, was born in South Carolina, Oct. 7, 1821,
and was graduated from West Point in 1842, serving later
with the 2nd Dragoons. He was in the Mexican War, was
promoted captain in March, 1855, and was named major of
cavalry when he entered the Confederate service, March 9,
1861. On July 19, 1861, he was promoted brigadier-general.
At Seven Pines he commanded Longstreet's division very
creditably, which doubtless influenced Longstreet in his
behalf. His commission as major-general was dated July 14,

Longstreet is a Capital soldier. His recommendations hitherto have been good, & I have confidence in him—Unless Huger had other duty,[3] I do not know where to get a division for Genl. A— yet awhile. I have called for returns, but have not yet rec^d them. I have also sent a circular to Division Commanders to see what can be done as to reorganizing brigades by states.[4] I fear the result. Nor do I think it the best organization. I would rather command a brigade composed of regts from different states. I think it could be better controuled, more emulation would be excited & there would be less combination against authority. I can understand why officers looking to political preferment would prefer it, & it may be more agreeable to the men. The latter consideration has much weight with me. But as it is your wish & may be in conformity to the spirit of the land, I will attempt what can be done. It must necessarily be slow & will require much time. All new brigades I will endeavour so to arrange.

As regards the petition of the officers of Whitings

1862. He was later lieutenant-general and corps commander in the Army of Northern Virginia (C. M. H., 1, 691 ff.).

[3] Benjamin Huger of South Carolina (1806–1877), was a graduate of West Point and in the Mexican War rose to the rank of colonel. He was made major-general in Confederate service in October, 1861, and commanded a division at Seven Pines. He was blamed for the partial failure of the first day's attack (Longstreet to Johnston, O. R., 13, 3, 580) but would seem to be acquitted by the evidence Alexander adduces (*Military Memoirs*, 78–79). For Huger's biography, see C. M. H., 5, 403 ff.

[4] Not found.

brigade I do not see how it can be complied with.[5]
It will leave him without a brigade.   He is still its
Commander, though at present in command of a
division.   The distribution of the brigade will have
the same effect.   The other matters to which you
allude I will call the attention of the Division &
Brigade Insp[r]s to.   I know none of the circumstances.

I am extremely obliged to you for your consideration for my comfort.   My horse does not fatigue
me.   He goes very comfortably & perhaps suits me
as I become more accustomed to him as well as any
I can get.   His gallop & walk are very pleasant.[6]

Very respy. & truly

R. E. LEE

His Exce[l]
President DAVIS.

No. 4.

HEAD QUARTERS
DEPT NORTH VA.

His Excellency   June 24th 1862.
President DAVIS
   SIR

I regret that I did not see you when you called

---

[5] Not found.   William H. C. Whiting (1824–1865) at this
time commanded G. W. Smith's division, composed of Whiting's, Hood's and Hampton's brigades (O. R., 13, pt. 3, 483).
His own brigade was composed of the 4th Alabama, 2nd and
11th Mississippi and 6th North Carolina, with Imboden's
and Reilly's batteries.   Whiting's career during the early
months of the war was most promising; his military qualities
at all times were high.

[6] Traveller is doubtless referred to.

this afternoon—I was called to the Williamsburg Road[1] where some heavy skirmishing was going on most of the day. One of the brigades, (Gen. Ransom's)[2] was new which rendered me more anxious of the result—The general behaviour of the troops was good, but the affair on the whole was not well managed.[3] This has caused me some anxiety—The enemy however was driven back from his advanced position. I have determined to make no change in the plan—I have ordered Genl. Huger to hold his lines at all hazards, and to advance if possible, making to-night every preparation to meet any attack of the enemy in the morning should he move against him—[4]

I have the honour to be
Very respectfully
Yours
R. E. LEE, Genl

---

[1] The Williamsburg road was one of the main thoroughfares from Richmond down the Peninsula. As its name suggests, its terminus was the ancient capital of the Commonwealth. The course of the road can be followed on practically all the military maps of the Richmond district.

[2] This was Robert Ransom's brigade, composed of the 24th, 25th, 26th, 35th and 49th North Carolina Infantry, with Burroughs' cavalry, two companies of North Carolina cavalry and Graham's battery. These troops had been on the south side of the James, near Petersburg, as a part of the defensive forces there but had been removed to join Lee when McClellan pressed him (O. R., 13, 3, 613). The brigade had been in service but two months (O. R., 13, 2, 792).

[3] See Ransom's report (O. R., 13, 2, 792). Part of his brigade was engaged from 11 A.M., until sunset. Casualties were small.

[4] Ransom's troops were serving with Huger's division at

No. 5.

H^D-QRS: 25 June '62

His Exce^l
Pres: DAVIS

I really do not know enough about W^m D.
Smith[1] to speak of his qualifications, or to say whether
he would answer for the position—He must know
but little of Coast defense. If Huger will answer
send him—Genl. R. H. Anderson can replace him—
There was an attack upon Hugers lines this mor^g &
he was absent I am told—Not at his qrs: this mor^g
I have just sent him an order to take his position
with his troops & to remain with them.[2]

Very resp^y
R. E. LEE
Genl.

---

this time, hence the order to the division commander (*Cf.*
O. R., 13, 3, 617.)

[1] William Duncan Smith of Georgia (1826–1862), West
Point graduate, colonel of the 20th Georgia regiment and
brigadier-general by commission of March 7, 1862. He was
placed in command of the district of South Carolina in June,
1862, but died of fever in October (C. M. H., 6, 437–38).

[2] Immediately after the battle of Seven Pines, Huger's
division had been placed in advance on the Williamsburg
road, occupying the ground abandoned June 2. He was not
disturbed until June 18, when the 53rd Virginia, serving on
picket line, was attacked. Little of importance transpired
until June 25, but on that day Ransom's brigade reinforced
Huger and participated in a brisk skirmish. A part of the
Confederate line was lost but was recovered later in the day.
Walker's brigade reached Huger on June 26 but was soon
moved, leaving Huger alone to defend the Confederate right

No. 6.

HEADQUARTERS
DOBBS HOUSE
26 June 1862

His Excell'cy
   Jeff^r. DAVIS
      Presid^t. &c

SIR

A note just received from General Jackson this morning states that in consequence of the high water & mud, his command only reached Ashland last night.[1] It was his purpose to resume his march this

---

when Lee began the Seven Days' Fight with an assault on the Federal right (*see* Huger's report, no. 307, O. R., 13, 2, 787 ff.).

[1] This letter was written at the beginning of the Seven Days' Fight, by which McClellan was driven from the Chickahominy to the James and was almost destroyed. Three days after the proposal that Jackson advance into Pennsylvania, and with no intervening correspondence to show the reasons for the change, it was decided that Jackson should join Lee and reinforce him in an attack on McClellan. Lee wrote on that day (June 8): "Should there be nothing requiring your attention in the valley, so as to prevent your leaving it for a few days, and you can make arrangements to deceive the enemy and impress him with the idea of your presence, please let me know, that you may unite at the decisive moment with the army near Richmond" (O. R., 11, 3, 582–83). Lee's plan for attacking McClellan had already taken shape and required the addition of reinforcements. To deceive the Federals, Lee determined to send troops to Jackson which should be permanently joined to his command but should at once be returned to Richmond to participate with the rest of Jackson's troops in Lee's assault. Accordingly Lawton with six regiments from Georgia and Whiting with nine regi-

morning at 2.30[2]. I fear from the operations of the
enemy yesterday that our plan of operations has
been discovered to them. It seemed to be his purpose, by his advance on our right yesterday, to discover whether our force on that front had been
diminished.[3] General Jackson writes that there

---

ments from Lee's army were dispatched to Jackson. The
latter was instructed to "leave your enfeebled troops to watch
the country and guard the passes covered by your cavalry
and artillery, and with your main body, including Ewell's
divisions and Lawton's and Whiting's command, move rapidly
to Ashland by rail or otherwise . . ." (O. R., 11, 3, 589,
June 11, 1862). Jackson obeyed orders, and, cleverly con-
cealing his intentions, moved his whole army from the Valley.
On Tuesday morning, June 24, the troops had reached Beaver
Dam on the Chesapeake and Ohio railroad, eighteen miles
from Ashland. Lee apparently expected Jackson to move on
the Ashland the same day, and from that place, to move to the
Stark Church, whence he was to begin his real advance at 3 A.M.,
June 26 (Alexander, 115–116; G. O., 75, A. N. Va., series
1862). General Lee's plan was for this movement to begin
an attack on McClellan's right which was expected to sweep
that part of his army down the Peninsula and destroy it.
Jackson's delay in making this advance, and his failure to
begin his movement from the Stark Church until 10 A.M.
instead of 3 A.M. has been the subject of much criticism.
Jackson makes no explanation in his official report (O. R.,
11, 2, 552) and the "high water and mud," here referred to
appear to be the only tenable excuse. For a full statement of
Jackson's side of the case, see Henderson.

[2] The official order said "at three o'clock, Thursday morning, 26th instant."

[3] This surmise was correct. Indeed, McClellan had learned
of Lee's general plan and of Jackson's approach on June 24.
A deserter from Jackson's army, who left his command near

was a movement on our extreme left beyond the Chickahominy. Our Cavalry pickets were driven in that direction, & the telegraph wire near Ashland was cut.

I am most respy

Your obt servant

R. E. LEE

Genl.

No. 7.

[*Telegram*]

HEAD QUARTERS
ARMY N. VA.
June 26th 1862.

His Excels
   President DAVIS
      SIR

The headquarters of the Commanding General today will be on the Mechanicsville Turnpike.

I have the honour to be

Very respectfully

Your obt Servt

R. H. CHILTON

A A G

[*Endorsed*]
   A. A. G. to
      Genl LEE
         HD QRS ARMY NO VA.
   June 26, 1862.

Gordonsville on the 21st, reported to McClellan that Jackson was moving to Frederick's Hall from Gordonsville, expecting

No. 8.

[Telegram]

HOGANS HOUSE June 27 62

GENL. HUGA [HUGER]

Genl. Longstreet's Brigade is on the road from
Hogans House to Dr. Gaines. Genl. A. P. Hill is
on the road from Walnut Grove Church to Cold
Harbor via Gaines Mill. Genl Jackson's command
supported by D. H. Hill is on the road to Cold Harbor turning Pohite Creek. I think it probable that
the enemy is in force behind Pohite Creek, crossing
the Chickahominy on his line to Gouldings by Fair
Oaks Station along your front. If he should diminish his forces in front of you or show a disposition
to abandon his works you must press him, cautiously
& hold your line at all hazards.' The New Bridge

---

to attack McClellan's rear on the 28th. Prior to this time,
McClellan seemed to have no idea as to the real plans of
Lee, and thought that Jackson was at Gordonsville, awaiting
reinforcements. Even on the 24th, after a vain effort to confirm the report of the deserter, McClellan telegraphed Stanton.
"I would be glad to learn at your earliest convenience, the
most exact information you have, as to the position and movements of Jackson, as well as the sources from which your
information is derived, that I may the better compare it
with what I have." Stanton's reply seemed to indicate, in a
maze of contradictory rumors, his belief that Jackson had
not joined Lee. On the evening of the 25th, however, McClellan had a fairly correct idea of the Confederate plan and was
already preparing to change his base to the James River
(McClellan's *Own Story*, 390 ff.).

    ' *Cf.* No. 5 *supra* and note thereto. As Huger held the
Confederate right, it was highly important that he should

Road is open to us & we must connect with Genl.
Magruder.

R. E. LEE

12 M. June 27 62.
Please send this to the Presd't.
[*Endorsed*]
Genl. LEE to Genl. HUGA.
HOGANS HOUSE
June 27, 1862.
(One enclosure.)

No. 9.

HEADQUARTERS &c
WᵐˢBURG ROAD
29 June 1862.

His Excy Presdᵗ Davis
Mʳ PRESIDENT
I have the honor to report for your information
that after the enemy had been driven from the left
bank of the Chickahominy on the 27th inst:,[1] he

---

make a show of strength and hold his position in case of attack.
His withdrawal from in front of McClellan would have overthrown Lee's entire plan. It would have enabled McClellan
to sweep his centre and left into Richmond before his right
could be driven past his lines.

[1] The action referred to here was the battle of Gaines'
Mill or first Cold Harbor. Owing to Jackson's tardiness on
the 25th and his delays on the 26th, this fight really opened
a battle which had been proposed for the previous day, the
26th. The attack was made by Confederate troops under
Jackson, A. P. Hill, D. H. Hill and James Longstreet against
a strong Federal force well directed by Fitz John Porter. The

seemed to have determined to abandon his position on the right bank & commenced promptly & quietly his arrangements for its evacuation—His intention was discovered but his proposed route could not be ascertained, though efforts were made all day yesterday with that view[2]—Having however discovered that no movements were made on his part to maintain or recover his communications with York river, which were entirely severed by our occupation of the York river railroad & the Williamsburg road; his only course seemed to me was to make for James

---

aim of this attack, as noted, had originally been to crumple up that part of McClellan's army on the left or northern bank of the Chickahominy River, drive the forces composing it down the Peninsula, break McClellan's line along the York River Railroad and force him to retreat at a disadvantage. But by reason of delays and misunderstandings which have been variously explained by different critics, Porter was allowed to escape, though heavily punished, and was enabled to join McClellan in moving his base to the James River.

[2] *Cf.* Alexander (*op. cit.*, 133): "On the Confederate side it was not yet clear what the enemy would do. Ewell's and Jackson's divisions had not been seriously engaged, and Ewell's was sent down the Chickahominy about seven miles to the Despatch Station, to see if they showed any disposition to cross the stream and retreat down the Peninsula." Lee was confident, early in the day, that no Federal troops remained on the north side of the river and, as Alexander points out, was only fearful lest McClellan might recross the river. Soon after Ewell's move, clouds of dust on the south side showed the Federals in motion; but as they occupied roads which might enable them to reach the lower bridges on the Chickahominy, Lee protected the approaches to the river and burned the bridges McClellan might have used (Lee's report, O. R., II, 2, 492–94).

river & thus open communications with his gun boats and fleet[3]—Though not yet certain of his route, the whole army has been put in motion upon this supposition—It is certain that he is south of the Chickahominy and can only cross it at or below Long bridges[4] Genl. Stuart is on the left bank watching his movements in that direction. General Jackson will cross to the right bank at Grapevine bridge. Genl. Magruder pursuing down the W^{m}s. Burg road. Genl Huger on the Charles City, & Genl Longstreet on the Darby town.[5] The Cavalry on the several roads south of the Chickahominy have not reported any of his forces in their front— I have directed the staff depts to send over to the battle ground north of the Chickahominy & secure all the public property left there of every description, & also that which has been abandoned by the enemy in his camp on the south side, where their tents are now still standing.[6] I request that these orders may be repeated by the Sec. of War[7]

---

[3] This, of course, was what McClellan did. Orders were issued to his supporting fleet to move into the James River. He joined them at Harrison's Landing after he stood off Lee's attack at Malvern Hill.

[4] This bridge was several miles below that which had been used during the previous engagements.

[5] The original of this order has not been found. See Lee's abstract of it in his report (*op. cit.*, 494).

[6] Orders not found. Several of the brigade commanders —Gregg, for instance—refer to the vast amount of military supplies left by the enemy on the field.

[7] George W. Randolph of Virginia, a grandson of Thomas Jefferson.

—Col. Lay[8] & Col. Harvey[9] have been charged with the execution of my directions in this matter on the north side of the Chickahominy—

I am with high respect

Your obt Servt

R. E. LEE.

No. 10.

HEADQUARTERS
2 July 1862.

His Excy Presd[t]. DAVIS

M[r]. PRESIDENT

The enemy this morning was found to have abandoned his position which he held yesterday[1]

[8] George W. Lay, at this time assistant inspector-general.

[9] Lieutenant-colonel Edwin J. Harvie, assistant inspector-general. Both Lay and Harvie were commended by General Lee in his report of the campaign (*op. cit.*, 498).

[1] General Lee's previous surmises as to General McClellan's change of base had been proved correct. Virtually all that he had anticipated in his No. 9, Lee saw fulfilled. The movements outlined by General Lee on the 29th were carried out, though Jackson was again delayed and Magruder did not attack with the vigor General Lee had expected. On the afternoon of the 29th, Magruder advanced and the so-called battle of Savage Station followed. The next day Jackson came up. Lee prepared to make the decisive attack of the campaign. Again, however, there was a delay which put the burden of the battle of Frazier's Farm on Longstreet and Hill alone, with no support from Jackson. On July 1, McClellan was found to be strongly entrenched at Malvern Hill and was struck by Lee's combined forces, acting now in comparative unity for the first time during the entire campaign. The final assault was so long delayed and the position of the enemy

The heavy rain, his extended cavalry, & some infantry, succeeded in keeping from us this information until arrangements could be made to collect our troops in some force, which owing to the battle of yesterday reaching into the night & unfavorable day required some time[2]—The cavalry is in pursuit. Genls. Longstreet & Jackson's commands will be formed to follow him rapidly, while the main body of the army will maintain its position to-day, to take care of the wounded, bury the dead & collect stragglers—Owing to the conflicting reports as to the course the enemy has taken, I have determined to send Genls Holmes & Wise's commands back to Drury's & Chafins Bluffs respectively.[3] Some re-

---

so strong that McClellan could not be dislodged. He retreated during the night.

[2] The final attack was not made until "night was approaching" and "it soon became difficult to distinguish friend from foe" (Lee). In connection with General Lee's statement that he did not promptly receive the news of McClellan's abandonment of Malvern Hill, it may well be noted that Lee regarded "the want of correct and timely information" as a prominent reason for his failure to destroy McClellan (Report, *loc. cit.*, 497).

[3] Chaffin's and Drewry's Bluffs were almost opposite on the south and north sides of the James. The Holmes referred to here was Major-General Theophilus H. Holmes, later lieutenant-general. On Sunday afternoon, June 29, Holmes moved three regiments of Colonel Junius Daniel's brigade, two light batteries and three companies of cavalry to the north side of the James across the pontoon bridge. He was joined the same evening by Brigadier-General J. G. Walker, with his brigade and two batteries. These had previously crossed from the southside on the 26th (Holmes' report,

ports state that a part of the enemy has crossed to the South side of James river with a view of joining Gen¹. Burnside. While from others it appears, he is fleeing down the north bank of the river, covered by his gun boats, to connect with his transports. I enclose you a note just received from Gen¹. Holmes⁴— Can a good commander be procured for Walker's brigade?⁵

I have the honor to be

Yr. obt svt

R. E. LEE

Genl.

No. 11.

HEADQUARTERS

Dᴿ POINDEXTERS HOUSE

3 July 1862.

His Excy JEFF DAVIS
&c &c

Mʳ PRESIDENT

I enclose you recent dispatches received from Gen¹. Stuart¹—They leave little doubt in my mind

---

O. R., 11, 2, 906). Henry A. Wise, on his own responsibility but as Holmes' suggestion, sent two regiments from Chaffin's Bluff—the 26th and 46th Virginia—and two batteries of artillery, Andrews' and Rives', to join Holmes (See Wise's report, *op. cit.*, 2, 916).

⁴ Not found.

⁵ Composed of the 30th Virginia, 3rd Arkansas, 2nd Georgia and 27th, 46th and 48th North Carolina regiments.

¹ Not found. Stuart's report, however (O. R., 11, 2, 519), makes it plain that he had become convinced that the Federals

even as to the possibility of the truth of Gen¹. Mᶜ-
Clellans grand movement across the James river to
Richmond. Such a movement on his part is hardly
possible, but in the uncertainty as to whether they
will be required in advance, I have determined to
retain for the present in their present positions the
commands of Magruder, Huger, D. H. Hill & Ran-
som²—I shall probably myself go farther down the
river in the course of the day, unless other information detains me here—

I have the honor to be

Your obt. servt—

R. E. Lee

Genl.

No. 12.

Headquarters &c

Phillips House

4 July 1862.

His Excy. Jeffⁿ. Davis
   President &c.
Mʳ. President
   I have just returned from examining the ground

---

were still moving toward deep water along the northern bank
of the James and had no intention of crossing.

   ² In other words, instead of sending his army farther down
the river, with no definite ideas as to McClellan's line of movement, Lee preferred to keep the troops where they could easily
be moved across the James in case McClellan proceeded
thither. They might, from the positions which they then
occupied, have been moved back either to the Richmond

at Westover occupied by the enemy.[1] I enclose a rough sketch[2]—The enemy is strongly posted in the neck formed by Herring creek & James river—The creek is not fordable, below where the road crosses it, except for a few hundred years; the rest is marshy & deep—Above it is fordable for infantry for about the same distance—The enemy's batteries occupy the ridge along which the Charles City road runs, north of the creek, and his gunboats lying below the mouth of the creek sweep the ground in front of his batteries—Above his encampments which lie on the river, his gunboats also extend; where the ground is more favorable to be searched by their cannon. As far as I can now see, there is no way to attack him to advantage; nor do I wish to expose the men to the destructive missiles of his gunboats—Our troops are posted in line in his front & closer examinations of the ground are being made.[3]

---

defences or thrown across the James to meet an attack from the southside. It is worthy of note that the movement which Lee here decided that McClellan did not intend to make was precisely that by which a greater general than McClellan, Grant, extricated himself from a situation somewhat similar to that in which McClellan found himself after his assault on Richmond had failed.

[1] Westover on the James, where McClellan made his head-quarters after his retreat from Malvern Hill, was the ancestral home of Colonel William Byrd and was one of the most famous seats on the river. It is still standing and in an excellent state of preservation.

[2] Not found.

[3] Upon his withdrawal from Malvern Hill on the night of July 1, McClellan proceeded to Westover and Harrison's

I fear he is too secure under cover of his boats to be driven from his position—I discover no intention of either ascending or crossing the river at present— Reinforcements have joined him[4] & his sick, wounded and demoralized troops have been sent down the river.[5]

I am most respecty

Your obt servt

R. E. LEE

General.

Landing where his gunboats were already anchored. Though hard pressed by Lee's cavalry, McClellan was greatly pleased at this last phase of the campaign and particularly at the small losses he suffered in men and munitions (McClellan, *Own Story*, 438).

[4] Lee appears to have been mistaken in supposing that McClellan had received reinforcements in any considerable numbers. In his dispatch to Lincoln of July 2, 5:30 P.M. (O. R., 11, 3, 287–88), McClellan says: "I thank you for the reinforcements." But subsequent correspondence makes it seem probable that the only troops who actually joined him at this time were those spared from the crews of his gunboats. For Davis' reply to this dispatch, approving Lee's decision not to attack, see O. R., 11, 3, 631–32.

[5] Appended to the correspondence of this date is the following letter. From its careful preservation, one can estimate the value placed upon it by Mr. Davis. It was captured and sent by General Lee to the President, Aug. 24, 1862 (O. R., 11, 3, 295; 12, 3, 942). For McClellan's reply, see *ibid.*, 11, 3, 306.

HEAD QUARTERS ARMY OF VIRGINIA

WASHINGTON, D. C., July 4 '62

GENERAL

As you have doubtless been informed I was a few days since assigned by the President to the command of the forces &

No. 13.

HEADQUARTERS
ARMY N. V^{A.}
July 9th 1862.

His Excellency President DAVIS
SIR

After a thorough reconnaissance of the position taken up by the enemy on James River, I found him

---

Departments lately under the command of Generals Fremont, Banks & McDowell—I avail myself of the first moment after ascertaining the strength positions & condition of the force thus assigned me to communicate with you—I beg you to understand that it is my earnest wish to co-operate in the heartiest & most energetic manner with you & that there is no service, whatever the hazard or the labor which I am not ready to perform with this army to carry out that object— That you may understand precisely what means are at my disposal for such a purpose & what is expected of me I will proceed to give you in detail all the information which will enable you to understand precisely my situation and the power I have to aid your operations—Do not hesitate to suggest frankly & freely to me any views and wishes you may entertain in regard to the assistance I can give you—Be assured that your suggestions will be received with all kindness & as far as possible adopted,—I am guided & shall be, by an earnest wish to contribute by every possible means within my control to the success of your operations.

You know the history of late peculiar operations in the Shenandoah Valley & that Genl Fremont has retired from his command by reasons unnecessary to set forth. The forces lately under his command & those of Genl Banks all collected in the neighborhood of Strasburg & Middletown—They are greatly demoralized & broken down & unfit for much active service for the present—Of some use they *can* be, but not much

strongly posted and effectually flanked by his Gunboats—In the present condition of our troops I did
not think proper to risk an attack, on the results of
which so much depended—I caused field batteries

for the present—They are scattered about and seem to be in
a constant "stampede"—They number about 23000 men of
all arms—

The Army corps of McDowell is about 19000 strong, is by
far the best, & in fact the only reliable portion of my command
—One Division is at Manassas the other at Fredericksburg—

Genl. Sturgis is in command of the forces within & outside
of the entrenchments near Washington.

They number about 17000 men mostly raw recruits &
fragments of broken regiments in no condition for service—

My first object is to concentrate all these forces as far as
practicable in advance of this place both to put them in
condition for active operations & to have them in hand
—In this arrangement the security of the Valley of the
Shenandoah and of the city of Washington must be held in
view—

I have therefore broken up the Depots on the Ohio river
& on the Baltimore & Ohio road, establishing my depots &
base of operations at Alexandria—I am concentrating the
two corps of Fremont (now Sigel) & Banks at Luray Gap
(Sperryville) Banks about five or six miles east of that place—
The Division of McDowell now at Manassas to move forward
to Warrenton & take post with his cavalry Brigade at Warrenton junction & strong cavalry pickets south of the Rappahannock—The division at Fredericksburg pickets the country
twenty miles in advance of that place—A good stone turnpike
connects Luray with Warrenton—It was my purpose before
the news of your critical situation reached here to concentrate the two divisions of McDowell at Orange Court House,
& the corps of Banks & Sigel at Stannardsville—Thence to
occupy Gordonsville long enough to destroy entirely the
Virginia central road between that place & Hanover Court

to play on his forces, and on his transports, from points on the river below. But they were too light to accomplish much, and were always attacked with superior force by the Gunboats—I have caused the

---

House—& to move in Charlottesville or a point just east of that place with my whole force united—So destroy the railroad between Lynchburg & Charlottesville and also by pushing cavalry in various directions toward it to destroy the railroad from Lynchburg to Richmond—To move down to James river at Columbia & to pursue the north (left) bank of the river toward Richmond at least as far as Tuckahoe creek—To take up a strong position behind that creek & throw bridges over the James river or secure those now existing within the proposed lines so as to be able to return my whole force across to the south side whenever it became necessary—Having secured these objects to aid you in anyway in the immediate operations against Richmond—

The occurrences of the last few days have deranged their plan & I am holding my forces at the points I have designated so as to be able by marching rapidly in Gordonsville & Charlottesville to cut off any force which may penetrate into the Valley of the Shenandoah from the direction of Richmond and at the same time be able to concentrate my whole force rapidly in front of Washington in case of necessity—These positions I shall hold until some definite news is received & some well defined plan of operation and of co-operation be determined on—It seems to me that it will not be difficult for the enemy at Richmond to detach fifty thousand to march rapidly in Washington if it be uncovered by the movement of the forces now under my command—

Much of my cavalry I am keeping in the Valley of the Shenandoah, and as soon as my forces are established as I have designated they will be pushed as far south as Swift run Gap & Harrisonburg—

I have entrenched a Brigade of Infantry with our battery

army to fall back to a position higher up the river, in order to meet the enemy should he again advance on Richmond, leaving the cavalry to watch his movements below—I have returned to my old quar-

---

at Winchester—A somewhat smaller force will be posted in like manner at Romney—The small posts at Clarksburg, Beverly Buckhannon &c all placed under charge of Genl Kelly who has some force also on the railroad—The care & protection of the road has been assigned to Genl Wood so that I am foot loose in that region—I have directed Genl Cox who has about 12000 men in the Kanawha Valley near Lewisburg to maneuvre so as to get Heth & Humphrey Marshall between himself and Lexington or Lynchburg & then to follow them through to Lexington by the Turnpike & open communication with Staunton or Charlottesville abandoning entirely his line to Pt Pleasant on the Ohio & calling in his small posts —Of course this movement will depend upon whether my operations toward Charlottesville and Richmond are carried out—

You now know my position & resources—A moveable force of forty three thousand men (nineteen thousand effective) posted as I have detailed to you are all I have and I am made responsible for the security of this city—

I trust you will communicate your wishes to me & give me the benefit of any views & suggestions which will enable me to aid you—I need not repeat that I stand prepared to do all in my power for that purpose.

I am very respectfully
Your obt servt
JNO POPE
Maj Genl Comd
Army of Virginia

MAJ GENL G. B. McCLELLAN
    Comd Army of the Potomac
       on James river

ters at Dobb's house, & will proceed at once to reorganize our forces for active operations.[1] We have
lost many valuable officers whose places must be
supplied, and our thinned ranks must be filled as
rapidly as possible—

I have the honour to be

Very respectfully

Your obt servt.

R. E. LEE

Gen.

---

[1] The order for "the army to fall back to a position higher
up the river" had been given the previous day, July 8, 1862.
Jackson was to take position on the Mechanicsville turnpike,
north of Richmond, Longstreet on Cornelius creek, between
the Central railroad and James river, D. H. Hill was to resume his former position of the Williamsburg road and Stuart
was left to watch McClellan (O. R., 11, 3, 636–37). As
this dispatch practically concludes the Seven Days' campaign
it may be noted here that General Lee never explained in
detail or complained of the reasons for the miscarriage of his
plans. In a sense he had achieved a most remarkable victory.
McClellan's boasted attack on Richmond had ended in a
hurried retreat and a campaign of conquest had degenerated
into a scamper for the protecting cover of gunboats. The
whole aspect of the war in Virginia had been changed and
the enemy had been driven from positions which they were
not to resume for two years. Yet General Lee insisted in his
published report and critics have maintained ever since that
while much was gained, as much more might have been
achieved. In the opening attack at Gaines' Mill, at the battle
of Savage Station and, to a less degree at Malvern Hill,
golden opportunities, readily discerned by General Lee, had
been lost by lieutenants. Had Lee's campaign been carried
out as planned, it would have been possible with precisely
the resistance encountered, to have virtually annihilated

No. 14.

H^D QRS. DOBBS' HOUSE

To   11th July 1862.

H. E. The President

SIR,

In reference to my conversation with you when I had last the honour of seeing you, should Genl R. H. Anderson be promoted as then recommended,[1] I would respectfully recommend Col: M. Jenkins to be made Brigadier General in his place. Col Jenkins has been repeatedly recommended for promotion by officers with whom he has served, and his conduct at the battle of the Seven Pines, was worthy of all commendation. He has also in the recent battles, shown great skill. Since the battle of the Seven Pines, four Colonels junior to him have been appointed Brigadier Generals, I would therefore suggest if practicable, that Col. Jenkin's promotion be dated from the battle of the Seven Pines,

---

McClellan's army. Alexander, who is in some respects the best critic of this campaign, frankly places the blame for the miscarriage of Lee's plan on General Jackson. He has strong evidence and good reasoning to support his case. Be that as it may, General Lee was certainly disappointed but he refrained from censure and would not be drawn into a controversy with Magruder on the subject. And if Jackson was not himself during this campaign, he more than made amends in that which followed—Second Manassas.

[1] On July 4, 1862, Richard Henry Anderson (see *supra*, No. 3) was promoted major-general and was assigned to the command of a division under Longstreet, composed of Armistead's, Mahone's and Wright's brigades.

31st May, so as to restore him to his relative rank.[2]

I have the honor to be
With high respect
Your obt· Servt
R. E. LEE,
Genl.

No. 15.

Hᴰ Qʀs. 25 July 1862.

His Excel JEFFN. DAVIS
President C. S.
SIR
I have had the honour to receive your letter of today in reference to the disposition of the Louisiana

---

[2] Micah Jenkins of South Carolina (1839–1864) came to Virginia as commander of the 5th South Carolina, D. R. Jones' brigade. He was recommended for promotion by Beauregard and Longstreet but fought R. H. Anderson's old brigade during the Peninsula campaign while ranking as colonel. On July 22, 1862, the commission requested by Lee in this letter was issued Jenkins. His brigade became attached to Longstreet's corps a little later and its commander grew to be a great personal friend of Longstreet. In the second day of the Wilderness fight, May 6, 1864, Jenkins was mortally wounded while riding with Longstreet. The latter (from Manassas, etc., 566) pays this feeling tribute to him: "But Micah Jenkins, who fell by the same fire, was no more. He was one of the most estimable characters of the army. His taste and talent were for military service. He was intelligent, quick, untiring, attentive, zealous in discharge of duty, truly faithful to official obligations, abreast with the foremost in battle and withal a humble, noble Christian. In a moment of highest earthly hope he was transported to

troops. In accordance with what I understood to be your wishes yesterday I had directed the 5ᵗ-6ᵗ-7ᵗ-8ᵗ & 14ᵗ regts; Wheats Battⁿ & Gerardeys field battery to constitute the brigade under Genˡ Taylor with Jackson.[1] If Huger is promoted a Brigadier & Genl. Taylor detached, it will accord with the views of your letter to-day—The 1ˢᵗ 2ⁿᵈ & 10ᵗ regts; the Zouave Chasseurs Col: Coppens the 3ʳᵈ battⁿ Col: Pendleton to constitute the brigade in this Army under such officer as you may appoint[2]—I shall assign it to the division of Genˡ McLaws.

In regard to sending at once the 10th regt: to

---

serenest heavenly joy; to that life beyond that knows no bugle call, beat of drum or clash of steel. May his beautiful spirit, through the mercy of God, rest in peace! Amen!"

[1] In the organization reported July 23, 1862, Richard Taylor's brigade, Ewell's division, T. J. Jackson's "command" (corps) was composed of the 6th, 7th, 8th and 9th Louisiana regiments with the 1st Louisiana special battalion, Captain Harris. The 5th Louisiana was attached to the brigade of General Paul J. Semmes, McLaws' divisions, and the 14th Louisiana was in Pryor's brigade, Longstreet's division. Girardey's battery was with R. H. Anderson's division.

[2] This would have been a brigade drawn from various existing commands. The 1st Louisiana belonged to A. R. Wright's brigade, R. H. Anderson's division, the 2d Louisiana to Cobb's brigade, McLaws' division, the 9th to Taylor's brigade, Jackson's division, the 10th to Semmes' brigade, McLaws' division, Coppens' battalion to Pryor's brigade, Longstreet's division and the 3rd battalion to J. R. Anderson's brigade, A. P. Hill's division. The 3rd battalion became the 15th regiment. The question was finally settled by making the 1st, the 9th, the 15th (3rd battalion), Coppens' battalion and the 2d and 10th into a brigade of McLaws' division.

La: that you must direct as you judge best.   I think though agreeable to the regt: it will create dissatisfaction with those that remain, & establish in other regts: a precedent for granting their claims to return home which have not been recognized.   It will also diminish the strength of this army by 607 good men.[3]

In regard to detaching Gen[l.] Taylor, his presence in La; will no doubt hasten the enrolment & expedite the recruiting of regts: If it should establish his own health, it will be an additional benefit to the service.   I would therefore on the latter ground alone recommend it.[4]   The remnant of Wheats batt[r] had better be placed under Capt. Atkins—

If you have any other directions to give on this subject please state them.

I am most resp[y]

Your obt servt.
R. E. Lee   Genl

No. 16.

Head Quarters
Army N. V[A].
July 25th

His Excellency
    President Davis
M[R] President
    I have read with care the telegram signed J.

---

[3] The regiment remained with the army (S. O. No. 163, A. N. Va., series 1862, paragraph 2, O. R., 13, 3, 656).

[4] General Taylor was Richard Taylor of Louisiana (1826–1879), only son of President Zachary Taylor. He came to

Walker from Hanover Junction [1]—His statements differ from those of two spies (Texans) who arrived from Washington to-day—These say that Pope with the greater portion of his forces is at Warrenton; that there are but three Regiments of infantry about Fredericksburg, (at Falmouth) the cavalry being on this side the river. They estimate Pope's force at about thirty five thousand men, and report about eight thousand men in Washington and Alexandria,— and further that seven heavy guns of the fourteen commanding the approaches to the Long Bridge, have been sent to McLellan since he reached James River. [2]

I have the honour to be
with the highest respect
Your obt servant
R. E. Lee
Genl.

Virginia as colonel of the 9th Louisiana but quickly assumed command of Walker's brigade with which he served through the Seven Days' Battle. On Jackson's recommendation he was promoted major-general. In accordance with this letter, he was sent to Louisiana as commander of the forces in that State west of the Mississippi. In this difficult position he acquitted himself admirably.

[1] Not found.

[2] This is the first letter of the series relating to the Second Manassas campaign. Following the collapse of McClellan's Peninsula campaign, the Federal forces were reorganized for a new attack by way of Northern Virginia. On June 26, Major-General John Pope had been assigned to the command of a new army styled the "Army of Virginia" and composed of the forces under Fremont, Banks and McDowell The immediate purpose of this change was to consolidate the

No. 17.

H^D-QRS: 26^h July '62.

His Exce^l. JEFF^N DAVIS
        President C. S.

MR PRESIDENT
    I enclose for your information a letter from Genl
Jackson.[1] He seems to be of the opinion that he

---

scattered forces and to place under a stern leader soldiers whose
discipline had become lax. The Federal government aimed
to use this army, when ready, to defend Washington in case
Jackson should again advance, to keep the Shenandoah
Valley under Federal control and to harass Lee's line of
communications around Gordonsville. Early in August,
the bulk of McClellan's army was directed to join Pope in
a new forward movement. Before this could be launched,
however, Lee was free from the necessity of watching McClellan and moved northward. The battle of Second Manassas
followed. The spies' information cited by General Lee in
this letter was erroneous in every essential detail. Pope was
in Washington; his main army was around Sperryville, not
Warrenton; instead of three regiments at Fredericksburg,
King's entire division was there. Pope had not 35,000 men
but about 43,000. Others were coming forward.

    [1] Not found, but see Lee's reply, O. R., 12, 3, 917. Pope
began his movement against Gordonsville on July 14 by
ordering Brigadier-General Hatch to advance from Culpeper
with his cavalry and destroy the Virginia Central railroad
around Gordonsville. Hatch understood the order to be for
the advance of his entire command and was so handicapped
by the slow progress of his troops along muddy roads that he
did not reach Madison C. H. until July 17 (O. R., 12, 3,
23–24). In the meantime, on July 13, Lee had ordered
Jackson to proceed from Mechanicsville to Louisa C. H., and
thence to Gordonsville to meet the Federal advance (S. O.

is too weak to encounter Pope & I fear Pope is too strong to be allowed to remain so near our communications. He ought to be suppressed if possible. I would have sent A. P. Hill['s] division as I stated to you, but have no one to command it. Branch is the Senior Brigadier & I cannot trust the division to him.[2] I feel that it will be necessary to reinforce him before he can do anything & yet I fear to jeopardize the division of this army, upon which so much depends.[3]

If the impression made by Morgan in Kentucky could be confirmed by a strong infantry force, it

---

A. N. Va., No. 150, series 1862, par. 3, O. R., 12, 3, 915). Jackson's vanguard reached Gordonsville on July 16 and Jackson himself made his headquarters near-by on July 19 (see his report, O. R., 12, 2, 181). His force at the time consisted of his own and Ewell's divisions. Although Hatch's attempt was abortive, Jackson foresaw a general advance and asked for reinforcements.

[2] Hill's "light division" was sent to Jackson the next day (O. R., 12, 3, 919). The General Branch mentioned here was Lawrence O'Brian Branch of North Carolina (1820–1862) who commanded a brigade composed of the 7th, 18th, 28th, 33rd and 37th North Carolina infantry. The implied criticism of General Branch was doubtless based on that officer's comparative inexperience. It certainly could not have been founded on any distrust of his bravery or ability, for Branch had fought most creditably during the Seven Days' campaign and had led a command conspicuous for its bravery. When Branch was killed at Sharpsburg, the same year, Hill declared "he was my senior brigadier and the one to whom I could have intrusted the command of the division with all confidence" (C. M. H., 4, 299–300).

[3] McClellan, it must be remembered, was still at Harrison's Landing.

would have the happiest effect [4]—If he is obliged to fall back, the reaction may produce the same result as in Mo: Where is Genl Marshall? [5] Now is the time for him to go in—But if Bragg could make a move, [6] or with E. K. Smith & Loring, it would produce a great effect. [7] Do you think anything can be done. I go to Drurys bluff to-day

Very resp^y

R. E. LEE

Genl

No. 18.

H^{D.} Q^{RS.} DEP. N. VA.

30th July 1862.

H. E. The President
     Richmond,
S^R,

   I have the honor to acknowledge the receipt of

---

[4] John H. Morgan, acting brigadier, had left Knoxville on July 4, 1862, with 900 men and had made a most successful raid through those parts of Kentucky under Federal domination. At the time of this letter he had aroused the Federals almost to a panic, had "travelled over one thousand miles, captured 17 towns, destroyed all the government supplies and arms in them, dispersed about 1,500 home guards and paroled near 1,200 troops." His losses had been about 90.

[5] Brigadier-General Humphrey Marshall, a powerful political figure in Kentucky and a great force with the people. He had resigned June 16, 1862, but had been reappointed by Mr. Davis four days later. Cf. Lee to Randolph; Loring to Randolph, O. R., 12, 3, 922.

[6] Braxton Bragg had assumed command of the army of Tennessee on June 17, 1862, and was at this time near Tupelo, Miss., preparing for a campaign into Tennesseee.

[7] E. Kirby Smith was in command of an independent army

the letter of Col. Smith 49th Va. Reg^t referred to me by you.[1]

In reply to a letter from Col. Smith to myself on the same subject, I informed him that I could not detach his reg^t. so as to give him an independent command, and that I could only gratify his wishes so far as to order his reg^t. to the army of Genl. Jackson as soon as an opportunity occurred. I have now written to Col. Smith informing him that I would attach his reg^t. to the brigade of Genl. Early, if that will meet his views.[2] I deem it inexpedient to divide the army by creating independent commands especially at a time when we require the united efforts of all the forces we can collect at the principal points threatened by the enemy. Should you think it proper however to direct that his regiment be detached as an independent command, it will give me pleasure to carry out your wishes.[3]

I have the honor to be,
Very respectfully
Your obt Servt.
R. E. LEE
Genl. Comm.

---

in East Tennessee and W. W. Loring was in command in Southwest Virginia. Both were adjacent to the territory in which Bragg proposed to operate.

[1] Not found.

[2] Smith's command had already been changed from one brigade to another. On the Peninsula defences, the 49th Virginia had been in the brigade commanded by Brigadier-General W. S. Featherstone, Rains' division. During the Seven Days' Fight, it was attached to Mahone's brigade, R. H. Anderson's division. The regiment was later joined to Early's brigade.

[3] Back of this letter and of William Smith's request for an

No. 19.

H$^\text{D}$-Qrs: 31 July '62

His Exce$^\text{l}$. Jeff$^\text{N}$ Davis
        Pres: C. S.
M$^\text{R}$ President

I enclose a letter for your private perusal just rec$^\text{d}$ from Gen$^\text{l}$ Jackson.   He seems to be in trouble about his Cav$^\text{ly}$ Commander.   The field of service will be too extended to be properly superintended by Genl Stuart, unless he is relieved from the command here.[1]   I cannot spare Gen$^\text{l}$ Fitz Lee, as by so doing it will defeat the object of his promotion. Viz his services here.[2]   I have written to Jackson to

---

independent command is a rather interesting chapter in Confederate history.   Smith, who had been Governor of Virginia, was a brave, true man but had not had military experience. At the outbreak of the war, he offered his services to the government and was accepted.   He rose to the rank of brigadier-general and was later named as major-general, retiring to become Governor of Virginia again.   But like so many politicians of his day, he wished the opportunity of distinguishing himself by a separate command.   Thus Wade Hampton, Cobb and Wise all organized "legions" at the first call to arms.   All these separate commands, except those like Mosby's Rangers, were later put into the line and did good service. General Lee steadfastly declined to encourage such separate organizations.   A biography of Smith has been written by J. W. Bell (N. Y., 1891).

[1] The "extended" "field of operations" was from the lower Richmond defences on the James River to the outposts beyond Gordonsville, where Jackson had three divisions.

[2] Fitzhugh Lee, nephew of Robert E. Lee, had been assigned on July 28, 1862, to the command of the second cavalry bri-

know if there is any one in his Command that he would prefer to Robertson. Probably Jackson may expect too much, & Robertson may be preparing his men for service, which I have understood they much needed. With uninstructed officers, an undisciplined brigade of Cav^l is no trifling undertaking & requires time to regulate[3]— Please return me the enclosed letters—

With high esteem   Your obt. servt

R. E. LEE

Genl.

---

gade, comprising the 1st, 3rd, 4th, 5th and 9th Virginia regiments.

[3] The point at issue is not clear, as the letter to Lee from Jackson does not appear. Beverley H. Robertson was a graduate of West Point and had been colonel of the 5th Virginia cavalry. Serving with Jackson in the Valley he had been made brigadier-general after the battle of Kelly's Ford and had been given command of Ashby's famous "Laurel Brigade," reorganized as the 2nd, 6th, 7th, and 12th Virginia cavalry and the 17th Virginia cavalry battalion. It would appear that Jackson was dissatisfied with Robertson's command of his troops and wished him displaced by Col. W. E. Jones. On Aug. 8, General Lee wrote Jackson: "As regards General Robertson, I will to-day see the Secretary of War. That subject is not easily arranged, and without knowing any of the circumstances attending it except as related by you, I fear the judgment passed upon him may be hasty. Neither am I sufficiently informed of the qualifications of Col. W. E. Jones, though having for him a high esteem, to say whether he is better qualified" (O. R., 12, 3, 926). *Cf.* No. 37, *infra.* It should be noted that Robertson acquitted himself gallantly in the Second Manassas campaign and won special mention from General Lee for a gallant charge (*ibid.*, 2, 558–59; for

No. 20.

H^D Qrs: 2 Aug. '62.

His Exce^l. Jeff^N Davis
      Pres: C. S.
MR President

In communicating to Genl McClellan your instructions to me relative to alleged murders Committed, on our citizens by officers of the U. S. Army, in the cases of Wm B. Munford & Col: John Owen &c &c, & in relation to the cartel for a general exchange of prisoners [&]c, would it be proper, or is it your desire, for me to send the copies of those papers, or shall I embody their contents in a letter from myself—

The reason I ask is, if the papers sent me are frw^d—they may carry mine aright. But there may be objections to this course.[1]

I am with great respect

R. E. Lee
Genl.

Robertson's report, see *ibid.*, 2, 746). It is not improbable that Robertson, who retained his command, had experienced difficulty in disciplining the Laurel Brigade which, while brave to the point of foolhardiness, had not previously adjusted itself to the strict regimen of military life.

[1] Davis' instructions were included in his letters of July 31, 1862, and Aug. 1, 1862, the latter covering a letter of June 29, 1862 (O. R., series 2, 4, 630, 635, and 792). These related to murders committed by Federals in New Orleans and Missouri and to violation by the Federals of the cartel for the exchange of prisoners agreed on between Generals D. H. Hill, C. S. A., and John A. Dix, U. S. A.

No. 21.

H^D Q^RS A. N. Va.
4th Aug. 1862.

H. E. The President,
     Sir,
     In reply to your letter of the 2nd inst; I have the
honor to inform you, that upon reflection, I deemed
it proper to embody your letters to myself, in letters
over my own signature, addressed to the Genl.
Command^g U. S. A. I thought this course preferable to sending copies of your letters to the enemy.[1]
     The two communications were sent yesterday
morning by flag of truce.
     I am Sir; very respectfully,
                    Your obt. servt.
                         R. E. Lee
                              Genl.

No. 22.

H^D-Qrs: 14 Aug '62.

His Exce^l Jeff^n Davis
     Pres: of the C. S.
Mr President
     I have made all arrangements for the well being
of the troops around Richmond. I have given

---

[1] Davis in his letter of Aug. 2, 1862 (O. R., series 2, 4, 838),
left to General Lee "the best method of conducting a correspondence relating to military matters." He added: "It was
my intention that copies of the letter . . . should be embodied
in your own letter to the Federal general, but if you think it
better to modify the arrangement I will be glad to have you
do so."

instructions to Genl Smith,[1] & Col: Gilmer[2] in reference to the defences & have placed the former in Command of the troops on both sides of the river— The aggregate of the four divisions, present & absent, amounts to 72.047 men.

From every account that reaches me the enemy is accumulating a large force in Culpeper.[3] Three

[1] Gustavus W. Smith, major-general and senior officer on the James after the removal of a large part of the army to Gordonsville. For Lee's instructions to him, see O. R., 11, 3, 677. General Lee wrote in part: "From your general knowledge of the affairs of this army, its objects and position, I deem no instructions necessary, beyond the necessity of holding Richmond to the last extremity should an attack be made upon it. The lines of defence on both sides of the river should be completed as soon as possible, and every attention given to the organization, instruction and discipline of the troops. . . . Should you be able to ascertain whether General McClellan is diminishing his force at his present position, please let me know and to what points they are being sent. It may be necessary in that event to reduce your force correspondingly or to withdraw it entirely. I wish you to keep this constantly in view."

[2] Colonel J. F. Gilmer, chief of the engineering corps, who was especially instructed to make a careful examination of the fortifications of Richmond and Petersburg (O. R., 11, 3, 668, 679–80).

[3] The movement here outlined marked the beginning of the Second Manassas campaign. When he had retired to Westover and Harrison's Landing at the close of the Seven Days' Fight, McClellan had insisted that if reinforcements were sent him he could march on Richmond and capture the city. While he was arguing the matter with the War Department, Pope was recalled from the West, as mentioned above, and was entrusted with the reorganization of the Federal forces in Northern Virginia. Unable to agree with Halleck, now virtual commander-in-chief, as to the number of new troops

deserters from Burnside came in to-day, & report
that he reached Fred[ericksbur]^g with 12000, &
rec^d 21 regts: after his arrival there. They were
old troops & came via Aquia creek. They did not
know where from. What do you think of the propriety of withdrawing R. H. Andersons division from
here to Gordonsville?[4] It amounts to 13,142 aggregate. This would leave an aggregate here of about

---

necessary to take Richmond, McClellan pleaded for a forward
movement against Lee, who, he insisted, had 200,000 men.
Halleck would not approve such a project and expressed his unwillingness to venture an attack on the line of the James when
he could not promise McClellan the troops the latter insisted
he must have. It was thereupon decided to withdraw the
army from the James and to begin another movement from
the Rappahannock. On August 13, 1862, McClellan began
to send his troops away on transports. In the meantime, as
has been noted, Lee, had sent a part of his forces to Gordonsville to meet the threatened advance from that direction.
Two weeks after Jackson moved, A. P. Hill was ordered to
support him and the two met Pope at Cedar Mountain, repulsed him and won a victory. On the very day that Mc-
Clellan began to withdraw, Longstreet went to reinforce
Jackson. As this letter makes plain, Lee was not sure of the
general advance from the North until about this time, but
he had concluded that McClellan would leave the James
(see O. R., 11, 3, 675–76). As it was necessary, however, to
strike Pope before he became too strong, Lee had to hazard
a possible movement up the James. He felt, in a word, that he
had more to lose by allowing Pope to assemble a large army and
advance from the Rappahannock than he had to risk by leaving only a small force to watch McClellan. This letter is his formal request for authority to make his dispositions accordingly.

[4] Anderson was ordered to withdraw the next day (O. R.,
11, 3, 679).

60,000. In addition to the four divisions above
stated, the two N. C. regts: from Salisbury & Lynchburg are ordered to D. H. Hill.[5] This will add about
1300 men to his strength. I thought they would
do better then, having not yet been in the field &
give them a better opportunity for instruction & to
pass through the camp diseases. I did this in anti-
cipation of the necessity of withdrawing Hill or M̱c-
Laws— Unless I hear from you to the Contrary I
shall leave for G—— at 4 A.M. tomorrow.[6] The
troops are accumulating there & I must see that arrangements are made for the field. I rec^d a letter
from Longstreet to-day requesting my presence.[7]
I will keep you informed of everything of importance
that transpires—When you do not hear from me,
you may feel sure that I do not think it necessary
to trouble you. I shall feel obliged to you for any
directions you may think proper to give.

I learn that Genl Johnston will soon return to
Richmond. He is riding on horseback every day
& he is gaining his strength rapidly.[8]

Wishing you every happiness & prosperity

I am with high esteem

Your obt. servt

R. E. LEE, Genl.

---

[5] The 42nd, Col. G. C. Gibbs, and the 57th, Lt.-Col. H. C.
Jones.

[6] Lee's correspondence of Aug. 15 is dated from Gordonsville.

[7] Not found, but see Lee to Longstreet, Aug. 15, 1862
(O. R., 11, 3, 676).

[8] General Joseph E. Johnston, whom Lee had succeeded
when the former was wounded at Seven Pines.

8 P.M.

P. S.—A note just rec^d from Genl G. H. Hill says
he has sent reliable scouts to ascertain M^cl—'s
[McClellan's] condition, & that there can be no
doubt but that Porters corps has left⁹ REL

No. 23.

GORDONSVILLE
16 Aug '62

His Exce^l JEFF^N DAVIS
      Pres: of the C. States
MR PRESIDENT

I think it certain that Gen^ls Burnsides & King
with their troops from Fred^g have joined Genl Pope
at Culpeper Ct House.¹ Their numbers are variously estimated, reaching as high as 40,000.² Putting them at 20,000, Popes force according to Genl
Jacksons estimate will be between 65,000 & 70,000—
This corresponds with accounts of intelligent men
from Culpeper. Two citizens who had been taken
prisoners made their escape from Culpeper Ct House
yesterday & say from overheard conversations the

---

⁹ This information was correct. Porter's (Fifth) Corps
had started its movement on this date (O. R., 12, 2, 465).

¹ On Aug. 1, 1862, Burnside left Newport News under orders
from Halleck and on the night of Aug. 3 reached Aquia Creek.
He took position at Falmouth, near Fredericksburg, and his
whole command, 12,000 effectives, was in place on Aug. 9
(O. R., 12, 3, 554). He moved forward on Aug. 12. King's
division left Falmouth on Aug. 9–10 and joined Pope late in
the afternoon of Aug. 11 (O. R., 12, 3, 560, 562, 565–66).

² Lee's estimate of 20,000 in the next sentence, was about
correct.

federals estimate themselves at 92,000.[3]   They report nothing but provisions coming by R. R. from
Alex[a] which is constantly arriving—No troops unless
they are drawing men from M[c]Clellan.   I do not see
where they will get them at present.   I hope to
hear every day of Imbodens success in his attempt
on the B. & O. R. R.   He started from Stanton
sometime since with about 600 men & by his own
calculations would have reached the trestle work
four or five days since.   We must make allowance
for delays & difficulties.[4]   I hope he will be in time
to arrest troops from the West— Report from Genl.

---

[3] It is not easy to state precisely Pope's strength from time
to time during this campaign, owing to his habit of consistently
understating his forces.   Longstreet (*Manassas*, etc., 195)
thinks Pope had 63,000 men at the time of battle of Second
Manassas, while Alexander (*Memoirs*, etc., 191) states that
Pope's whole army numbered 90,000.   On Aug. 20, four days
after this letter was written, Pope telegraphed Halleck that
he had 45,000 men for duty (O. R., 12, 3, 603).   This is
manifestly an understatement since McDowell's corps (Third),
which Pope stated to be 18,000 on Aug. 20, reported 23,765
as the aggregate present on Aug. 16 (*ibid.*, 580).   Others
were in proportion to this difference.   In his official report,
Pope stated that his forces on Sept. 1 numbered 62,000
(*ibid.*, 2, 44).

[4] Col. John D. Imboden, commanding the 1st Virginia
Partizan Rangers, had gone into Western Virginia in the hope
of striking the line of Federal communications with the west
by tearing up the Baltimore and Ohio railroad.   He was
joined on Aug. 22 by Brigadier-General A. G. Jenkins; but,
though they met with considerable success, they did not have
enough men to tear up the railroad.   Imboden filed no report,
but see his letter to C. W. Russell, Sept. 1, 1862, O. R., 12,
3, 949 ff.   Jenkins' report is in *ibid.*, 2, 757.

French to-day McClellan is still sending off troops, [5] & I see a letter published in the Phil^a Enquirer of the 13th from its Fort Monroe correspondent, stating that the mail boat from Harrisons landing had reached Old Point 11 Aug. & that the indications were that a movement of the whole or a large part of the army was about taking place. If it was going up the river, I suppose it would have been discovered before this. If down, they must again be about to change their base of operations—It may be that this part of the country is to be the scene of operations. In that event the War will for a season at least be removed from Richmond & I would recommend that the troops be removed too. The Garrisons can be kept up & the defences in every particular perfected. The completion of the Richmond should be pushed forward with all vigour & in a short time she would clear the river. I think the health as well as discipline of the Army will be benefited by a change to the Country from the town & the city itself receive a more healthy atmosphere— If it can be ascertained that McClellan is moving, unless his quarters can be beaten up, I would recommend that another division follow Andersons. [6]

I am with great respect
Your obt servt
R. E. LEE, Genl.

---

[5] *Cf*. S. G. French to S. Cooper, A. G., Aug. 16, 1862: "A lieutenant . . . reports that from 1 P.M. yesterday up to this morning 108 vessels passed down the river and 8 up; only 5 are reported with troops" (O. R., 11, 3, 680).

[6] The last of McClellan's troops left Aug. 16, 1862, the

No. 24.

[Telegram]

Received at Richmond Aug 25
By Telegraph from Jefferson 24   To Presdt DAVIS
            Via Rapidan '25
Have written you my views today and ordered Genl
Smith to join me with all the troops available subject
to Your approval.[1]
23 Coll 92   *[Endorsed]*   R. E. LEE.
    Aug 24, 1862.
        Genl R. E. LEE
        Jefferson, Va.

No. 25.

[Telegram]

Rec'd at Richmond Aug 26, 1862.
By Telegraph from Jefferson 25th
        Via Rapidan 26th
            To Presdt JEFF^N DAVIS
I believe a portion of McClellans army has Joined
Pope expedite the advance of our troops[2]
16 Coll 64   *[Endorsed]*   R. E. LEE.
    Recd Aug 26
        Jefferson, Va
            Augt 25, 1862
                Gen. R. E. LEE.
    In reference to McClellans army

---

date of this letter (see McClellan's report, O. R., 11, 1, 90).
Smith was ordered to send forward his division the next day
(*ibid.*, 3, 680).
    [1] For Davis' answer, see O. R., 12, 994; Aug. 25, 1862.
    [2] Davis hardly credited this report: he said that new troops

No. 26.

HEADQRS DEPT. N. VA.
26 August 1862.

His Excy JEFF[N] DAVIS
President C. S. A.

MR PRESIDENT

I send you herewith a letter written by A. A. Tomlinson an officer of the Federal Army, which was picked up on the road by which they had marched, & which contains some facts in relation to the battle near Cedar run which may be interesting & which shew how they regarded the issue of that engagement.[1]

I would suggest, that as the letter is of wholly a private character, that no publicity be given to the name of the writer, though the facts could be made known if you deem fit for its publication would in all probability injure him without materially benefitting us—

I am very respecty
Your obt svt
R. E. LEE
Genl.

---

had been sent to Point Comfort, but he ordered Hill and McLaws to support Lee. The latter, it need scarcely be remarked, was right in his information: Pope, as has been pointed out, had been heavily reinforced from McClellan.

[1] Tomlinson's letter not found. The battle of Cedar Run or Cedar Mountain was fought Aug. 9, 1862, when Winder's and Hill's divisions under Jackson, supported by Field's and Stafford's brigades repulsed an attack by Banks' corps and drove the enemy back with a loss of about 2,400 men. Tomlinson had probably expressed the amazement of the Federals

No. 27.

[Telegram]

Rec'd at Richmond Aug 28
By Telegraph from 2½ miles of Salem 27
    Via Rapidan 28th
        To Presdt DAVIS
The advance under Genl Jackson last night broke up the Orange and Alexandria R.R. at Bristoe Station capturing three (3) trains of Cars and prisoner's This was Genl Trimbles Brigade captured Manassas taking Eight Guns provisions and prisoner's

    Parts of Hookers and Sickles Brigades have joined Pope at Warrenton from Alexandria.

    Other troops from Acquia I particularly require Hampton's Cavalry expedite the reinforcements ordered.[1]

              R E LEE
              General

63/252
[Endorsed]
    Genl R. E. LEE
      Near Salem.

---

at this unexpected blow and had described movements in a manner prohibited by the army regulations. It was typical of Lee that he had time to think, during this busy week, of the possible hardship to the Federal officer the publication of this letter might work. The writer of the letter forwarded by General Lee may have been Abia A. Tomlinson, later Colonel of the 5th W. Va. infantry, Hayes' brigade, Scammon's division.

    [1] This dispatch spoken of as "not found" in O. R., 12, 3, 946; for Davis' answer, Aug. 28, 1862, see *ibid.*, 946. This action was the first step in the Second Manassas campaign, for which see Dispatch 29 and notes thereto.

No. 28.

[Telegram]

Recd at Richmond Aug   at 9 o'clock.
By Telegraph from Head Quarters
    Manassas Junction
        9 o'clock P.M. 29
            Via Rapidan 30

To Presdt DAVIS

So far this Army has steadily advanced and repulsed the frequent attacks of the enemy.   The line of the Rappahannock and Warrenton has been relieved. Many prisoners are captured and I regret quantities of stores to be destroyed for want of transportation.[1] Anderson not yet up and I hear nothing of those behind.   We have Ewell, Trimble and Taliaferro wounded.   The latter slightly, the others not mortal.[2]

R. E. LEE

67 Coll 268
    J 4

---

[1] Jackson's first attack, it must be remembered, was made without support and in circumstances which made it impossible for him to remove any of the stores the Federals had accumulated.   Bitter were the complaints of the soldiers at having to give to the flames so much that was valuable, both to wear and to eat.

[2] The three officers named were Richard S. Ewell, later corps commander in Lee's army until incapacitated in the early summer of 1864, I. R. Trimble, who was later captured, and W. B. Taliaferro, a Virginian who was subsequently transferred to South Carolina.

No. 29.

HEADQRS. Sept: Nº. VA.
NEAR GROVETON VA.
30 August 1862

His Excy JEFFᴺ DAVIS
    President C. S. A.

MR PRESIDENT

My dispatches will have informed you of the march of this portion of the army. Its progress has been necessarily slow, having a large and superior force on its flank; narrow & rough roads to travel, and the difficulties of obtaining forage & provisions to contend with. It has so far advanced in safety and has succeeded in deceiving the enemy as to its object. The movement has, as far as I am able to judge, drawn the enemy from the Rappahannock frontier and caused him to concentrate his troops between Manassas & Centreville—My desire has been to avoid a general engagement, being the weaker force, & by manœuvring to relieve the portion of the country referred to[1]— I think if not overpowered

---

[1] The significance of General Lee's movements and the wisdom of the plan of campaign he here explains are apparent. Jackson's advance to Cedar Mountain had been a military necessity for the protection of the Virginia Central railroad. It was also made in the hope that the Confederates might meet Pope's advance in detail as it moved from its base to Culpeper. Various delays had, however, brought these plans to naught and, after the battle of Cedar Mountain, had placed practically the whole of Pope's army in front of Jackson. The latter hoped that the Federals would attack, for his position was very strong, but he could not tempt his opponent to take the offensive. Accordingly, on Aug. 12,

we shall be able to relieve other portions of the country, as it seems to be the purpose of the enemy to

Jackson decided to withdraw toward Gordonsville in the hope
that Pope would follow. In such an event Jackson believed
he would have time to fortify himself and could strike Pope
at a distance from his base. Pope seemed inclined to pursue
and would probably have done so, with results that can only
be surmised, had not Halleck put his veto on the plan. As
it was, Pope remained behind the Rapidan and waited for the
coming of McClellan's army. When Lee was advised, on
Aug. 16, that McClellan had withdrawn from the James, he
saw the immediate necessity of striking Pope's line—stretch-
ing from Raccoon Ford on the Rapidan to Robertson's River
—before the seasoned troops from the James could unite with
Pope. Lee planned to take the offensive at once, to cross the
Rapidan, turn Pope's flank and cut off his retreat. Delays in
the advance of the Confederate cavalry and the capture of an
important message prevented such action. But Pope became
alarmed, evacuated his position, crossed the Rappahannock
and took up his line on the north side, where he was practically safe from an attack and could wait in safety for the
arrival of all of McClellan's army. Lee was equal to the emergency and determined to hazard the issue on a single bold
throw. He detached Jackson and Stuart with 24,000 men
on Aug. 25 and sent them around Pope's flank to Manassas
Junction. With the rest of the army, Lee determined to hold
the Rappahannock in case Pope should advance. A more
daring plan was hardly conceivable: Jackson had to march
fifty miles through a rough country while Lee, with less than
half his army, had to face possible destruction. If the march
was prompt and the blow on Pope's flank and rear was decisive, Jackson might so alarm Pope and so threaten his communications as to compel a general withdrawal. But if Jackson
was delayed, if he failed or if Pope's reinforcements came up
too quickly, the annihilation of the divided Confederate
forces was not improbable. Pope learned that Jackson was
moving but did not surmise his destination until the Con-

collect his strength here— This morning General Anderson's division arrived[2] and Col Lee's reserve batteries.[3] The partial contests in which both wings

---

federate forces had passed Thoroughfare Gap and were within striking distance of Manassas. Before Hooker, who was sent to investigate, could locate the Confederates, Jackson destroyed the Federal stores at Manassas on Aug. 27. Pope immediately left his lines and turned to face Jackson, to whom, in the meantime, Lee was sending strong reinforcements under Longstreet. For the moment the campaign hinged on the rapidity with which the two lines could move by different routes to the same point. By the time Pope was ready to attack Jackson, he found the whole Confederate army in his front. The result of the engagements of Aug. 28–30 was a decided victory for the Confederates (Alexander, *op. cit.*, chapter xi.; Longstreet, *op. cit.*, chapters xiii. and xiv.; O. R., 12, 2; Lee's report, *ibid.*, 551 ff.). The letter here printed, written apparently on the morning of the decisive day's fighting, discloses the interesting fact that Lee wished to avoid a general engagement and aimed primarily at relieving the pressure on the Rappahannock. This is contrary to the accepted view that Jackson's advance to Manassas was intended as a general turning movement. From his request for supplies, a little further down in this letter, Lee seemed to think that the engagements through which he was passing were but preliminary to a general offensive campaign.

[2] R. H. Anderson's division, Longstreet's corps, composed of Armistead's brigade (9th, 14th, 38th, 53rd and 57th Virginia regiments and the 5th Virginia battalion), Mahone's brigade (6th, 12th, 16th, 41st and 49th Virginia regiments) and Wright's brigade (3rd, 22nd, 44th and 48th Georgia regiments). These troops had been on the Richmond defences, had been moved to the next base at Gordonsville and were among the last to leave the old line when Lee moved to Manassas.

[3] Stephen D. Lee's battalion, composed of Eubank's, Grimes',

of the army have been obliged to engage has reduced
our ammunition, & the reinforcements seem to be
advancing slowly — I have heard of none on the
road except Gen¹ Ripley,⁴ one mile south of Amissville on yesterday evening— In order that we may
obtain the advantages I hope for, we must be in larger
force; and I hope every exertion will be made to create
troops & to increase our strength & supplies—Beef,
flour & forage may be obtained in the back country by
proper exertions in the different departments; & it
will be far better for us to consume them than to leave
them for the enemy—We have no time to lose & must
make every exertion if we expect to reap advantage—
    I have the honor to be
        With high respect
          Your obt servant
            R. E. LEE
              Genl.

No. 30.
[Telegram]

Recd at Richmond Sept 1st, 1862.
By Telegraph from Hd Qrs Army N. Va.   Groveton
  30th Aug.   10 o'clock P.M.
     Via Rapidan 1st.
          To Presdt DAVIS
This Army achieved today on the plains of Manassas

Jordan's, Parker's and Taylor's Virginia and Rhett's South
Carolina artillery. It is worthy of note that Colonel Lee,
advancing during the night of Aug. 29–30, found himself at
dawn on the scene of the previous day's fight and close to the
Confederate division then on picket duty.
  ⁴ R. S. Ripley of South Carolina who, it would appear, did

a signal victory over combined forces of Genls
McClellan and Pope.   On the 28th and 29th each
wing under Genls Longstreet and Jackson repulsed
with valour attacks made on them separately.   We
mourn the loss of our gallant dead in every conflict
yet our gratitude to Almighty God for his mercies
rises higher and higher each day, to Him and to
the valour of our troops a nations gratitude is
due.[1]

R. E. LEE

82 Coll 328
74
[*Endorsed*]
Aug 29 and 30, 1862
Genl R. E. LEE
Manassas.

---

not arrive in time for the final engagements, as he is not
mentioned in any of the reports.
[1] With the correspondence of this date is filed in the De
Renne papers a copy of Lee's dispatch to Pope, Aug. 31, 1862,
declining a truce but consenting that ambulances be sent to
remove the Federal wounded within their lines.   The copy
is marked "respectfully forwarded for the information of the
War department, Sept. 3, 1862, R. H. Chilton, A. A. G."
Among the dispatches of this period the originals of which
are in the De Renne papers and copies of which are printed
in the Records from the headquarters letterbook appears the
dispatch of Lee to Davis, Chantilly, Sept. 3, 1862.   In paragraph 3, line 12 of the printed text (O. R., 12, 2, 559) the
blanks should read "Jenkins."   The blank in the next line
should read "Means."

No. 31.

[Telegram]

Recd at Richmond Sept 8, 1862
By Telegraph from Montgomery Co., Md.

To Presdt DAVIS

13 miles from Frederick town Md. 6th. [1]

Two divisions of the army have crossed the Potomac. I hope all will cross today navigation of the canal has been interrupted and efforts will be made to break up the use of the Baltimore and Ohio railroad.

R. E. LEE.

[Endorsed]

Sept 6, 1862.
Genl R. E. LEE
near Frederick, Md.

---

[1] On this date General Lee issued his proclamation to the people of Maryland inviting them to unite with the South and thus formally began the Antietam campaign,—the third and not the last that he was to wage within the seven months he commanded the army during 1862. The De Renne correspondence contains the originals of practically every dispatch forwarded by General Lee to the President during the entire progress of the campaign in Maryland. But as all of these are printed in the *Official Records*, they are omitted here. In order not to lose the continuity of Lee's movements, a few words descriptive of the advance into Maryland may not be out of place. The engagement of Aug. 30, the final day of Second Manassas, did not end until 9 P.M., when the last of Pope's routed army was driven beyond Bull Run. Realizing now that what he had expected to be little more than a diversion had become a notable victory, Lee was naturally desirous

of pressing his advantage. But the Stone Bridge had been destroyed and the darkness of the night made the fords uncertain. The next morning the Federals were located at Centreville, in a strong position, from which position Lee prepared to drive them by a turning movement on their right flank, directed along the Little River Turnpike. Again on September 1, Pope paused on the heights of Germantown and struck at Lee's front and right flank in order to cover a general withdrawal, which he completed the same night. "The great advantage of the advance of the army," wrote Lee in summarising his movements, "is the withdrawal of the enemy from our territory and the hurling back upon their capital of their two great armies from the banks of the James and Rappahannock rivers" (Lee to Davis, Sept. 3, 1862). The moral effect of the successive defeats of McClellan and Pope was great: for the first time since the first advance of the Federals, Virginia was practically free of invaders and could breathe easily. Anxious to take advantage of this public confidence, Lee forthwith proposed an invasion of Maryland. It seems perfectly plain from his first dispatch suggesting this advance that he did not anticipate a great victory. He merely believed that if he were to take his army into Maryland, it would have a salutary effect upon that State, would hearten Confederate sympathisers there and might influence the European governments which seemed at the time not unfavorably disposed to a recognition of the independence of the Confederacy. Mr. Davis readily approved the plan. It was announced to the troops. Preparations for the advance were speedily completed and on September 4–7, the first columns, as stated in this dispatch, crossed the Potomac. Lee did not hesitate, in carrying out the plan of an advance, to divide his forces. Jackson was ordered to move on Harper's Ferry where some 12,000 men, from sheer foolhardiness, had been left by the Federals. He was to capture the town and was then to move into Maryland where the rest of the army was expected to be by that time. Unfortunately for Lee, a copy of his plan, addressed to D. H. Hill, fell into Federal hands and was carried to McClellan, restored by this time to command of the army. The Federal commander at once realized that by crossing South Mountain and moving quickly he might be able to divide the two Confederate armies and destroy them. He had merely to cross the mountains before Jackson could come from Harper's Ferry and he would be between Lee's advance and his base of supplies. Ere Jackson could reach Lee, the latter's army might be crumpled up. Or, if this failed, McClellan would still have the advantage of a strong, united army facing two weak opposing armies. Lee did not know that McClellan had captured his letter to Hill, but when he learned on Sept. 13 that Harper's Ferry had not fallen, he saw at once that he must either withdraw to the Potomac or so strengthen the forces holding the gaps in the mountains as to prevent the Federals from crossing. He at once dispatched Longstreet to reinforce Hill at Turner's Gap. After a sharp engagement on Sept. 14, the Federals forced their way over the mountains and advanced to cut off Lee. But the latter, fully apprised of his danger, lost no time in falling back to Sharpsburg (Antietam), before the Federals could cut him off. Fortunately for the Confederates, Harper's Ferry surrendered on the morning of September 15, with 12,000 prisoners, thousands of small arms, 73 pieces of artillery and many stores. Leaving only the necessary guard at Harper's Ferry, Jackson at once pushed forward to join Lee. The latter was now in a strong position around the village of Sharpsburg and was at least safe from immediate destruction. By the time his supporting columns reached him on the morning of September 17, he had approximately 50,000 men,—sufficient to hold off the 75,000 whom McClellan had available on the field. The battle which followed witnessed probably the heaviest losses of any single day's fighting during the war, but its close left Lee in his original position, thanks to the arrival of A. P. Hill at a time when the Federal attack was hottest. At a council of war held that night, many of Lee's lieutenants were for a retreat across the Potomac, but they could not prevail upon the commander-in-chief, who was con-

fident that McClellan would not renew the attack the next
day. He seems even to have contemplated a movement
beyond the Federals' right in an effort to double them up but,
Longstreet alleges, was dissuaded by him. Lee waited a full
day for a renewal of the attack and then withdrew across the
Potomac without difficulty. He had suffered heavily and
some of his best regiments had been practically destroyed,
but he was still intent on taking the offensive. On Sept. 21,
he wrote Davis: " . . . it is still my desire to threaten a
passage into Maryland, to occupy the enemy on this frontier,
and if my purpose cannot be accomplished, to draw them into
the Valley where I can attack them to advantage." Few
campaigns of General Lee have been more minutely discussed
than this, and few of his dispositions have been more severely
criticised than those by which he hazarded the existence of
his army by dividing it. General Longstreet, who was never
lacking in ability to view an event in retrospect, states that
he opposed the plan and expected disaster from it. On the
other hand, it must be remembered that the acute danger to
which Lee's army was subjected on September 14 and 15 was
due not so much to the daring of his plan as to its accidental
detection by McClellan. There is little reason to believe that
McClellan would have moved against the passes in South
Mountain with even the tardiness he displayed, had he not
had General Lee's own statement as to the position of his
forces. But for this accident, it is not improbable that Jackson would have joined Lee after the capture of Harper's Ferry
and would have united with him in an offensive movement
the results of which might have been highly advantageous.
It is true that Lee took chances. But it is also true that he
won the first advantage in the Seven Days' Fight, the decisive
victory at Second Manassas and the no less decisive triumph
at Chancellorsville by taking at least equal chances. Lee's
congratulatory order to the army, at the end of the campaign,
is not a boastful summary of its achievements: "Since your
great victories around Richmond, you have defeated the enemy
at Cedar Mountain, expelled him from the Rappahannock,

No. 32.

[*Telegram*]

Recd at Richmond, Oct. 28, 1862.

By Telegraph from Hd Qrs A. N. W. 28

To His Excellency The Presdt JEFF DAVIS.

Your dispatch of 25th[1] rec'd will make the arrangement you desire as soon as practicable.

R. E. LEE.

15/160 Coll free from S.

[*Endorsed*]

Oct. 28, 1862

Genl R. E. LEE.

---

and, after a conflict of three days, utterly repulsed him on the plains of Manassas and forced him to take shelter within the fortifications around his capital. Without halting for repose, you crossed the Potomac, stormed the heights of Harper's Ferry, made prisoners of more than 11,000 men and captured upwards of 75 pieces of artillery, all their small arms and other munitions of war. While one corps of the army was thus engaged, the other insured its success by arresting at Boonesborough the combined armies of the enemy, advancing under their favorite general to the relief of their beleaguered comrades. On the field of Sharpsburg with less than one-third of his numbers, you resisted from daylight until dark the whole army of the enemy and repulsed every attack along his entire front of more than 4 miles in extent. The whole of the following day you stood prepared to resume the conflict on the same ground and retired the next morning without molestation across the Potomac. . . . History records few examples of greater fortitude and endurance than this army has exhibited. . ." (G. O. 116, A. N. Va., Oct. 2, 1862; O. R., 19, 2, 644).

[1] In his dispatch of Oct. 25, General Lee warned the government against attacks on the Petersburg and Weldon Railroad

No. 33.

[*Telegram*]

Recd at Richmond Nov. 20, 1862.

By Telegraph from Fredericksburg 20 To His Excellency JEFF DAVIS

I think Burnside is concentrating his whole army opposite Fredericksburg.[1]

R. E. LEE.

10/130 pd
D Mc.

[*Endorsed*]

Nov. 20, 1862
Genl R. E. LEE
FREDERICKSBURG

(O. R., 1, 19, 681). Davis' dispatch to Lee, which has not been located, may have related to the same subject.

[1] The De Renne correspondence contains nothing of importance on the brief but brilliant campaign that ended hostilities for the year in Virginia. McClellan seemed bewildered after the battle of Antietam by the "tremendous strength" of the Southern army and insisted that he could not advance without heavy reinforcements and supplies. Given these, he proposed a plan based upon the disposition of Lee's army after the return to Virginia. Probably in accordance with his announced purpose of drawing the enemy into the Valley—a fact that seems to have been overlooked by most critics of the campaign—Lee divided his forces. Jackson he sent into the Valley, between Winchester and Strasburg; Longstreet he placed at Culpeper. McClellan learned of this and suggested that he make an effort to attack Lee in detail, using against the Southern commander the tactics so disastrously employed by Lee at Second Manassas. It seems probable, Longstreet to the contrary nowithstanding, that Lee would have liked nothing better than that McClellan advance into

No. 34.

[Telegram]

FREDERICKSBURG [, Nov.] 25 [, 1862]
To Col. [JOSIAH] GORGAS
What long range guns on siege carriages can you
send me from Richmond?[1]

R. E. LEE

---

the valley after Jackson. He certainly was not as much
concerned at the Federal plan as Longstreet would indicate.
In any event, he was saved such a campaign by the removal
of McClellan from the supreme command and the elevation of
Ambrose E. Burnside, one of the most gallant but clearly
the most incapable of all the captains who opposed Lee. The
lines had gradually been withdrawn as the fall went by and
the Federals were again on Virginia soil. Burnside promptly
rejected McClellan's plan, wasted his cavalry in futile diver-
sions and moved on Fredericksburg as his prospective base
for a new march on Richmond. He predicted that he would
eat his Christmas dinner in Richmond, but his high hopes only
aroused ridicule in the enthusiastic Confederate ranks. The
campaign that followed was short and disastrous. Burnside's
movements, as indicated by the dispatch here printed, were
anticipated by Lee, who moved his army gradually along the
Rappahannock and took up a position on the hills just south
of Fredericksburg. With amazing recklessness, Burnside
threw his army across the river and without any coherent
plan assaulted Lee's fortified position on December 13, 1862.
The Federals showed noble dash and courage but they were
mowed down by brigades. After a single day's fighting,
Burnside abandoned the effort and gave Lee little trouble
during the rest of the winter. The Federals admitted a loss
of 1,284 killed, 9,600 wounded and 1,769 missing; the Confederate loss was but little more than one-third as heavy.

[1] Gorgas, chief of ordnance and one of the most valued of
the Confederate officers replied as follows: "We have two

[*Endorsement of Dispatch No. 34*]
  Nov. 25/62
    Telegrams
Genl LEE to Col GORGAS
Col GORGAS to Genl LEE
  President's despatch letter book Page 222

No. 35.

CAMP FRED^G 6 Jany 63.

M^R. PRESIDENT

Allow me to congratulate you & the country upon your safe return to Richmond.[1]   I trust your health has been invigorated,[2] & that you have enjoyed great satisfaction as well as comfort from the condition of affairs in the great west.   I know that your visit has inspired the people with confidence, & encouraged them to renewed exertions & greater sacrifices in the defense of the Country, & I attribute mainly the great victory of Genl Bragg to the courage diffused

---

thirty pounder Parrott guns on the lines.   No others disposable."   The reply is on the same sheet with the telegram from Lee.

  [1] Just before the battle of Fredericksburg, Mr. Davis began a somewhat extended tour of Tennessee and Alabama.   He returned to Richmond early in January.   Lee's correspondence with him during this time was carried on through the Secretary of War (See O. R., 1, 21, 1062 ff.).   Mr. Davis resumed direct correspondence with General Lee on January 12, 1863 (*ibid.*, 1088).

  [2] Mr. Davis had suffered severely during the autumn of 1862, particularly with his eyes.   His general physical condition was poor.

by your cheering words & presence.[3]   I hope it will result in driving the enemy beyond the Ohio. We have also much to do in the East. My letters to the Dept. will inform you of the condition of affairs here. I am more uneasy at the state of affairs in North Carolina. Wilmington which I think is the real point of attack ought to be defended to the last extremity.[4] It can be reinforced by Beauregard, & North Carolina ought to turn out every man in the State for its defence & the protection of its Eastern frontier.[5] Genl D. H. Hill is suffering greatly in health, & seems depressed in spirits.[6]   Do you think he could be of service in arousing his people & in calming conflicting political views, which the Secy of War & Genl G. W.

---

[3] The reference is doubtless to the battle of Murfreesboro, fought Dec. 31, 1862, though this could hardly be viewed as a "great victory."

[4] This policy, it will be recalled, was adopted and the defence of Wilmington was one of the most vital features of the Confederate military programme.

[5] Lee had been relying upon the help to be given by North Carolina for several weeks. *Cf.* his letter to G. W. Smith, *ibid.*, 1060, Dec. 12, 1862: ". . . As regards Wilmington, troops from South Carolina could be thrown there upon an emergency, and recalled to their position when no longer required.   But I have been in hopes that North Carolina would turn out all the troops within her borders at this time, and which could operate to such advantage on her eastern frontier.   I think that if you will write to General Martin, he will make an effort to have this done. . . ."

[6] General Hill had three horses killed under him at Sharpsburg and had been at Fredericksburg.   He was sent to North Carolina in accordance with the suggestion in this letter (see O. R., *loc. cit.*, 1093; S. O., 1863, No. 14, §1).

Smith seems to think threaten disastrous consequences? If so I will detach him from this army. I know you will have much to occupy your attention. I will not trespass farther on your time, but wishing you all happiness & prosperity, & many returns of the New Year, remain with great esteem, your obt. servt

R. E. LEE

His Exc^y Jeff^N Davis
Pres: of the Confed. States.

No. 36.

HEADQUARTERS AN VA.
Jan 11th 1863.

His Excellency
President JEFFERSON DAVIS
MR PRESIDENT

I have the honour to have received your letter of 7th inst, with the two inclosures from Col. Imboden. In accordance with your instructions I have addressed a communication to Gen. Halleck upon the subject, a copy of which I enclose herewith. I have taken the liberty of extending the time for his response to ten days, as I ascertain that five days would be too short a period for the investigation to be made, and the reply to reach this point.[1]

I have the honour to be
Very respectfully
Your obt servt

R. E. LEE
Genl.

---

[1] This correspondence related to General Milroy's so-called assessment orders, references to which are given in a note in

No. 37.

H^D-QRS: FRED^G 24 Feb^y '63

His Excy JEFF^N DAVIS
    Pres: C. S. RICHMOND VA:
MR PRESIDENT

Before selecting a camp of refreshment for Genl
Hamptons brigade,[1] Genl Stuart was directed to
cause an examination to be made to ascertain where
forage could be procured.[2] The object was to place

O. R., 1, 21, 1054. On Jany. 10, 1863, General Lee wrote
Imboden: "With regard to the orders of Milroy, you must
endeavor to repress his cruelties as much as possible. I will
recommend to the Secretary of War that prisoners taken from
his command be not exchanged, but held as hostages for the
protection of our citizens (O. R., loc. cit., 1086). Again
on Jany. 20, 1863 (ibid., 1102), Lee wrote Imboden: "By the
direction of the President, I have written to General Halleck
on the subject of Milroy's orders. He replies that these
orders are unauthorized, and if on investigation he finds them
authentic, he will order Milroy to change his course. I do
not think retaliation upon the Union people of the northwest
would help our cause in that region." A copy of Lee's letter
to Halleck, Jany. 10, 1863, is in this collection, certified by
W. H. Taylor, A. A. G.

[1] Hampton's brigade, as reported in the organization of the
Fredericksburg campaign, was composed of the following
regiments: 1st N. C., Col. L. S. Baker; 1st S. C., Col. J. L.
Black; 2nd S. C., Col. M. C. Butler; Cobbs's (Georgia) Legion,
Lieut.-Col. P. M. B. Young; Phillips' (Georgia) Legion, Lieut.-
Col. W. W. Rich (O. R., 21, 544).

[2] Correspondence with J. E. B. Stuart not found. Genl.
Stuart, by orders of Feb. 13, 1863, had been directed to begin
independent cavalry movements in the Valley against Genl.
Milroy (O. R., 25, 2, 621).

it in a region containing forage, the consumption of which would not interfere with the supplies for the rest of the army.   The Staff officer sent to Page Co. reports favourable.   It is contiguous to Culpeper, but one County intervening,[3] has not been occupied by troops & the consumption of the forage there does not affect the supply for the main army.   The brigade is relieved from duty at present.   I should think the horses would recuperate sooner than if sent at this time to N. C.   Corn can be procured in Eastern N. C. but the chief Q^rM^r of the Army informs me long forage is scarce.   Genl Hampton's brigade was originally assigned to duty in Culpeper because it was the most important line— It was the largest brigade & he was the Senior $Brig^{r4}$— There has been great scarcity of forage in the whole army, & it requires the greatest care of officers & men to keep the horses in condition.   The horses in best condition in the Army are those of Genl W E Jones[5] in the Shenandoah Valley— It is my great desire to recuperate the Cav^y & if I know where in Eastern N. C. Hamptons brigade could be better provided, would gladly send it

---

[3] Rappahannock, with easy passes through the Blue Ridge.

[4] The four brigades of Maj.-Gen. Stuart's cavalry division at this time were those of Wade Hampton (organization as above); of Brig.-Gen. Fitzhugh Lee (1st, 2nd, 3rd, 4th Virginia, and 5th Virginia during part of the autumn); of Brig.-Gen. W. H. F. Lee (2nd N. C. and 9th, 10th, 13th and 15th Va.) and of Brig.-Gen. W. E. Jones (6th, 7th, 12th Va. regiments and 17th Va. Battalion, Lieut.-Col. Funston, and Maj. E. V. White's battalion of Virginia cavalry).

[5] William E. Jones was a native of Washington County, Virginia, and was born in May, 1824.   Educated at Emory

there. It will not be more than a month before it will be again wanted. Fitz Lee's brigade is on the upper Rapp^k & W^m. F. Lees on the lower^6

I am with great respect

Your obt servt

R. E. LEE

Genl

No. 38.

H^D-QRS: FRED^G 7 March '63

MR PRESIDENT

I have conversed with Col Lee in reference to the

---

and Henry College, he graduated at West Point in 1845, served in the extreme west during the years before the war, but retired from the army ere hostilities began. He raised a company of cavalry before the ordinance of secession was passed and was at First Manassas. His subsequent military record was brilliant and his services at Brandy Station and during the Pennsylvania campaign were particularly notable. He was killed in battle, June 5, 1864. The brigade to which reference is here made was the famous Laurel Brigade, formerly commanded by Robertson and composed largely of men who had been with Turner Ashby in his memorable early campaign (see C. M. H., 3, 616 ff.).

^{6} Hampton's brigade richly deserved the rest General Lee planned for them. In addition to serving in the great campaigns of the year, these men had been engaged in a number of small engagements and skirmishes, including those at Dumfries, Dec. 12; at Dumfries and Fairfax Station, Dec. 27–29, at Hartwood Church, Nov. 28 and at Occoquan, Dec. 19, 1862 (see Hampton's reports, O. R., 15, 690, 695, 735). The achievements of this and the other cavalry brigades were made the subject of a general order to the Army of Northern Virginia, Feb. 28, 1863 (O. R., loc. cit., 1114). "These

proposed organization of the Art^y for this Army.[1]
I have considered the subject well & it is the best plan
I can submit. I had hoped to have gotten your views
on the subject, but finding I could not leave my post,

---

deeds," announced Lee, "give assurance of vigilance, activity,
and fortitude and of the performance of still more brilliant
actions in the coming campaign."

[1] Probably G. W. C. Lee, General Lee's eldest son, for some
time aide to President Davis. Colonel Stephen D. Lee,
later lieutenant-general, the only other officer to whom General
Lee might have reference, had left the Army of Northern
Virginia in the fall to go to Vicksburg. From this letter it
would appear that President Davis had sent Colonel G. W. C.
Lee to General Lee's headquarters to discuss the proposed
organization of the artillery. The subject was one which
had been carefully considered and matured with no little
difficulty. On Feb. 11, after conference with Cols. S.
Crutchfield and E. P. Alexander, Brig.-Gen. W. N. Pendleton forwarded to General Lee an elaborate plan for the
"better organization of our artillery" (O. R., 25, 2, 614 ff.).
In this plan, General Pendleton explained the respects in which
a battalion organization of the artillery was preferable to the
regimental system, though his arguments are not the same
as those advanced in this letter. With his plan, General
Pendleton submitted a list of artillery officers for whom promotion, transfer, etc., was proposed, which list is extremely interesting in the estimate it places on the different officers. Four
days later (Feb. 15, 1863) in G. O. No. 20, General Lee promulgated the substance of this plan to the army, though he
did not name the company officers or announce the promotions. The next day (O. R., loc. cit., 628) General Pendleton
proposed some minor changes and asked General Lee's construction of the law governing the number of officers he might
have (see note 3 below). On the 19th (ibid., 633), General
Lee wrote Jackson and probably Longstreet asking their
opinion and comment on the changes. In his reply, General

& wishing to get the Art^y in the most efficient condition before the opening of the campaign thought it best not to delay. Any improvement you may suggest, I shall be thankful for. I think the batt^n organization for Art^y better than the regimental.

Jackson forwarded the statement of his chief of artillery, Col. S. Crutchfield, and made objection to some features of Pendleton's plan on the ground that he wished to remain with him and to have promoted those artillery officers who had seen service in his corps. In particular, he objected to the promotion of Maj. H. P. Jones and Capt. J. G. Barnwell. General Longstreet, in a letter of Feb. 24, 1863 (*loc. cit.*,641),approved the recommendations of General Pendleton, thought it best that the senior captain of the Washington artillery should be promoted and asked General Lee to wait until the opinion of Colonel Walton could be given. On Feb. 27, 1863, General Lee replied to General Jackson that he did "not concur altogether with the principle there laid down [in Jackson's letter] regulating claims to promotion. I think the interest of the service, as well as justice to individuals, requires the selection of the best men to fill vacant positions." Jackson's reply was rather crisp (*ibid., loc. cit.,* 645–46). He apparently withdrew his objection to Major Jones and hoped that "Captain Barnwell will not be promoted into the artillery of my corps. I know nothing of his qualifications." He added significantly: "I have had much trouble resulting from incompetent officers having been assigned to duty with me regardless of my wishes. Those who assigned them have never taken the responsibility of incurring the odium which results from such incompetency." To this General Lee apparently made no reply, but from correspondence between Crutchfield and Jackson it appears that the promotion of Major Jones was acquiesced in by Crutchfield and Jackson (*loc., cit.,* 655). On March 2, General Lee communicated the proposed organization to President Davis and raised the question as to the number of officers to be commis-

Two field officers to a batt[n] in my opinion are necessary. Any one of the proposed batt[ns] in time of
action, occupy a greater space, require more care &
attention, & are more difficult to command in time of
battle, than a regt: of Inf[y], which experience shows
require three field officers. The two batteries have
frequently to be detached— If you have not an officer
of judgment & experience to send forward select the
position, prepare the way &c., the captains have to
leave their batteries or lead them blindly forward.
This results in exposure or delay. A Captain should
always be with his battery. The six Comp[y] batt[ns]
would be better with three field officers. I did not
wish to fill every post, but to leave opening for promotion. The Art[y] officers deserve great credit for their
Conduct & advancement in their profession. They
have rec[d] but little promotion in comparison with
other arms— Young Inf[y] and Cav[y] officers have
sprung into Brigadier & Major Gen[ls][2]— But if the
law does not allow the officers as proposed, that puts

---

sioned for these commands (O. R., *loc. cit.*, 651). It was
probably in response to this letter that Colonel Lee was sent
to discuss the matter with him, after which conference this
letter was written.

[2] This was notably true. Promotions in the artillery
service were so slow that colonels in this army were frequently
outranked by men who had been captains at the time the
artillery officers received their three stars. It is worthy of
comment, however, that in the Army of Northern
Virginia, artillery officers, regardless of rank were highly
esteemed and had splendid opportunities for detached
service. Incidentally, the standard of efficiency was very
great.

an end to the subject.[3] I thought I had kept below
the limit of the law. According to my acceptation
of its provisions, the 264 guns would authorize 11 Lt
Cols: In the proposed organization only 7 were provided for. I was undetermined as to which of the
majors was most entitled to promotion at the date
of my former letter. Since then, upon the recommendations of Col Crutchfield, Genl Pendleton &
Genl Jackson, I have concluded that Major H. P.
Jones should be.[4] I therefore request if it can be
done, that he be promoted to Lt. Col; This will
give 8 Lt Cols; & leave 16 majors— The latter is the
exact number authorized for 264 guns. The captain
of the Washington Art[y] proposed to be promoted was
not named in my former letter— Genl Longstreet
desired Major Walton[5] to select him, & he is still

---

[3] General Lee refers to this law in his letter of March 2
(*loc. cit.*) as "act No. 39, approved January 22, 1862." The
position he takes in his construction of this act is that of Pendleton in his letter of Feb. 16, 1863. Pendleton said: "The
law authorizes field officers in the proportion of a major for
every sixteen guns, a lieutenant-colonel for every twenty-
four, a colonel for every forty and a brigadier for every eighty.
Does not this permit us to have 6 colonels, 11 lieutenant-
colonels and 16 majors? The 6 colonels we have; of lieu-
tenant-colonels we have only 8. . . . Of majors we should
have just 16."

[4] Hilary P. Jones appears as lieutenant-colonel of Jones'
battalion, artillery, second corps, in Special Orders 106,
par. 14; April 16, 1863. His batteries were Carrington's,
Garber's, Latimer's (Tanner's) and Thompson's. He was
attached to Ewell's corps after Jackson's death.

[5] General Lee gives Walton the wrong title here, though he
states it correctly later in the dispatch. J. B. Walton was

absent. I fear by this means the Louis[a] captain
will lose rank. They are all good officers—Gen.
Longstreet thinks the Senior, which is Capt Eshel-
man,[6] should be promoted. From all that I have
heard my own impression is that Capt W. C. Squires
is the better officer.[7] I wish Col: Walton was here
to decide the matter.

You are aware that the present law authorizes you
to appoint a Brig[r] Genl for every 80 guns. That
would give three for this army. I named no one for
the positions, for I wished to consult you first on the
subject. I presume from what I have heard that
applications will be made to you, & to prevent annoy-
ance it may be better to consider the matter. Genl
Elzy if his health & habits do not interfere would
make a good chief of Art[y]— He has always been in
that service— Is brave & attentive & ought to be well
informed. My opinion is based upon my acquaintance
with him in his early service. Since the Mexican

Colonel, commanding the Washington artillery, the reserve of
Longstreet's corps. It was to him that Longstreet wrote the
famous "Let the batteries open" order of July 3, 1863 (*From
Manassas*, etc., 390).

[6] The name is usually spelled Eshleman, the officer being
B. F. Eshleman, senior captain, 1st company, Washington
Artillery.

[7] The initials are "W. C." in the *Official Records*. Of him,
in his letter of Feb. 11, Pendleton wrote "Captain Squires is
understood to have been especially recommended for promotion by Colonel Walton. He would, no doubt, make a good
field officer for this battalion." Neither Eshleman nor
Squires was immediately promoted, though Eshleman later
became major.

War I have seen little of him. If the law allows, he might be assigned with his present rank. Gen'l Pendleton could be assigned to Jackson's corps—[8] Genl Longstreet would recommend Col: Walton for his corps. Col: Walton is a brave steady & good officer in battle & maintains good discipline in his batt^n. I could not say from my own knowledge that he is the best selection for the place. His knowledge of Art^y especially its science, must be limited, & I think his knowledge of ground defective, & his selection of positions not good.[9] I have had during the past campaign, before & in battle to employ Col Long in selecting positions for Art^y examining fields &c &c. I consider him better qualified for those

---

[8] This is Arnold Elzey, later major-general, a native of Maryland (b. 1816) and a West Point graduate of the class of 1837. He had been an artillery officer during the Seminole and Mexican wars and had been promoted brigadier-general on the field of First Manassas for gallantry in action. He had been wounded during the Valley campaign, while he was serving with Jackson, and had been sent to command the Richmond defences. General Lee doubtless remembered Elzey's former connection with Jackson's command in recommending him for service with that officer. A little later (May 4, 1863) General Lee recommended Elzey to take command of Trimble's division. General Elzey was not sent forward to General Lee on either request, but served continually around Richmond until practically incapacitated by a serious face wound at the battle of Cold Harbor. He recovered and commanded the artillery of Hood's army during the Tennessee campaign (see C. M. H., 2, 157 ff.). Elzey died in Baltimore in 1870.

[9] Colonel J. B. Walton, mentioned above, commander of the Washington artillery. Colonel Walton was not promoted, though he served gallantly.

duties than any officer with me, & would make a
better Genl of Art^y— I know the difficulty of appointing him, & the objection to taking any one in his
position & promoting them over men serving in the
field. Yet he is the best man I can name—¹⁰   I have
written down hastily the above remarks for your
consideration. I regret I have not time to condense
them—

I remain most resp^y your
Exc^y obt servt.

R. E. Lee
Genl.

His Exc^y Jeff^n Davis
Pres: C. States.

No. 39.

H^d-q^rs: 11 March '63.

Mr President

I have rec^d your despatch of yesterday & will
comply with your instructions as soon as possible.¹
The Storm of yesterday which is still raging, will so
much augment the difficulties of transportation, that

---

¹⁰ This was Colonel A. L. Long, later chief of artillery,
second corps; at this time General Lee's military secretary.
To him the country owes the *Memoirs of General Lee*, a well-
known biography, written when General Long was blind.

¹ Not found. The *Official Records* contain no correspondence for these days other than order for an independent movement by General John D. Imboden, which was postponed until
April 20. No action of importance occurred during March
except the engagement at Kelly's Ford on the 17th, for which
see Stuart's report and enclosures, O. R., 25, 1, 58.

I wish to see that the necessary provisions & forage can be supplied to the Army. It may require till the end of the week

I am with great respect
Your obt servt
R. E. LEE
Genl

His Exc^y JEFF^N DAVIS
Pres: Conf. States.

No. 40.

CAMP NEAR FRED^G 21 March '63

MR PRESIDENT

Upon an examination of the Senate bill presented by Genl Sparrow for the organization of the staff of the army, I think some changes might be made to advantage.[1] These will readily occur to you & I will therefore allude to them generally. I think it important & indeed necessary to simplify the mechanism of our army as much as possible, yet still to give it sufficient power to move & regulate the whole body. Our armies are necessarily very large in comparison with those we have heretofore had to manage. Some of our divisions exceed the army Genl Scott entered the city of Mexico with, & our brigades are larger than his divisions. The greatest difficulty I find is in causing orders & req^ns to be obeyed. This arises not from a spirit of disobedience, but from ignorance.

---

[1] Printed in O. R., series 4, 2, 447, but entered here as illustrative of the problems of organization confronting General Lee in the winter of 1862–63.

We therefore have need of a corps of officers to teach others their duty, see to the observances of orders, & to the regularity & precision of all movements. This is accomplished in the French Service by their staff corps, educated instructed & practised for the purpose. The same circumstances that produced that corps exists in our own army. Can you not shape & form the staff of our army to produce equally good results? Although the staff of the French army is larger than that proposed by Senate bill, I am in favour of keeping ours down, as it is so much easier to build up than to reduce, if experience renders it necessary. I would therefore assign one Genl Off^r to a Genl Comm^g an army in the field, & give to his Inspr Genl, Q^r Mr Genl, Comm^g Genl, Chief of Ordnance & Med^{cal} Director provisional grade of Col: of Cav^y—I would reduce his aids & give to his chief of staff & Insp^r Genl assistants, or they will never be able to properly attend to their outdoor & indoor work, which from the condition of our army, as before stated is very heavy. I would apply the same principles to the division & brigade staff— placing their chiefs on an equal footing & giving each a complete organization in itself, so that it can manuevre independently of the corps or division to which it is habitually attached, & be detached with promptness & facility when required. Each therefore in addition to its Genl Staff should have a surgeon, Q^r M^r & Commd^{d}'s ordnance officer— If you can then fill these positions with proper officers, not the relatives & social friends of the Comm^{ds}—who however agreable their Comp^y are not always the most useful

you might hope to have the finest army in the world—
I beg you will excuse the liberty of my suggestions,
& believe me with great respect

Your obt svt

R. E. LEE
Genl.

His Excel JEFF^N DAVIS
Pres. C. S.

No. 41.

[Telegram]

HEAD QUARTERS FREDS. 26th March 63
Genl S COOPER
Adjt Insp. Genl RICHMOND, VA.
Gen,

On the 25th inst. Capt John S. Mosby attacked
and routed a body of the enemy's cavalry, on the
little river turnpike, near Chantilly. He reports ten
killed and wounded, and a Lieutenant and thirty-five
men, with their horses, arms, and equipments captured. He sustained no loss.[1]

I have the honour to be

Your obedt Servant

(Signed) R. E. LEE
Genl.

[Endorsed]
Genl LEE
Hd Qrs Fredericksburg
March 25, 1863

---

[1] For Mosby's report, see O. R., 25, 2, 71–73.

No. 42.

[Telegram]

Recd at Richmond April 2, 1863
By telegraph from Fredericksburg 2
                    To His Excellency JEFF DAVIS
    I believe Burnside with his corps has gone to
Kentucky.[1] He has assumed Command of Depart-
ment of Ohio. No troops in my opinion have left
Hooker's army for Tennessee will write by mail.
                                        R. E. LEE
[Endorsed]
    April 2, 1863
        Genl R. E. LEE
            Fredericksburg
    Movement of Burnside and corps to Kentucky.
33/99 D. A.

No. 43.

[Telegram]

Recd at Richmond Apl 29, 1863
By telegraph from Fredericksburg 29
                    To His Excellency JEFF DAVIS.
    If any troops can be sent by rail to Gordonsville
under a good officer I recommend it Longstreet's
Division if available had better come to me and the
troops for Gordonsville and protection of Rail Road

---

    [1] General Lee had reported this movement on March 28
(*cf.* O. R., 15, 689).

from Richmond and North Carolina if practicable. Genl Howard has six (6) batteries with him. Please order the forwarding of our supplies.[1]

R. E. LEE

[*Endorsed*]
Telegram from
Genl LEE
Fredericksburg Va.
April 29, 1863

No. 44.

[*Telegram*]

Received at Richd Apl 30th 1863 at 8:50 A.M.
By telegraph from Fredericksburg 30
To His Ex Presdt DAVIS
Dispatch of 11.30 P.M. yesterday received. Genl Stuart is supposed to have crossed Rapidan last Night to interrupt Enemys column at Germania. He cut it in the afternoon near Maddens North of

---

[1] Reprinted in Cooper to Longstreet (O. R., 25, 2, 758), with this addition after the word "Howard": "of the enemy's force, making toward Gordonsville." The movement announced here was one of the preliminaries of the Chancellorsville campaign, described in notes to Dispatch 45, *infra*. As the Federal cavalry was moving on Lee's flank and as a strong infantry force was suspected to be moving beyond Lee's left toward Gordonsville, it was highly important that the Virginia Central Railroad be protected, in case the Federals could not be turned back. T. S. Rhett's command, some 1,400 effectives, was rushed to Gordonsville and other troops were ordered from Staunton. Longstreet's old division had left Lee and gone to Suffolk to watch a threatened movement from Norfolk.

Rapidan. He captured prisoners from 5th, 11th, and 12th Corps.[1]

[*Endorsed*]

> Telegram from
> Genl LEE
> Hd Qrs Fredericksburg
> April 30th 1863.

No. 45.

[*Telegram*]

Translation of Despatch.

FREDKSBGS HD QRS [Apr. 30? 1863] 12 o'clock

Learning, yesterday afternoon, that the enemy's right wing had crossed the Rapidan, and its head had reached the position assumed on our extreme left to arrest their progress, I determined to hold our lines in rear of Fredericksburg with part of the force and endeavor with the rest to drive the enemy back to the Rapidan. Troops were put in motion last night and will soon be in position

I hear nothing of the expected reinforcements.[2]

> (Signed) R. E. LEE
> Genl

Official

> JAS. CAREY, Lt.

[*Endorsed*]

> Genl LEE
> Hd Qrs Fredericksburg
> 12 o'clock.

---

[1] See notes to Dispatch 45, *infra*.

[2] The few unpublished dispatches of this correspondence

No. 46.

[Telegram]

Received at Richmond May 7 1863
By telegraph from Fredericksburg to His Excely
Prest. DAVIS
I desire Genl Rodes to command D. H. Hill's old

---

that relate to Chancellorsville do not throw any new light on
a battle which differed from all those Lee had fought after
assuming command in Virginia only in that it deepened the
general gloom in the North and resulted in a reverse for the
Federals as serious as any that they had received. Following
the fiasco at Fredericksburg and Burnside's futile "mud
march," Virginia was given a respite. With their outposts
along the Rapidan, the Confederates went into winter-quarters
and devoted their energies to improving the fighting-force of
their Virginia armies. Debated questions of organization
and of rank were settled, many men were given furloughs and
allowed to go home, the gaps caused by the bloody fights of
1862 were filled up, the ordnance was improved and every
preparation was made for a spring campaign, which, it was
hoped, would end the war and secure the independence of the
South. In April the Federals began to move once more, this
time under the command of Joseph Hooker, a most successful
and dashing division commander but a man incapable, as it
developed, of handling a large army in the field. Hooker's
plan was worked out after he had spent some time in raising
the courage of the dispirited troops. He proposed first to
send his cavalry across the Rappahannock and around Lee's
left and rear to cut his communications and to harass his line.
The main army was to be divided into two columns, one of
which was to make a feint below Fredericksburg while the other
carried the fords above the town and then moved down the
right bank to catch Lee on his left flank. The whole plan was
carried out with more expedition than the Federals had shown

Division. He is a good soldier behaved admirably
in the last battles and deserves promotion. Genl
Johnson will command Trimbles Division.[1] Genl

---

since the beginning of the war. The cavalry did little and was
no match for the troopers Lee could spare to follow them and
to strike back at the Federals. But the infantry crossed the
Rappahannock in good form and moved forward promptly.
As announced in this dispatch to the President, Lee proceeded
once more to divide his forces. Early he left at Fredericksburg to hold that city and to prevent an advance along the
line of the Richmond, Fredericksburg and Potomac railroad;
with Jackson and the rest of the army, he fell back to that
tangled section known as the Wilderness. On April 30,
Hooker reached Chancellorsville, a little settlement about
12 miles west of Fredericksburg and there took a good position. For reasons which have never been explained, however,
he did not advance and found himself confronted by Lee on
May 1. It is not improbable that Hooker hoped that Sedgwick, who had been sent against Early at Fredericksburg,
would drive back his opponent, confuse Lee's right and enable
him to trap the Confederates. In any event, Lee made the
most of the delay. In conference with General Jackson, he
determined once more to divide his little army and to send
Jackson by a forced march around Hooker's right and rear.
How brilliantly that movement was completed and with
what disastrous results to the Federals is familiar to all.
While Lee kept up a show in Hooker's front, with a force that
might have been crushed by a single well-directed blow, Jackson with more than 25,000 of the finest soldiers in Lee's army,
moved through a wooded country by obscure roads, and late
in the evening struck Hooker's rear. The blow was staggering, the losses were heavy and Hooker, after another day's
uncertainty, hurried back across the Rappahannock. Splendid as was Lee's victory, he felt and the country felt that it
was dearly bought by the fatal injury to General Jackson.

[1] These assignments were made by S. O., 125; O. R., 1, 25,

Trimble is still disabled and I fear will not be able to take the field.

R. E. LEE

Genl

[*Endorsed*]
  Telegram from
    Genl LEE   47/141
      Fredericksburg
        May 7 1863

---

787.   Robert E. Rodes (1829–1864) was a native of Virginia and a graduate of the Virginia Military Institute, who brought an Alabama regiment to the front in 1861 and was in large measure identified with the troops of that State.   His brigade in October, 1861, was composed of the 5th, 6th, 12th and 61st Alabama infantry and the 12th Mississippi.   The last named regiment was transferred and its place was taken by the 3rd and 26th Alabama regiments.   He was wounded at Seven Pines, but served at Antietam, and at Chancellorsville commanded the foremost division of Jackson's corps in its assault of May 2nd.   When Jackson and A. P. Hill were both wounded he assumed command of the corps but yielded it the next morning to General J. E. B. Stuart.   For his gallantry at Chancellorsville, Rodes was made major-general and served with distinction at Gettysburg.   He was fatally wounded at Winchester, Sept. 19, 1864 (C. M. H., Ala., 441 ff.).   Edward Johnson (1816–1873), here recommended for the command of Trimble's division, was a native of Kentucky, a graduate of West Point and had an admirable record for valor in the Mexican War.   His services in the Confederate army during the first two years of the war were largely confined to Western Virginia where he acquitted himself with credit.   As requested by General Lee, he was now assigned to the command of a division composed of Steuart's, Nicholls', J. M. Jones' and

No. 47.

[Telegram]

Recd at Richmond May 7, 1863.
By telegraph from Fredericksburg 7
To His Ex Prest DAVIS

After driving Genl Sedgwick across the Rappahannock on the night of the fourth (4) inst I returned
on the 5th to Chancellorsville with the divisions of
Genls McLaws and Anderson. Their march was
delayed by a storm which continued all night and the
following day. In placing the troops in position on
the morning of the sixth (6) to attack Genl Hooker
It was ascertained he had abandoned his fortified
position The line of skirmishes was pressed forward
until they came within range of the enemys batteries
planted north of the Rappahannock which from the
configuration of the ground completely commanded
this side. His army therefore escaped with the loss
of a few additional prisoners[1]

R. E. LEE
Genl

---

the Stonewall brigade. He served with Lee until captured
at the Bloody Angle, and when exchanged was assigned to
Hood's Tennessee army. After much stiff fighting, he was
again captured and did not see further service.

[1] This dispatch succinctly states the outcome of the Chancellorsville campaign after the events described in the note to
Dispatch No. 45, *q. v.*

No. 48.

H^D Q^{RS} Fred^G 25 May 1863

MR President

I beg leave to return you my thanks for your prompt consideration & action on my letter of the 20th [1]—I may have misled you in my remarks upon Genls Heth & Pender as to my views regarding their promotion. I desired to call your attention to the fact, that if Genl A. P. Hill was promoted, a Commander for his division, would be required, & to bring to your consideration the merits of the two principal candidates in the division. If this was your understanding & you decided in favour of Heth, it was all I intended— I have a high estimate of Genl Heth. But Genl Pender has proved himself a capable officer. Has been conspicuous in every battle, won the confidence of the division, & would seem to be entitled to the promotion— On announcing yesterday to Genl Hill, the promotion of himself & Gen Ewell, & my intention to divide the army into three corps, he in the afternoon addressed me the accomp^y letter. You will see his opinion of the two officers. I had always intended to have taken two of the six brigades of A. P. Hills division & to have united them with Ransoms & Cookes & formed a division, forming another division of the remaining four— I think it will be better to give this latter to Pender & the former to Heth—should it be thought better to promote him, rather than Ransom. Pender has long been identified with those four brigades—

---

[1] Lee to Davis, O. R., 25, 2, 810. Davis to Lee, not found.

Has at times been in Command. His conduct in the
last battle was most gallant & I fear the effect upon
the men of passing him over in favour of another not
so identified with them.[1]

           I am very resp^y your obt servt

                         R. E. LEE

                            Genl

His Excy JEFF^N DAVIS
    Pres C. States.

---

[1] The fatalities at Chancellorsville made new appointments
and promotions necessary. As early as May 4 (O. R., *loc.
cit.*, 774), General Lee had telegraphed Mr. Davis that he was
in need of two major-generals and recommended R. E. Rodes
for D. H. Hill's old division and Elzey for Trimble's division,
unless Edward Johnson could take the field. Rodes and
Johnson were named accordingly (O. R., *loc. cit.*, 787;
S. O., No. 125, pars. I and II. See also, *supra*, No. 46).
Soon thereafter, James A. Walker and William Smith were
appointed to the commands previously held by Generals
Paxton and Early, the rank of the new commanders being
that of brigadier-general (*ibid.*, 809; S. O., No. 135, §§ X
and XI.). On the following day, General Lee wrote regarding minor promotions and suggested that the corps be reorganized and made smaller. He proposed that Ewell be given
a corps composed of three divisions of Jackson's old corps and
that a new corps be formed of one of Longstreet's divisions,
A. P. Hill's old division and a new division to be composed
of Ransom's, Cooke's and Pettigrew's brigades. He added:
"In this event I also submit to you whether it would not be
well to promote Ewell and A. P. Hill. The former is an
honest, brave soldier, who has always done his duty well.
The latter, I think upon the whole, is the best soldier of his
grade with me. . . . R. H. Anderson and J. B. Hood are also
capital officers. They are improving, too, and will make good
corps commanders, if necessary." Regarding the proposed

promotions to fill the place of A. P. Hill, he wrote that he presumed a major-general would be wanted for Hill's division. He said: "Heth is the senior brigadier in the division. I think him a good officer. He has lately joined this army, was in the last battle [Chancellorsville] and did well. His nomination having been once declined by the Senate, I do not know whether it would be proper to promote him. Pender is an excellent officer, attentive, industrious and brave; has been conspicuous in every battle, and I believe wounded in almost all of them." All the officers mentioned in this correspondence are well known in military annals. Richard S. Ewell (1817–1872) was a West Point graduate (1840) and gained his captaincy in the Mexican army. He was named brigadier-general in Confederate service June 17, 1861; became major-general in October, 1861, and lost a leg at Groveton, Aug. 28, 1862. He was promoted to lieutenant-general in May, 1863, taking charge of the 2nd corps, as had been proposed by General Lee, with the divisions of Early, Johnson and Rodes. Ambrose P. Hill (1825–1865) graduated in the West Point class of 1847 and was named as colonel when the Virginia troops were organized in 1861. Commissioned brigadier-general in Feb., 1862, he was promoted to the next rank, May 26, 1862, and, on May 24, 1863, was made lieutenant-general, his divisions being those of Anderson, Heth and Pender. Distinguished in every engagement, his death in front of Petersburg, April 2, 1865, was a serious loss to the army. Upon him as perhaps upon none of his other young officers, except Stuart, General Lee implicitly relied, and to him the memory of the great commander seemed to revert on his deathbed, for among his last words were: "Tell A. P. Hill he *must* come up." Harry Heth (1825–1912) was a Virginian, West Point class of 1847, and colonel of the 55th Virginia until January, 1862, when he was promoted brigadier-general. He had won particular fame for his activity at Chancellorsville and was made major-general as suggested in this letter. His command was his own brigade, Archer's, Pettigrew's and Cooke's (O. R., 25, 2, 840; S. O. 146, §I.). William D. Pender (1834–

No. 49.

HEAD QRS. ARMY No. VA.
26th. May 1863.

His Excy JEFFN DAVIS
    President Confed. States.
MR. PRESIDENT

Since my letter of the 20th inst.¹ in which I stated
that I would assign General Gordon to the command
of Rodes' old Brigade, I have received the enclosed
petition of all the commissioned officers of Lawton's
Brigade.   I respectfully submit it to your better
judgement, whether it will not be best, if General
Lawton is still unfit for the field (as it would that he is
from a late letter I have received from him) to keep
General Gordon in his present position where he is so
acceptable, and where he is entirely willing to remain, being a Georgian by birth.²   If you decide that

_____

1863) was a North Carolinian, a West Point graduate of 1854,
—a classmate of J. E. B. Stuart,—and entered the Confederate
service as colonel of the 3rd N. C.   His commission as brigadier-general was dated June 3, 1862, and that as major-
general, May 27, 1862.   His new division was composed of the
brigades of Pender, Lane, Thomas and McGowan.   Pender
was fatally wounded at Gettysburg and died at Staunton,
July 18, 1863.   Of him A. P. Hill wrote: "No man fell during
the bloody battle of Gettysburg more regretted than he,
nor around whose youthful brow were clustered brighter rays
of glory" (C. M. H., 4, 337).   The letter of General Hill,
to which Lee refers in this communication does not appear in
this correspondence or in the *Official Records*.

¹ O. R., 25, 810.
² Brigadier-General A. R. Lawton (1818–1896) had been
seriously wounded at Sharpsburg and was at this time incapa-

this is best, then a brigade commander will be necessary for Rodes' Brigade. In reference to this I enclose Genl Rodes' letter upon that subject. Col. Morgan is highly spoken of by General Rodes. He formerly commanded an Alabama Regiment of Infantry, but retired before the reorganization. Col. O'Neal is the Senior officer in the brigade, and commanded it in the late battles, and had commanded it four or five months. I am not acquainted with anyone of the three officers mentioned by General Rodes, but would recommend the appointment of Col. O'Neal as perhaps the most fit—as he has been identified with his regiment and the brigade by long service as Lieut. Col. and Colonel.[1]

I am with great respect
Your obt. Servt.
(Sgd.) R. E. LEE
General.

---

citated for military service. He was later appointed quartermaster-general and did not again join the army in the field though he much preferred active command to the burdensome duties assigned him. Brigadier-General John B. Gordon, later lieutenant-general and one of Lee's corps commanders, had been in charge of Lawton's brigade during the absence of the commander and was being urged by the officers to keep it. He was made major-general on May 14, 1864.

[1] This was a case that caused correspondence at a later time (see No. 81, *infra*). Colonel O'Neal was here recommended by General Lee, though not in very glowing terms. In the sketch of his life in the C. M. H., it is stated that he was appointed brigadier-general at this time but did not receive his commission. But in writing to Mr. Davis on April 6, 1864, General Lee seemingly overlooked the fact that he had recommended Colonel O'Neal. "Colonel Morgan" was

Official Copy [*of Dispatch 49*]
W. H. TAYLOR A. A. G.
[*Endorsed*]
HEAD QURS. A. N. V.
26th May 1863.
R. E. LEE
General

Recommending Col. E. A. O'Neal 26th. Ala. Regt. for the position of Brig. Genl. and that he be assigned to the command of Rodes' (old) Brigade.

No. 50.

HᴰǪʀꜱ: FREDᴳ 28 May '63.

Mᴿ PRESIDENT

I have had the honour to receive your letter of the 26 Inst:[1] & regret that I should not have been more explicit in my former communication—[2] I think Genl Pender deserves promotion on account of valour & skill displayed on many fields, & particularly at the battle of Chancellorsville— I have so stated in my remarks on a letter of Genl A. P. Hill, forwᵈ to the A. & I. Genl—[3] He has worked so faithfully with

later Brigadier-General John Tyler Morgan of Alabama, Senator in the Congress of the United States after the war and one of the most respected men in the South. For General Lee's recommendation of Colonel Morgan, see *infra*, No. 123, which dispatch explains the conflicts as to the appointment of Colonel O'Neal to the rank of brigadier-general.

[1] O. R., 51, 2, 716.
[2] *I.e.*, Lee to Davis, May 25, 1863, *supra*, No. 48.
[3] Not found.

the division in which he is, that to pass him over in
the selection of a Commander for it, might be injurious to the division & discouraging to other officers—
I have therefore recommended him for promotion—[4]
As the other division will be composed of Heths,
Archers, Pettigrews & one other, either Ransoms,
Cookes or Perrys if I can get no other,[5] I have rec-
omm^d Heth the Senior— I should be very glad to
have a division for Ransom, & should dislike to lose
him from this army— I think he will make a fine
division Commander— Under the circumstances I
do not think any better arrangement can be made
than what you propose— Send Genl French[6] to
Mississippi & put Ransom in his place— Genl
French wishes to go to Mississippi & if he could serve
with Art^y I think would be useful— From Genl

---

[4] Pender's commission was of May 27, his assignment to his
command was on May 30, 1863 (O. R., *loc. cit.*, 840).

[5] Cooke's was the one ultimately chosen. Heth's brigade was
the 40th, 47th, 55th regiments and the 22nd battalion, Virginia Infantry; Archer's the 13th Alabama regiment, the
5th Alabama battalion, and the 1st, 7th and 14th Tennessee
regiments; Pettigrew's the 11th, 26th, 47th and 52nd North
Carolina regiments; Perry's the 2nd, 5th and 8th Florida
regiments; Cooke's the 15th, 27th, 46th, 48th and 59th North
Carolina regiments; Ransom's the 24th, 25th, 35th and 49th
North Carolina regiments.

[6] Samuel G. French, a native of New Jersey and a graduate
of West Point, class of 1843. In accordance with this suggestion General French was sent to Mississippi. The Ransom
here mentioned is Robert Ransom, Jr., of North Carolina, a
West Point graduate of 1850, who first served in the Confederate army as colonel of the 1st North Carolina regiment. He
was promoted major-general at this time (C. M. H., 4, 344 ff.).

Longstreets account while under his command & as
far as I have been able to judge from a distance he
has no experience with Inf^y— I have forw^d Genl D.
H. Hills report of his operations below Kinston.
One of his regts: on picket was surprised & behaved
badly— He moved down with two brigades & drove
the enemy within their trenches, but could accomplish no other benefit— He thinks Genl Foster has a
large force there still— I can get no satisfactory information of the force of the enemy at West Point or
of their purpose— Genl Elzys scout places his
strength at 15,000, which I cannot believe— From
the division of the Federal dept. into three districts
under Naglie, Prince & Wessells, I have thought
it probable that Genl Foster might be transferring
his force to W[est] P[oint]. But that is not conclu-
sive as Genl F—may still be retained in Command
of the whole— I am glad to hear that the accounts
from Vicksburg continue encouraging— I pray &
trust that Genl Johnston may be able to destroy
Grants army— I fear if he cannot attack soon, he
will become too strong in his position— No time
should ever be given them to fortify.[7] They work so
fast. Yet I know how hard it is to be ready with our
means. If the organization you propose of local
forces in the different States can be successfully
carried out, it will add greatly to our strength— I

[7] This is the first reference in this correspondence to the
adversary against whose attacks Lee was to wage his last
campaign. "They work so fast" is a terse but a worthy
tribute to the army with which General Grant gained the
capitulation of Vicksburg on July 4, 1863.

hope your Exc^{ys} health will continue to improve & that you may soon be restored— With great esteem Your obt servt

R. E. LEE
Genl

His Exc^y President DAVIS

No. 51.

[Telegram]

Received at Richmond May 29th. 1863.
By telegraph from Fredericksburg
To His Excellency Prest. DAVIS
I gave Genl Hill Discretionary orders from Richmond to apportion his force to the strength of Enemy and send what could be spared. He declined to act and requested positive orders. I gave such orders as I could at this distance. Now he objects. I cannot operate in this manner. I request you to cause such orders to be given him as your judgment dictates.[1] Pickett has no Brigade in place of Jenkin's

---

[1] This dispatch was in substance repeated by General Lee on May 30 (O. R., 25, 2, 832). The Hill mentioned here was D. H. Hill (1821–1889), a native of South Carolina but closely identified with Virginia and North Carolina. He graduated from West Point in 1842, won the brevet rank of major in the Mexican War and retired from the army in 1849 to accept a professorship in Washington College. At the outbreak of the war he became colonel of the 1st North Carolina and led it at the battle of Bethel. Promoted in September, he speedily rose to be major-general and was distinguished during the Seven Days' Fight. He had been at Sharpsburg but had been

so Genl Longstreet reports. Genl Hill has retained
one Regt. from Pettigrew and one from Daniels.[2]

R. E. LEE

89/267
    D A
[*Endorsed*]
    May 29/63
       Genl R. E. LEE

No. 52.

[*Telegram*]

Received at Richmond June 4th. 1863.
From Fredericksburg June 4th. 1863.
   Hon. JAS. A. SEDDON:
    Reports from Genl Pickett and Major Collins[1] on
the lower Rappahannock state that the Enemy from
York River have crossed at Urbanna and are pro-

---

sent to meet the threatened invasion of North Carolina. Despite the sharp tone of this dispatch from General Lee, Hill
possessed and deserved his confidence. Later friction with
General Bragg led to his practical dismissal, although he held
at the time the rank of lieutenant-general.

   [2] Daniel's brigade was commanded by Junius Daniel of
North Carolina (1828–1864) and was composed of the 32nd,
43rd, 45th and 53rd North Carolina regiments and the 2nd
North Carolina battalion. For a sketch of his life, see C.
M. H., 4, 306–07. He was killed during the Spotsylvania
campaign. Pettigrew's brigade is listed on p. 97, note 2.

   [1] Major C. R. Collins, commanding detached cavalry below
Fredericksburg.

ceeding up the Northern Neck.[2]   I presume to join
Genl Hooker.

(Signed) R. E. Lee

Copied for the President
    By direction of the Secy of War
    R. G. H. Kean
        Chf of Bu of War
[Endorsed]
    Genl R. E. Lee
    Fredericksburg.

No. 53.

[Telegram]

Received at Richmond June 7th 1863.
By Telegraph from Fredsby 7th.
    To His Excellency Jeff^N Davis Presdt. &c.
    Genl Elzey reports reinforcements have been sent
to Genl Hooker's army from Suffolk, Yorktown and
West Point.   I require all troops that can be spared.
Pickett[1] has been ordered to Culpepper.   I advise

---

    [2] These were part of the force which had been on a raid
along the Mattaponi. See H. A. Wise's report O. R., 27, 2,
783–784.
    [1] Cf. Lee's report to Davis, June 7, 1863, O. R., 27, 2, 293.
General Lee wished Pickett's division united with his army
and thought that J. R. Cooke's brigade should go to Hanover
Junction.   Micah Jenkins' brigade could take Cooke's place.
He adds: "If it is true, as reported by General Elzey, that
only 1,500 of the enemy remain in Suffolk, Ransom's brigade
will be more than sufficient for that line.   West Point being

Cook's brigade be sent immdy to the Junction[2] and
Jenkins take its place. The Cavalry reported South
of South Anna and West of the Junction must be our
own, possibly a Regt. from North Carolina, though
I have heard of its being on the march.

R. E. Lee
Genl

78/234
> AV.

[*Endorsed*]
> Genl. R. E. Lee
> Fredksburg.

No. 54.

[*Telegram*]

June [15] 1863

By telegraph from Culpeper 15th.
> To His Excellency Jeff. Davis
> God has again crowned the valor of our troops
with success.   Early's division stormed the Enemys

---

evacuated, and the force at Yorktown reduced, there is nothing
to be apprehended from that quarter and Cooke and Jenkins
should be directed to follow me as soon as you think it safe
for them to do so." For further information on the situation
in the Peninsula at this time, see Seddon to Lee, June 9, 1863,
O. R., 27, 3, 874.

[2] Hanover Junction on the Virginia Central Railroad, from
which point troops might easily be moved either to the south
and east of Richmond or back to General Lee's army.

entrenchments at Winchester capturing their artillery &c.[1]

R. E. LEE
Genl.

23/92
TT.
[*Endorsed*]
Genl R. E. LEE
Culpepper

No. 55.

[*Telegram*]

Received at Richmond July [10] 1863
By Telegraph from Near Hagerstown via Martinsburg 10th.
To His Excellency JEFFN. DAVIS

Your telegram of July 9th. has been received. I thank you for the troops sent.[2] My letter[3] will inform you the state of things, the army is in good health and condition and hold a position between Hagerstown and Williamsport. The Enemy is gradually making appearance against us. I have

---

[1] Genl. Jubal A. Early's report of the capture of Winchester is to be found in O. R., 27, 2, 459 ff. With this message is another, undated, marked "Orange C. H. 6" as follows: "If Pickett is no longer wanted in North Carolina he had better be drawn towards Richmond."

[2] Davis to Lee, O. R., 27, 3, 986, in which Davis notified Lee that Sam Jones with 3,000 infantry and two batteries of artillery had been ordered to Winchester to receive orders from Genl. Lee.

[3] Probably the one printed in O. R., 27, 2, 300, July 10, 1863. With this dispatch begin those which General Lee wrote after

sent all the prisoners and most of the wounded
across the river.

R. E. LEE.

65/collect 260
  D. H. to Staunton.

[*Endorsed*]
  Genl. LEE
    Martinsburg.

---

the Gettysburg campaign.   The most important unpublished
item of the De Renne collection, in its new light on Gettysburg, is Dispatch No. 60, *infra*.   The collection, while rich
in Gettysburg dispatches, contains many that are already in
print and are accordingly omitted.   The Gettysburg campaign
followed Chancellorsville even more naturally than the Maryland campaign of 1862 followed Manassas.   Hooker's defeat
was an extremely heavy blow to the North not so much in the
actual losses, serious though they were, as in the confirmation
it gave to the widespread belief that the South could not be
subdued.   Never had the spirit of the North sunk so low as
when Hooker's broken corps limped back to safety across the
Rappahannock.   Many who had frantically proposed opposition to peaceable secession in 1863 were willing, in June, 1863,
to let the "erring sisters" of Scott's figure "go in peace."
Moreover, the victory over Hooker raised enthusiasm in the
South above anything that had been known even after Second
Manassas or Fredericksburg.   It was felt that a single direct
blow, aimed at the vitals of the North, might end the war and
bring peace.   On June 5, General Lee moved his headquarters
to Culpeper and took most of his army with him.   A. P. Hill's
corps was left at Fredericksburg with orders to watch Hooker,
then just across the river, to call for reinforcements from
Richmond if the enemy threatened and to follow Hooker
should he leave his position.   Ewell went ahead up the valley,
Longstreet followed and Hill came on as soon as Hooker moved
to keep between Lee and Washington.   After manœuvres too

No. 56.

[Telegram]

Received at Richmond July 16th. 1863.
By Telegraph from Near Martinsburg 14th. Via Staunton 16th.
To JEFF. DAVIS Presdt.
After remaining at Hagerstown long enough to

---

well known to need repetition here, the opposing hosts clashed at Gettysburg, July 1–3, 1863. General Lee's Dispatches, Nos. 55–59 inclusive, relate to the details of the return movement to Virginia soil. General Lee's first report of the "unsuccessful issue" of Gettysburg was contained in a dispatch of July 4. On the 7th, he wrote more fully and explained at some length the reasons for his return by the route he chose. He said in part: "Finding the position too strong to be carried and being much hindered in collecting necessary supplies for the army by the numerous bodies of local and other troops which watched the passes, I determined to withdraw to the west side of the mountains. This has been safely accomplished with great labor and the army is now in the vicinity of this place [Hagerstown]. One of my reasons for moving in this direction after crossing the mountain was to protect our trains with the sick and wounded which had been sent back to Williamsport and which were threatened by the enemy's cavalry. Our advance reached here yesterday afternoon in time to support our cavalry in repulsing an attempt of the enemy to reach our trains. Before leaving Gettysburg, such of the sick and wounded that could be removed were sent to Williamsport, but the heavy rains that have interfered so much with our general movements, have so swollen the Potomac as to render it unfordable and they are still on the north side. Arrangements are being made to ferry them over today."

cause the enemy to concentrate his forces in that vicinity and finding he was fortifying himself in his position I thought it advisable in the present uncertain stage of the river to withdraw the army to the south side of the Potomac which was done last night without molestation.   We should have nothing to regret had not Genl Pettigrew received a severe wound in a feeble attack of the enemy's cavalry upon our rear guard as he was being withdrawn this morning across the river.[1]

R. E. LEE.

94/collect 376
CV.
[*Endorsed*]
July 14th. 1863.
Genl. R. E. LEE
Near Martinsburg, Va.

No. 57.

[*Telegram*]

Received at Richmond July 24th. 1863.
By Telegraph from Culpeper 24th.   To His Excellency JEFFN. DAVIS.
I reached here this morning with Longstreet's Corps. I expect Hill's Corps to arrive within ten

---

[1] This was Brig.-Genl. J. J. Pettigrew, mentioned in previous dispatches. He had been wounded by a pistol shot in crossing the Potomac on July 14 and died on July 17, as reported by Lee to Seddon, O. R., 27, 3, 1016. "The army has lost a

(10) miles this evening. Ewell's will come by
Thornton Gap.[1]

R. E. LEE.

25/100
PC.
[*Endorsed*]
   July 24th. 1863
     Genl. R. E. LEE
     Culpepper.

No. 58.

[*Telegram*]

Received at Richmond July 25th. 1863.
   By Telegraph from Culpeper 25th. To His Excel-
     lency JEFFN. DAVIS
   The wish expressed in your telegram of 22nd. has
been anticipated.[2] Surgn. Mitchell is now on leave
to visit his mother.

R. E. LEE.

22/28
DV.
[*Endorsed*]
   July 25th. 1863
     Genl. R. E. LEE.

---

brave soldier and the Confederacy an accomplished officer,"
wrote the great commander.
   [1] *Cf.* Lee to J. E. B. Stuart, July 24, 1863; O. R., 27, 3, 1037.
This was the formal end of the return from Gettysburg.
   [2] Not found.

No. 59.

[Telegram]

Received at Richmond July 31st. 1863.
  By Telegraph from Culpeper 31st. To Hon.
JEFFN. DAVIS President C. S.
  Reports from Scouts indicate movements of
Enemy to Fredericksburg. I am making corres-
ponding movements.[1]

R. E. LEE.
Genl.

14/56
VB.
[Endorsed]
  Telegram from Genl. LEE
    Culpepper C. H.
      July 31st. 1863.

No. 60.

Unofficial

CAMP CULPEPER 31 July '63

His Excy JEFFN DAVIS
    President Confed. States
Mr PRESIDENT
  Your note of the 27th enclosing a slip from the
Charleston Mercury relative to the battle of Gettys-
burg is recd—[2] I much regret its general censure

---

[1] See Lee to Davis, Aug. 1, 1863, No. 61, *infra.*

[2] Not found. The *Mercury* was notorious for its anti-
administration sentiments and in this article apparently
blamed General Heth for the failure at Gettysburg.

upon the operations of the army, as it is calculated to do us no good either at home or abroad. But I am prepared for similar criticism & as far as I am concerned the remarks fall harmless. I am particularly sorry however that from partial information & mere assumption of facts that injustice should be done any officer, & that occasion should be taken to asperse your conduct, who of all others are most free of blame, I do not fear that your position in the confidence of the people, can be injured by such attacks, & I hope the official reports will protect the reputation of every officer. These cannot be made at once, & in the meantime as you state much falsehood may be promulgated. But truth is mighty & will eventually prevail. As regards the article in question I think it contains its own contradiction. Although charging Heth with the failure of the battle, it expressly states he was absent wounded.[3] The object of the writer & publisher is evidently to cast discredit upon the operations of the Gov^t & those connected with it & thus gratify feelings more to be pitied than envied —To take notice of such attacks would I think do more harm than good, & would be just what is desired. The delay that will necessarily occur in receiving official reports has induced me to make for

---

[3] Heth's report of the action of his division will be found in O. R., 27, 2, 637 ff., and the report of Brig.-Genl. Joseph Davis, commanding the division on the second day, will be found in *ibid.*, 650 ff. Heth was wounded on the first day of Gettysburg and had no part in the action of the two following days. His division was commanded by Brig.-Genl. Pettigrew and Brig.-Genl. Joseph Davis during this time.

the information of the Dept: a brief outline of operations of the army, in which however I have been unable to state the conduct of troops or officers.[4] It is sufficient to show what was done & what was not done. No blame can be attached to the army for its failure to accomplish what was projected by me, nor should it be censured for the unreasonable expectations of the public—I am alone to blame, in perhaps expecting too much of its prowess & valour. It however in my opinion achieved under the guidance of the Most High a general success, though it did not win a victory. I thought at the time that the latter was practicable. I still think if all things could have worked together it would have been accomplished. But with the knowledge I then had, & in the circumstances I was then placed, I do not know what better course I could have pursued. With my present knowledge, & could I have foreseen that the attack on the last day would have failed to drive the enemy from his position, I should certainly have tried some other course. What the ultimate result would have been is not so clear to me. Our loss has been very heavy, that of the enemys is proportionally so. His crippled condition enabled us to retire from the Country, comparatively unmolested. The unexpected state of the Potomac was our only embarrassment.[5] I will not trespass upon your

---

[4] See Lee's report to Genl. S. Cooper. A. and I. G., July 31, 1863, *loc. cit.*, 305–311.

[5] This letter, to be appreciated, must be read in connection with the fervid utterances of other Confederate commanders. Writing, it will be observed, in a spirit of frankness, General

Exc^{ys} time more.   With prayers for your health &
happiness, & the recognition by your gratified country
of your great services.

I remain truly & sincerely yours

R. E. LEE.

Lee casts no aspersions on any of his subordinates.   Neither
Heth, Longstreet, Ewell, nor Stuart,—the four officers most
frequently blamed for the defeat,—receives a word of criticism.
The reader who cares to study the controversy evoked by the
failure of the campaign has abundant literature.   The reports
of all the Confederate officers who survived are printed in
O. R., *loc. cit.*   General Longstreet's defence and his virtual
attack on Lee's generalship during the campaign will be found
in his *Manassas to Appomattox*, chapters xxv–xxviii.   Justice
to Longstreet requires us to remember that the writer of this
questionable narrative was an old man, soured by failure and
embittered by circumstances.   The Longstreet of 1865 could
not have written this book.   A valuable critique of the battle
is that of Brig.-Genl. E. P. Alexander, *Military Memoirs of a
Confederate.*   As chief of artillery in Longstreet's corps,
Alexander had every opportunity of seeing the battle and of
measuring the responsibility of those concerned in it.   Colonel
John S. Mosby has defended Stuart's part in the campaign
in his *Stuart's Cavalry in the Gettysburg Campaign.*   The articles on the campaign in *Battles and Leaders of the Civil War*
will be found valuable.

The criticisms to which General Lee refers in this letter probably made a deeper impression on the great commander than
he himself realized.   In his letter of Aug. 8, written nine days
afterwards, he declares in memorable terms: "I know how
prone we are to censure and how ready to blame others for the
non-fulfillment of our expectations.   This is unbecoming in
a generous people, and I grieve to see its expression.   The
general remedy for the want of success in a military commander
is his removal.   This is natural, and in many instances, proper.
For, no matter what may be the ability of the officer, if he

No. 61.

[Telegram]

Received at Richmond August 1st. 1863.
By Telegraph from Culpeper 1st.   To Hon. JEFFN.
DAVIS
Reports of enemy moving to Fredericksburg are
not confirmed to-day.   On the contrary they appear

---

loses the confidence of his troops disaster must sooner or later
ensue.   I have been prompted by these reflections more than
once since my return from Pennsylvania to propose to Your
Excellency the propriety of selecting another commander for
this army.   I have seen and heard expression of discontent
in the public journals at the result of the expedition.   I do
not know how far this feeling extends in the army.   My
brother officers have been too kind to report it, and so far
the troops have been too generous to exhibit it.   It is fair,
however, to suppose that it does exist, and success is so necessary to us that nothing should be risked to secure it.   I therefore, in all sincerity, request Your Excellency to take measures
to supply my place.   I do this with the more earnestness
because no one is more aware than myself of my inability for
the duties of my position.   I cannot even accomplish what I
myself desire.   How can I fulfill the expectations of others?
In addition I sensibly feel the growing failure of my bodily
strength.   I have not yet recovered from the attack I experienced the past spring.   I am becoming more and more incapable of exertion, and am thus prevented from making the
personal examinations and giving the personal supervision to
the operations in the field which I feel to be necessary.   I am
so dull in making use of the eyes of others I am frequently
misled.   Everything, therefore, points to the advantages to be
derived from a new commander, and I the more anxiously
urge the matter upon Your Excellency from my belief that
a younger and abler man than myself can readily be attained.

to be advancing on this route. Have crossed columns of infantry on pontoon bridges at Ellis' and
Kelly's Fords and Rappahannock Bridge. Their
cavalry have pressed ours this side of Brandy

I know that he will have as gallant and brave an army as ever
existed to second his efforts, and it would be the happiest day
of my life to see at its head a worthy leader—one that would
accomplish more than I could perform and all that I have
wished. I hope Your Excellency will attribute my request
to the true reason, the desire to serve my country, and to do
all in my power to insure the success of her righteous cause.
I have no complaints to make of any one but myself. I have
received nothing but kindness from those above me, and the
most considerate attention from my comrades and companions in arms. To Your Excellency I am specially indebted
for uniform kindness and consideration. You have done
everything in your power to aid me in the work committed to
my charge, without omitting anything to promote the general
welfare. I pray that your efforts may at length be crowned
with success, and that you may live long to enjoy the thanks
of a grateful people" (O. R., 51, 2, 752–53). Davis' reply to
this letter is a tribute to the character and judgment of the
Confederate President. It will be found printed in O. R. 29,
2, 639–40). The most significant part of the dispatch printed
in the text is that which relates to the "might-have-beens"
of the campaign. Careful as is General Lee's statement, it
contains these important facts: (1) that he regarded his plan
of campaign as practicable, (2) that he believed it "would have
been accomplished" "if all things could have worked together,"
(3) that he did not see on July 31, almost a month after the
battle, what "better course" he could have pursued on July
3 with the information he then had and (4) that *with his
present knowledge*" (*i.e.*, on July 31) *and* could he "have foreseen that the attack on the last day would have failed," he
would have tried "some other course." These statements
have been dissected and arranged in order because their

Station.[1]   Their camp seems to be in motion.   I
shall not fight a battle north of the Rapidan, but
will endeavor to concentrate everything behind it.
It would be well to send all reinforcements in Richmond to Orange C. H.

R. E. LEE.

86/364
   VM.
[*Endorsed*]
   August 1st. 1863.
   Genl. R. E. LEE
      Culpepper.

---

substance has been controverted by General Longstreet.   The
latter claims that General Lee told him, in a private letter,
"had I but followed your advice, instead of pursuing the
course that I did, how different all would have been!"   Longstreet also cites the testimony of Col. T. J. Goree of Texas
that General Lee remarked to him that if he had permitted
Longstreet to carry out his (Longstreet's) plans, instead of
making the attack on Cemetery Hill, the campaign would have
been successful (*Manassas*, etc., 400).   It would be easy to
criticise these statements and to dispute the authority upon
which they rest.   But General Lee's own words seem a
sufficient contradiction of Longstreet's remarkable claim.
General Lee believed the attack would succeed when he
ordered it; he did not believe, on July 31, that it should have
failed had "all things worked together."   Only in the knowledge which neither he nor Longstreet possessed on July 3
and in the realization that the attack which should not have
failed did fail, was he prepared to admit that he would have
followed a different course.

   [1] See Lee's detailed comment on these movements, O. R.,
27, 2, 324.   See also Hill's report, *ibid.*, 609.   It is worthy of
note that General Lee's announced purpose not to fight north

No. 62.

HEAD QUARTERS AN. VA.

August 1st 1863

His Excy JEFFERSON DAVIS
    President Conf States
Mᴿ PRESIDENT

I have the honour to recommend Brig. Gen. C. M. Wilcox to the command of the division lately under Gen. Pender ¹— This division is composed of two brigades from N. Carolina under Genl Lane & Scales, one from So. Carolina (Gen. MᶜGowan's) and one from Georgia² (Gen. Thomas')— Gen Lane the senior brigadier of the division is not recommended for promotion³—Gen Thomas the next in rank, a

---

of the Rapidan was carried out the next year when he "concentrated everything" south of the river and met General Grant there. The reasons were the same in both cases: north of the Rapidan Lee had to defend a line too long for his weakened army. South of the river he could operate on a shorter line, nearer his base.

¹ William D. Pender, major-general, had been mortally wounded by a bursting shell on July 2 and died at Staunton, Va., July 18, 1863. Pender was generally regarded as one of the staunchest, most aggressive men in the Confederate service.

² This had been a very large and strong division. J. H. Lane's brigade was composed of the 7th, 18th, 28th, 33rd and 37th N. C. regiments, E. L. Thomas' the 14th, 35th, 45th and 49th Georgia; A. M. Scales' the 13th, 16th, 22nd, 34th and 38th North Carolina; S. McGowan's the 1st S. C. ("Orr's") rifles, 1st S. C. provisional army and the 12th, 13th and 14th South Carolina.

³ This was James H. Lane, familiarly known as the "little General" or as plain "Jim Lane." He was a graduate of the

highly meritorious officer if promoted it is thought
might create dissatisfaction.[4]   Gen. Wilcox is one
of the oldest brigadiers in the service, a highly
capable officer, has served from the commencement
of the war and deserves promotion.   Being an officer
of the regular army he is properly assignable any-
where.[5]   I think it probable that some meritorious
officers who have been on duty in Gen. Johnston's
Department may be without a command.[6]   If Gen.
Stephen D. Lee is in this situation I would recommend that he be ordered to this army to take charge
of Wilcox's brigade in case of the latter's promo-

Virginia Military Institute and was engaged in teaching prior
to the outbreak of the war.   He entered as major of the 1st
North Carolina regiment, the so-called "Bethel" regiment,
was elected colonel of the 28th N. C. and was promoted brigadier-general, Nov. 1, 1862, which rank he held until the end.
After the war he returned to educational work.

[4] Edward L. Thomas of Georgia, a graduate of Emory
College and a soldier during the Mexican War, where for
gallant service he was promoted lieutenant from the ranks.
At the outbreak of the war he raised a regiment (the 35th Va.)
and was commissioned colonel, Oct. 15, 1861.   He was made
brigadier in 1862.

[5] Cadmus M. Wilcox, born in North Carolina but raised in
Tennessee, was a West Pointer, class of 1846, and saw service
in the Mexican War.   Serving for some years as instructor at
West Point (1852–57) he was an authority on rifles.   His first
commission in the Confederate army was that of colonel of
the 9th Alabama (July 9, 1861) and his promotion to the rank
of brigadier came on Oct. 21, 1861.   In accordance with the
recommendation of General Lee in this letter, he was made
major-general Aug. 9, 1863.

[6] Owing to the capture of Vicksburg.

tion[7]—Col. Flournoy of this brigade is represented as an excellent officer and worthy of promotion, but he is now absent badly wounded and it is said will not be fit for duty in six months.[8] But for that, I should recommend him for promotion. Should Gen. S. D. Lee not be available, Col James Deshler of Alabama a graduate of the Military Academy and I believe, a good officer, might be obtained.

I am with great respect

Your oby servant

R. E. LEE

Genl.

---

[7] Stephen D. Lee remained with the army in the far South and attained the rank of lieutenant-general. Wilcox's brigade (A. P. Hill's [3rd] Corps, Anderson's division) was composed of the 8th, 9th, 10th, 11th and 14th Alabama regiments.

[8] The name "Flournoy" is undoubtedly a *lapsus pennæ* for Forney. No Flournoy commanded a regiment in Wilcox's brigade but Colonel William H. Forney had led his regiment, the 10th Alabama, at Gettysburg, where he was wounded in the arm. General Lee apparently did not know it but Colonel Forney had been captured and was in the hands of the enemy (*see* infra, No. 65). He was not exchanged until the autumn of 1864 when he was commissioned brigadier-general, as here recommended, and assigned to Wilcox's brigade which he led with valor during the Petersburg campaign. General Forney was one of four distinguished brothers who held Confederate commissions—one as major-general, one as brigadier, one as lieutenant-colonel, one as major. This record is almost without an equal in the annals of the South, rivalling in the number of commissioned officers if not in rank the family of Lee, in which the father was general and virtual commander-in-chief, one son a major-general, one a brigadier-general and the other a captain.

No. 63.

H^D Q^{RS} A. N. Va.
5th Aug 1863

His Exc^y President DAVIS
  Richmond,
Mr. PRESIDENT,

I have the honour to return the letters enclosed in that of your Excellency's of the 4th inst^1; No arrangements have been made for consolidating the regiments as Col Holt supposes. It is a subject that would require time and to be beneficial, should be executed judiciously. I have thought it better to keep the regiments as they are for the present, and with brigades where it could be done to advantage. I should prefer to recruit the regiments if possible, and hoped that it could be done under your recent proclamation, calling all men under forty five with service. I cannot say now what is the exact strength of Col Holt's regiment, but it must be very desirable to recruit it up to the standard he proposes. To send it to Ga at this time for that purpose, I do not think advisable, as many other regts would consider they had equal claims to the same indulgence, and thus a large force would be taken from the army. At this time every man is wanted in the ranks that can be got there, and it would be far preferable that the accounts should be sent to the regiments. As to the propriety of converting Col Holt's into a cavalry regt, I think it had better be continued as infantry. If we could get horses for our dismounted cavalry

---

^{1} Not found.

we should have as many as could be supported. But getting horses is the difficulty. If they can be procured, I recommend that they be furnished to the cavalry already organized and partially instructed.[2]
I am with great respect,
Your Excellency's obt. servt.
R. E. LEE
Genl.

No. 64.

HEAD QUARTERS A N Va
Aug. 10th 1863

His Excellency JEFFERSON DAVIS
President Confederate States
M[r] PRESIDENT
The presence of Col Gabriel C. Wharton who has arrived with his regiment from the army of Gen S. Jones[1] enables me to make some changes in the

---

[2] The *Official Records* contain no correspondence on this subject and no reference to the proposed "consolidation." The officer mentioned is Col. Bolling H. Holt, 35th Ga. Infantry, Thomas' brigade, Wilcox's division, A. P. Hill's (3rd) corps. No orders regarding this command at the time of this dispatch have been located.

[1] Colonel Wharton, in command of a small brigade, had been serving with General Sam Jones in Western Virginia but had been sent to Winchester July 21 and had been ordered thence to General Lee's army on July 27 (O. R., 27, 2, 1031, 1041). He was speedily returned to service in the Valley. See No. 66, *infra*.

Virginia brigades which I think will be beneficial—
I propose therefore to transfer the 49th Va. Regt.
from Gen. Early's to Gen. Picketts division—[2]
This will strengthen Pickett a little and I believe
will be agreeable to the regiment— This regiment was
formerly commanded by Colonel now Genl W^m
Smith.[3] I propose also to transfer the 25th Va. from
Johnson's division[4] to Early's to replace the 49th—
this will be agreeable to all parties— In order to
compensate Johnson's division I propose to assign
Col. Wharton with his regiment[5] to the brigade
formerly commanded by Genl John M. Jones—and
to assign Gen. John M. Jones to the command of
Gen. W^m. Smith's former brigade in Early's division
—[6] This gives a good commander to this brigade,

---

[2] The 49th Va. Infantry, Lieut.-Col. J. Catlett Gibson,
belonged at this time to Smith's brigade, Early's division,
Ewell's corps. Pickett's division belonged to Longstreet's
corps.

[3] The famous "Extra-Billy" Smith mentioned above, several
times Governor of Virginia, member of the Confederate
Congress, who attained the rank of major-general, August
1863.

[4] The 25th Va., Colonel J. C. Higginbotham, belonged to
Jones' brigade, Johnson's division, Ewell's (2nd) corps. Jones'
brigade at this time was composed of six Va. regiments,—the
21st, 25th, 42nd, 44th, 48th and 50th.

[5] Wharton's old regiment was the 51st Va.

[6] Jones' brigade (see Note 4), while its commander was absent
wounded, was temporarily commanded by Colonel, later
General B. T. Johnson. Smith's brigade was composed of the
13th, 31st, 49th, 52nd and 58th Va. John M. Jones of Virginia
was a West Pointer, class of 1841 and had been an instructor
at the Academy. Serving as A. A. G. to General R. S. Ewell,

and leaves Wharton the Senior Colonel to command the brigade of John M. Jones— It also brings together troops from the same section and unites the 50th & 51st Va. Regts which were formerly under the command of Col. Wharton in Western Virginia and organized by him. I became acquainted with Col. Wharton in Western Virginia and think him an excellent soldier— He is one of the oldest Colonels and has commanded a brigade for a long time— I would therefore recommend him for promotion[7] to supply the vacancy occasioned by the resignation of Gen Wm Smith.[8]   By the arrangement which I propose he will be in command of a brigade in Johnson's division and Gen. John M. Jones transferred to a brigade in Early's division and I hope many difficulties will be reconciled.

The difficulty of supplying a commander to Wilcox's brigade provided he is promoted as has been recommended is not so easily overcome— The person best entitled and best qualified in my opinion is Col Forney of the 10th Alabama in that brigade— He is an officer of intelligence, energy and bravery and of long and faithful service.   Unfortunately he is badly wounded and in the hands of the enemy. He was first wounded at the battle of Williamsburg

---

he was promoted brigadier-general in 1863.   He was killed in action, May 5, 1864.

[7] Gabriel C. Wharton entered the service as major of the 45th Va. in July, 1861, and in August was made colonel of the 51st.   He was made brigadier-general as here proposed.

[8] Resigned to become candidate for Governor of Virginia, to which office he was elected.

in his arm. He had scarcely recovered from that when he was wounded in the same place at the battle of Gettysburg— He also received a wound in the other arm, this was comparatively slight though the ball struck him in the side— But he received a third wound in the foot which is represented as more serious breaking some of the bones— I fear therefore it will be a long time before he will be fit for duty— While I think it better to wait for the present and leave the brigade in command of a Junior Colonel now with it than to obtain a commander outside of it unless one of great excellence can be procured—[9] I enclose a letter from Gen. A. P. Hill on the subject and ask your Excellency to exercise your judgment in the case.[10]

> I am with great respect
> You obt servt
> R. E. Lee
> Genl.

No. 65.

> Head Qurs. A. N. Va.
> August 17th 1863.

His Excy Jefferson Davis
    President Confederate States
Mr. President
    The number of desertions from the army is so great and still continues to such an extent that unless

---

[9] This recommendation was carried out. Colonel L. C. C. Sanders of the 11th Ala. commanded the brigade during Forney's imprisonment. See *supra*, No. 62.

[10] Not found.

some cessation of them can be caused I fear success in the field will be seriously endangered. Immediately on the publication of the amnesty which I thought would be beneficial in its effects, many presumed on it and absented themselves from their commands choosing to place on it a wrong interpretation.[1] In one corps the desertions of North Carolinians and to some extent of Virginians has grown to be a very serious matter. The Virginians go off in many cases to join the various partizan corps in the state. General Imboden writes that there are great numbers of deserters in the Valley who conceal themselves successfully from the small squads sent to arrest them. Many cross the James River near Balcony falls enroute for the south along the mountain ridges. Night before last thirty went from one regiment and eighteen from another. Great dissatisfaction is reported among the good men in the Army at the apparent impunity of deserters.

---

[1] The amnesty recommended by General Lee was contained in A. and I. G's G. O. No. 109, Aug. 11, 1863, as follows:

"I. A general pardon is given to all officers and men within the Confederacy, now absent from the army, who shall, within twenty days from the publication of the address of the President in the State in which the absentees may then be, return to their posts of duty.

"II. All men who have been accused or convicted and undergoing sentence for absence without leave or desertion, excepting only those who have been twice convicted of desertion, will be returned to their respective commands for duty" (O. R., 29, 2, 641–42). This was communicated to the Army of Northern Virginia in General Lee's G. O. No. 82, August 12, 1863 (O. R., 51, 2, 754).

In order to remove all palliation from the offense
of desertion and as a reward to merit, I have instituted in the Army a system of furloughs, which
are to be granted to the most meritorious and urgent
cases at the rate of one for every hundred men
present for duty.[2]   I would now respectfully submit
to your Excellency the opinion that all has been done
which forebearance and mercy call for and that
nothing will remedy this great evil which so much
endangers our cause except the rigid enforcement of
the death penalty in future in cases of conviction.

I am with great respect
Your obt Servt.
R. E. LEE
General

No. 66.

[Telegram]

Received at Richmond Augt. 24 1863
By Telegraph from Orange C. H. 24
To Genl. S. Cooper

On application of Genl. Sam Jones, I have directed
Jenkins and Wharton's Brigades to report to him.[1]

R. E. LEE

---

[2] See G. O. No. 84, A. N. Va., August 16, 1 ,63 (O. R.,
51, *loc. cit.*).   Furloughs were to be at the rate of 2 for each
100 men present for duty and were to range from 15 to 30 days
according to the residence of the furloughed men.

[1] See Jones to Lee, August 21, 1863, asking for "Wharton's
command," also to Seddon, August 24, 1863, asking that he

Official copy of Telegram received and respt.
submitted to the President.

Jno. Withers

Asst. Adjt. Genl.

[*Endorsed*]

    Augt. 24 1863.

      Genl. R. E. Lee

      Orange C. H.

No. 67.

30 Aug '63

Mᴿ President

I think Genl Sam Jones can move forward on
that line—I will send to the Adjt. Genl to see if
he has any dispatches & will come & see you this
afternoon.[1]

Very respectfully

R. E. Lee

"order General Jenkins' and Colonel Wharton's brigades and
my three field batteries back to me" (O. R., 29, 1, 41–42).
See also Lee to Stuart, August 24, 1863 (*ibid.*, 2, 655). Jones
was hard pressed at the time.

[1] No correspondence bearing on this letter appears in the
Official Records. General Jones, commanding in Southwest
Virginia, had just met and repulsed Averell's raid (reports in
O. R., 29, 1, 44 ff.) and had received news that the Federal
advance on Knoxville threatened Eastern Tennessee and
Southwest Virginia. It was probably regarding Jones' ad-
vance to protect the frontier that this letter was written. See
Seddon to Jones, O. R., 29, 2, 681, August 31, 1863.

No. 68.

HEAD QUARTERS A N Va.

Sep 8th 1863.

His Excellency JEFFERSON DAVIS
    President Confederate States
MR PRESIDENT

I beg leave to forward to you directly the inclosed papers for your consideration as I think speedy action on the case of much importance to the efficiency of the brigade in question. I leave it to your better judgement to suggest what is best to be done in the matter.[1]

I am with great respect
Yours very truly
R. E. LEE
Genl.

No. 69.

[Telegram]

Received at Richmond Sept. 9 1863.
By Telegraph from Orange C. H. 9. To His Ex.
    JEFFN. DAVIS

Troops are on march Two divisions will reach Hanover Junction this morning. No trains yet.[2]

R. E. LEE

15/60
[Endorsed]
    Sept. 9/63.
        Genl. R. E. LEE.

---

[1] The papers referred to have not been found. Davis' reply not found.

[2] Amplified in same to same, Sept. 9, 1863, O. R., 29, 2, 706.

No. 70.

CAMP ORANGE CT. HS. 2 Oct. '63.

His Exc^y JEFF^N DAVIS
    Pres: of C. States—Richmond Va.
MR PRESIDENT

I know of no Georgia Brig^r to take command of
the Cav^y organized by Genl Cobb except Genl Iverson— I can spare him, but shall have to get a Brigadier to command the Louisiana Brigade, formerly
Nicholls, now temporarily commanded by Genl
Iverson[1]— I presume Genl. Nicholls will never be
able to take the field which I very much regret[2]—

These men were soldiers of Longstreet's corps *en route* to join
Bragg. See Longstreet's *From Manassas*, etc., chap. xxx.
The transportation of these troops as directed by Brigadier-
General A. R. Lawton, Quartermaster-General, was regarded
as one of the most notable achievements of that office during
the war.

[1] Nicholls' brigade was composed of the 1st, 2nd, 10th, 14th
and 15th Louisiana regiments, Johnson's division, Ewell's
(2nd) corps. Alfred Iverson was a native of Georgia, a graduate of the Tuskegee, Alabama, Military Institute and a
soldier in the Mexican War. Later entering the regular army
he was assigned to service in the West. Upon the outbreak
of the war he volunteered and was sent to North Carolina,
where he became colonel of the 20th regiment. He served in
various commands until made brigadier-general, Nov. 1, 1862.
From 1863 to the end of the war he served in Georgia and
nearby States. He is listed as commanding Nicholls' brigade
in the return A. N. Va., August 31, 1863.

[2] Owing to the amputation of a foot, resulting from a wound
at Gettysburg. Francis T. Nicholls was born in Louisiana in
1834 and was a West Point graduate of the class of 1851. He
helped to organize the 8th Louisiana, was made lieutenant-

It is considered by all the officers that there is no one in the brigade among the higher officers qualified for the command.[3]   To take a person from out of the brigade unless his qualifications justify it is apt to produce discontent.   As far as I can judge Col Stafford of the 9th La. Hays brigade is the most suitable person.[4]   Genl. Hays who ought to know his Cols: best I am told is very decided in his preference to him over Cols: Forno & Penn[5] the others that have been recommended.   Gen. Early also speaks highly of Col Stafford He has seen him in battle & commends his gallantry and good management.   I believe too he is the Senior Col. from La. in this army & has commanded Hays brigade in battle[6]—Col. Penn is considered the better drill

---

colonel in July, 1861, and became colonel of the 15th Louisiana on June 24, 1862.   His commission as brigadier-general was of October 14, 1862.   He never returned to active field duty with the Army of Northern Virginia after that time, but served as post-commandant at Lynchburg, Va., and later in the Trans-Mississippi department, (C. M. H., 10, La., 313.   See the order for his assignment to Lynchburg in O. R., 29, 2, 642; A. and I. G's. S. O. No. 190, par. 17, August 11, 1863).

[3] The colonels of these regiments were: 1st, W. R. Shivers; 2nd, J. M. Williams; 10th, Eugene Waggaman; 14th, Z. York; 15th, Edmund Pendleton.

[4] It is worthy of note that in choosing a brigadier-general for this brigade of Louisiana troops, Genl. Lee took care to follow the usual rule and to recommend a native of that state. Hays' brigade was composed of the 5th, 6th, 7th, 8th and 9th Louisiana regiments.

[5] Colonel Henry Forno, 5th Louisiana; Colonel David B. Penn, 7th Louisiana.

[6] Leroy A. Stafford entered the service as lieutenant-colonel

officer of the two & while Ewell's corps was under command of Genl Hill, Gen Edwd Johnson, to whose division Nicholls brigade belongs applied for the appointment of Col Penn, but as it was not recommended by Genl Hill, & not being satisfied on the subject myself I refrained till now. It is herewith enclosed & also an unofficial note just rec^d from Genl. Ewell.[7]

> I am with great respect your obt svt
> R. E. LEE.
> Genl.

No. 71

[Telegram]

By Telegraph from Orange C. H. 6   To His Excy. JEFFN. DAVIS.

The enemy is crossing at Morton's ford in large force of infantry. The country is so wooded it is difficult to ascertain his strength or intentions.[1] If Rodes is not wanted where he is I want him

---

of the 9th Louisiana, of which Richard Taylor, later lieutenant-general, was commander. In accordance with this recommendation of General Lee, Stafford was made brigadier-general, Oct. 8, 1863, (Cooper to Lee, O. R., 29, 2, 777).

[7] Not found.

[1] This was at the conclusion of the so-called "Mine Run" campaign, the reports of which appear in O. R., 29, 1, 823 ff.

back.² Please direct. Transportation must be
provided.

R. E. LEE

44/35²
Vn.
[*Endorsed*]
   Telegram
      Genl. R. E. LEE.
         Orange C. H. 6 Dec. 1863.

No. 72.

[*Telegram*]

Received at Richmond Dec. 7 1863.
By Telegraph from Orange C. H. 7   To His Excy.
JEFFN. DAVIS.
   Dispatch of sixth received. Can go if ordered.
Have written by mail.¹

R. E. LEE

11/44   Vb.
[*Endorsed*]
   Telegram
      Genl R. E. LEE
         Orange C. H. Dec. 7 1863

---

² Major-General Robert E. Rodes, whose report of his
operations at the time is printed in O. R., *loc. cit.*, 876 ff.
   ¹ Davis' message of Dec. 6, 1863, not found, but manifestly
along the line of his telegram of Dec. 6 which read: "Can you
go to Dalton, as heretofore explained?" (O. R., 29, 2, 861).
Lee, it will be recalled, had been in Richmond and had
probably discussed with the President the advisability of his
taking command of the Southern army. In his detailed reply

No. 73.

H^RQ^{RS}: 20 Jany '64.

MR PRESIDENT

I heard some days since that several men of this army mostly Louisianians that were in or passed through Richmond, were joining Genl Morgans Command. I wrote to the Secy. of War on the subject & requested it might be stopped. Since then I have rec^d other evidences of the fact. A member of my staff informs me that Dr T. W. Hancock of Jackson Hospital Richmond stated to him yesterday, that a recruiting officer of Genl Morgan has visited his Hospital, promised the men clothing & two months furlough, & that 25 or 30 convalescents whom he was about to send to this army, deserted & he understands were forwarded to Decatur Geo: Dr. Hancock also stated that he heard

---

(*loc. cit*) Lee wrote: "I can [go to Dalton] if desired, but of the expediency of the measure you can judge better than I can. Unless it is intended that I should take permanent command, I can see no good that will result, even if in that event any could be accomplished. I also fear that I would not receive cordial co-operation, and I think it necessary if I am withdrawn from here that a commander for this army be sent to it. General Ewell's condition, I fear, is too feeble to undergo the fatigue and labor incident to the position. I hope Your Excellency will not suppose that I am offering any obstacles to any measure you may think necessary. I only seek to give you the opportunity to form your opinion after a full consideration of the subject. I have not that confidence either in my strength or ability as would lead me of my own option to undertake the command in question." It is needless to add that this letter ended the question. Lee remained where he was.

from 200 to 250 men in other Hospitals had been ordered away. I am sure that Genl Morgan would neither countenance or authorize such proceedings, but I know how unscrupulous many men are in raising companies. You will see if this conduct is allowed, that all discipline is destroyed & our armies will be ruined.[1]

I have therefore to request that all these men be returned to this army, & that the officers, who have been engaged in this illicit conduct be punished.

I have the honour to be

Your obt servt

R. E. Lee

Genl.

His Excy. Jeffⁿ. Davis
Pres. Confed. States.

---

[1] The grievance of which General Lee here complains was a very serious one to the armies of the South. The exploits of General John H. Morgan, Colonel John S. Mosby and other so-called partisan leaders were very alluring to the men in the ranks. Not only did Mosby and his men, for instance, win great renown and meet with rare adventures but they had substantial advantages denied the soldiers with the regular armies,—good food, occasional plunder, booty and a bed to sleep in. Any young man of adventurous spirit counted himself lucky to find a place with Mosby's renowned rangers. A statement of the case from the standpoint of a regular officer is to be found in Thos. L. Rosser's letter to General Lee, Jany. 11, 1864, O. R., 33, 1081. In this letter Rosser wrote: "It is almost impossible for me to manage the different companies of my brigade that are from Loudoun, Fauquier, Fairfax, etc., the region occupied by Mosby. They see these men living at their ease and enjoying the comforts of home, allowed to possess all that they capture, and their duties mere pastime

No. 74.

[*Telegram*]

Telegram in cypher.

Received at Richmond, Feby. 3, 1864.

By Telegraph from Orange C. H., Feby. 3, 1864.

To

The President

Do you wish troops sent to Richmond.[1]

R. E. LEE

Genl.

---

pleasures compared with their own arduous ones; and it is a natural consequence in the nature of man that he should be dissatisfied under these conditions, . . . This is melancholy, but it is nevertheless true and it can only be, in my opinion, remedied by placing all men on the same footing who are of the same rank.   If it is necessary for troops to operate within the lines of the enemy, then require the commanding officer to keep them in an organized condition, to rendezvous them within our lines and to move upon the enemy when opportunity is offered."   This letter, forwarded by Genl. Stuart bears that officer's commendation of Mosby but contains this added sentence: "Such organizations [*i.e.*, partisan rangers] as a rule are detrimental to the best interests of the army at large." General Lee wrote on the same paper: "As far as my knowledge and experience extends, there is much of truth in the statement of General Rosser.   I recommend that the law authorizing these partisan corps be abolished.   The evils resulting from their organization more than counterbalance the good they accomplish."   Accordingly the Confederate Congress passed a law abolishing partisan rangers, the effect of which measure was to place Mosby's men, Morgan's command and other partisan corps in the regular service. See also Lee to Cooper, Apr. 1, 1864 O. R., 1, 33, 1252.

[1] No answer or related correspondence.   Several cavalry raids against Richmond were threatened during the winter,

[*Endorsed*]
        Telegram from
        Genl. R. E. Lee
    Orange C. H. Feby. 3/64.
        Movements of troops.
        Recd Feby. 4th. 64

No. 75.

[*Telegram*]

Received at Richmond, Va., Feby. 6 1864.
By Telegraph from Orange C. H. 6
            To Genl. S. Cooper

On the 30th. ulto. Genl. Rosser captured a train
of ninety three (93) wagons loaded with Commissary
stores & forage on way from New Creek to Petersburg, three hundred (300) miles, twenty prisoners.
The Guard of eight hundred (800) Infantry escaped
to the mountains. Our loss twenty five (25) killed &
wounded. Information of the advance upon Petersburg having been received the Garrison evacuated it
during the night. On the 2d. Rosser destroyed the
bridge over Patterson Creek & North Branch of
Potomac & Canal, and captured forty prisoners, Two
hundred and seventy prisoners, fifty wagons and
teams twelve hundred (1200) cattle & five hundred
(500) sheep have been brought off. Genl. Rosser

_____

one of which, under Dahlgren, caused some apprehension for
the time. That raid, however, was in March.

has shown great energy and skill, and his command
deserves great credit.[1]   R. E. LEE

Official copy of telegram received
and respy submitted to the President.

JNO WITHERS,
Asst. Adjt. Genl.

[*Endorsed*]
Genl. R. E. LEE
Tel. to A. & I. G.
Orange C. H. Feby. 6/64.
Captures by Genl. Rosser's
Brigade in N. Va.
Recd. Feby. 6/64.

---

[1] General Thomas L. Rosser's report of his expedition into
Hampshire and Hardy counties, West Virginia, will be found
in O. R., 33, 45 ff. For this expedition Rosser received much
praise. In his usual commendatory style, J. E. B. Stuart wrote
that it "furnishes additional proofs of General Rosser's merit
as a commander, and adds fresh laurels to that veteran brigade
so signalized for valor already." General Lee added to
Rosser's report: "General Rosser acquitted himself with
great credit in this expedition." Rosser was a native Virginian
who was in the Military Academy when the war began. At
once volunteering, he was commissioned lieutenant in the
regular army of the Confederacy and won promotion by his
skill as an artilleryman in destroying General McClellan's
observation-balloon during the Peninsula campaign. After
the Seven Days' Fight he was promoted colonel of the 5th
Virginia Cavalry, and in 1863 was made brigadier-general,
assigned to the command of the famous Laurel Brigade and
was serving with this command at the time of this campaign.
He was made major-general in November, 1864. A dashing
officer and personally most valorous he was one of the youngest
major-generals in the army and was of the type most dear to
the heart of cavalrymen.

No. 76.

[*Telegram*]

Received at Richmond Feby. 7 1864.
By Telegraph from Orange C. H. 7 To His Ex.
JEFFN. DAVIS
As far as could be ascertained at five A. M. this
morning the Enemy had retired to the north side of
the Rapidan at Morton's Ford.[1]   R. E. LEE
Genl.

26/208
V
[*Endorsed*]
    Telegram
Genl. R. E.LEE
Orange C. H. Feby. 7 1864.

No. 77.

Respy. returned— Commander Wood who had
the hardest part to perform did his part well— Hoke
seems to have done all he could, & it was not expected
that Dearing could do more than to occupy Fort
Bannington. But Genl Barton seems to have
altogether failed, which I hope can be satisfactorily
explained. It was competent for Genl Pickett to
have charged the mode of attack if circumstances
prompted it.[2]   R. E. LEE
Genl.

    HᴰQᴿˢ: 9 Feby. '64.

---

[1] On February 6, 1863, General Meade began a demonstration against General Lee's left, held by Ewell, at Morton's
Ford. He was met promptly and was driven back without
serious loss. The reports are in O. R., 33, 141 ff.

[2] Evidently the endorsement of a report of the New Bern,

No. 78.

[Telegram]

RICHMOND, VA., March 4th. 1864.
Orange C. H. March 3d. 1864.
To Genl. S. Cooper, A. & I. General
Genl Pendleton will be ordered to report to you
for the duty indicated in your telegram. [1]

(signed) R. E. LEE
Genl.

Respy. submitted to Genl. Bragg. [2]

JOHN W. RIELY
Capt. A. A. G.

N. C., expedition of Feb. 1, 1864. The full details are given
in the reports of Genls. W. H. C. Whiting, J. G. Martin, G. E.
Pickett, R. F. Hoke and S. M. Barton, C. S. A., O. R., 33, 82 ff.
General S. M. Barton was rather severely criticised by the
other officers engaged in this movement for his failure effectively to co-operate, to which failure they attributed the non-
success of the venture. A court of inquiry was ordered at
the direction of General Lee and at the request of General
Barton, though its report does not appear (see O. R.,
loc. cit., 100, 1187). General Barton was later relieved of
command by General Ransom for failure to co-operate in a
movement on May 10, 1864. A court was again ordered but
was later countermanded. General Barton remained in the
service in command of a brigade of reserves around Richmond.
His personal courage was never questioned. (For Ransom's
report, etc., see O. R. 36, 2, 213 ff. For Barton, see C. M. H.,
3, 579 ff.)

[1] Evidently Brigadier-General W. N. Pendleton, Chief of
Artillery, A. N. Va. Related correspondence not found.

[2] This is the first dispatch in this collection sent after
General Braxton Bragg had been appointed, Feb. 24, 1864, as
special military adviser to the President. In one sense,

[*Endorsed*]
Orange C. H.
3d March 1864.
　R. B. No. 31
　R. E. LEE
　　General
Concerning Genl. Pendelton.
Recd. Hd. Qrs. A. C. S.
　　　　4 March 64.

No. 79.

[*Telegram*]

Received at Richmond, Va., March 5th 1864.
　By Telegraph from Orange C. H. March 5th.
To General S. COOPER,
　A. & I. General.
　　The following troops have reinlisted for the war
since my announcement of 19th. Feby. most of them
before the law retaining all men in the service was

General Bragg occupied the position which General Lee had
held early in 1862,—a position of great possibilities but of an
anomalous character. As the President was himself titular
constitutional head of the army, the officer to whom he dele-
gated the immediate supervision of military affairs could not
directly serve as commander-in-chief and was at once subordinate to the President and not superior to officers of equal rank
in the field. Bragg's appointment seems not to have affected
General Lee in the slightest. Correspondence from the commander of the Army of Northern Virginia was addressed,
as in the past, to the President or to the War Department
and only on rare occasions to General Bragg himself. Most of
the letters and dispatches to General Lee came as they had

made known. Phillip's Legion Cavalry, Carrington's Battery, Garbers' Battery, Jeff. Davis' Legion, 1st. South Carolina Cavalry, 44th. Virginia Infantry, Louisiana Battery, Carpenter's Battery, 1st. North Carolina Regiment, 13th. Virginia Infantry, 58th. Virginia Infantry, 12th. Virginia Cavalry, Stafford's Brigade, 2d. North Carolina Cavalry, 10th. Virginia Infantry.[1]

(signed) R. E. Lee
Genl.

Official copy of telegram received March 6th. 1864 and respectfully submitted to Genl. B. Bragg

JOHN W. RIELY
Capt. & A. A. G.

[*Endorsed*]
    Orange C. H.
        5th. March 1864.
        R. E. LEE
        Genl.

Announcing reinlistments.
    R. B. 41
    Recd. 7th. March 64.

---

before General Bragg's appointment. Relations between Lee and Bragg seem to have remained entirely pleasant and were marked with uniform courtesy and deference until the end. It is to be noted that General Lee's dispatches to the War Department, copies of which had formerly been sent to the President, were now forwarded General Bragg and by him, it would appear, turned over to Mr. Davis. This, however, was not uniformly the case.

[1] During January and February, 1864, a general effort was made in the armies of the Confederacy to procure the re-

No. 80.

H^D Q^{RS} ARMY N VA.
25th March 1864.

His Excy JEFFERSON DAVIS,
 Presd^t Confd. States
  Richmond Va.
MR. PRESIDENT,
 I have the honor to acknowledge the receipt of the
letter forwarded to me by your directions, containing

---

enlistment of all men whose terms were expiring. Many had
already enlisted for the war,—indeed many entered the service
with no definite term of enlistment,—but the military situation
demanded that the strength of the armies be kept at the
maximum. Congress about this time passed an act authorizing the commanders indefinitely to hold men whose terms had
expired or would shortly expire, but as General Lee here points
out, many commands re-enlisted before the provisions of this
law were known. Other reports on the same subject are printed in O. R., 33, 1152, 1173, 1190, etc. The troops mentioned
in this communication were assigned as follows: Phillips'
cavalry legion belonged to Young's brigade, Wade Hampton's
division; Carrington's (Charlottesville) battery to Cutshaw's
battalion, 2nd corps; Garber's (Staunton) battery to the same
command; the Jeff Davis legion to Hampton's division of the
cavalry (Stuart's) corps; the 1st S. C. Cavalry was taken from
Lee's army in March and sent to reinforce General Beauregard. Its commander was Colonel Black. The 44th Virginia
infantry belonged to Jones' brigade, Johnson's division, 2nd
corps; the "Louisiana" battery was either Moody's, 1st corps,
or Landry's, 3rd corps, sometimes called respectively the
"Madison" and the Donaldsonville batteries. The Washington
artillery may possibly be meant. Carpenter's (Alleghany)
battery was of Braxton's (Brown's) battalion, 2nd corps; the
1st N. C. Infantry, Col. H. A. Brown, belonged to G. H.

the views of the writer as to the intentions of the enemy in the approaching campaign.[1]

I have read the speculations of the Northern papers on the subject, and the order of Gen Grant published in our papers yesterday, but I am not disposed to believe from what I now know, that the first important effort will be directed against Richmond. The Northern papers, particularly if they derive their information from official sources, as they profess, do not in all probability represent the real purpose of the Federal Govt. but are used to create false impressions. The order of Gen. Grant, closely considered, is not inconsistent with this idea. There was no apparent occasion for the publication at such a time and place of his intention to take up his H^d Q^{rs} with the army of the Potomac, and the announcement appears to me to be made with some hidden purpose. It will be remembered that northern papers of the 14th inst: represented Gen. Grant as en route for Tennessee to arrange affairs there preparatory to assuming immediate command of the

---

Steuart's brigade, Johnson's division, Ewell's (2nd) corps; the 13th Virginia Infantry Col. J. B. Terrill, was of Pegram's brigade, Early's division, Ewell's corps; the 58th Virginia Infantry was of the same brigade; the 13th Virginia Cavalry was attached to Rosser's brigade of Stuart's cavalry corps; Stafford's brigade (L. A. Stafford) was composed of the 1st, 2nd, 10th, 14th, and 15th Louisiana regiments and was a part of Johnson's division, Ewell's corps; the 2nd N. C. Cavalry belonged to Gordon's brigade, W. H. F. Lee's division, Stuart's cavalry corps; the 10th Virginia Infantry was of G. H. Steuart's brigade, Johnson's division, Ewell's corps.

[1] Not found.

army of the Potomac. What those arrangements were, we do not know, but if of sufficient moment to require Gen Grant's personal presence in the West just on the eve of his entering upon active duties with another army, it can not be probable that he had completed them by the time his order bears date, March 17th, especially, as several of the few days intervening between his departure from Washington and the publication of the order, must have been consumed in travelling. The establishment of an office in Washington to which communications from other armies than that which Gen. Grant accompanies shall be addressed, evidently leaves everything to go under the direction of the former authorities as before, and allows no room for inferences as to whether any army will be active or not, merely from the fact of the presence of Gen. Grant. There is to my mind an appearance of design about the order which makes it of a piece with the publications in the papers, intended to mislead us as to the enemy's intention, and if possible, induce corresponding preparation on our part. You will remember that a like ruse was practised at Vicksburg. Just before the Federal Army went down the river, the indications given out were such, that it was thought the attempt on Vicksburg would be abandoned, and that it was proper to reinforce Gen. Bragg, whose army it was supposed would next be attacked. It is natural that the enemy should try to conceal the point which he intends to assail first, as he may suppose that our armies, being connected by shorter lines than his, can concentrate more rapidly. In confirmation of these views, I cannot learn that the army of Gen. Meade has been reinforced by any organized troops, nor can I learn of any coming east over the B & O Rail Road which I have ordered to be closely watched. A dispatch from Gen. Imboden dated March 23rd states that it is reported that the enemy was moving troops westwards over that road all last week. The report is vague but if true, the troops referred to may be recruits, convalescents & furloughed men going to the corps from the east now serving in the West, or they may be reinforcements for the army of Tennessee. I have reiterated my order about watching the road, and directed the rumor above mentioned to be carefully investigated. From present indications, I am inclined to believe that the first efforts of the enemy will be directed against Gen Johnston or Gen Longstreet, most probably the former. If it succeed, Richmond will no doubt be attacked. The condition of the weather and the roads will probably be more favorable for active operations at an early day in the south than in Va. where it will be uncertain for more than a month. Although we cannot do more than weigh probabilities, they are useful in stimulating and directing a vigilant observation of the enemy, and suggesting such a policy on our part as may determine his. His object can be ascertained with the greatest certainty by observing the movements of his armies closely. I would advise that we make the best preparations in our power to meet an advance in any quarter, but be careful not to suffer ourselves to be misled by feigned movements into strengthening one point at the expense of others, equally exposed and equally important. We should hold ourselves in constant readiness to concentrate as rapidly as possible wherever it may be necessary, but do nothing without reasonably certain information except prepare. This information I have already said, can be best obtained by unremitting vigilance in observing those armies that will most probably be active in the campaign, and I trust that your Excellency will impress this fact, and the importance of energy accuracy and intelligence in collecting information upon all officers in a position to do so. Should a movement be made against Richmond in large force, its preparation will no doubt be indicated by the withdrawal of troops from other quarters, particularly the Atlantic Coast and West. The officers command^g in these regions should endeavor to get early and accurate information of such withdrawal.   Should Gen. Johnston or Gen Longstreet find the forces opposed to them reduced sufficiently to justify attacking them, they might entirely frustrate the enemy's plans by defeating him.   Energy and activity on our part, with a constant readiness to seize any opportunity to strike a blow, will embarrass, if not entirely thwart the enemy in concentrating his different armies, and compel him to conform his movements to our own.   If Gen. Johnston could be put in a condition to operate successfully against the army opposed to him, he would effectually prevent a combination against Richmond. In the meantime, to guard against any contingency, everything not immediately required should be sent

away from Richmond, and stores of food and other
supplies collected in suitable and safe places for the
use of the troops that it may become necessary to
assemble for its defence. I beg to repeat that the
utmost vigilance and circumspection, coupled with
active and energetic preparation are of the first
moment to us.[2]

With high respect,

Your obt. servt.

R. E. LEE

Genl.

---

[2] General Lee was for the time mistaken. Following his
appointment as commander of the armies of the United States
on March 10, 1864, General Grant had come East and on the
24th apparently began operations at Culpeper Court-House
(O. R., 33, 721). General Lee, however, speedily divined
the real purpose of the enemy, for on March 30 (*ibid.*, p. 1244),
he wrote President Davis that he expected Grant to make a
forward movement in Virginia. He said: "Since my former
letter [probably the one here printed] on the subject the indications that operations in Virginia will be vigorously prosecuted by the enemy are stronger than they then were. General
Grant has returned from the army in the West. He is at
present with the Army of the Potomac, which is being reorganized and recruited. From the reports of our scouts the
impression prevails in that army that he will operate it in
the coming campaign. Every train brings it recruits, and it
is stated that every available regiment at the North is added
to it. It is also reported that General Burnside is organizing
a large army at Annapolis, and it seems probable that additional troops are being sent to the valley. It is also stated
that preparations are making to rebuild the railroad from
Harper's Ferry to Winchester, which would indicate a reoccu-
pation of the latter place. The Baltimore and Ohio Railroad is very closely guarded along its whole extent. No

No. 81.

H⁰ Qʀˢ: Army N Va. 6 Apl. '64.

Mʳ President

I very much regret that you should be required to investigate complaints from members of this army. The one from Col: O'Neal 26ᵗʰ Alabᵃ—has been presented to me several times, & I think this is not the first occasion on which it has been brought to your attention. I have stated that I was aware of no injustice having been done Col: O'Neal that the recommendations for a commander to Rodes former brigade was made from military considerations, & that the action of the Dept. had conformed to my recommendations. I feel aggrieved at this repeated charge of injustice, & but that we are upon the eve of a campaign in which the presence & services of every one will be required, I should ask for a court

---

ingress or egress from their lines is permitted to citizens, as heretofore, and everything shows secrecy and preparation. Their plans are not sufficiently developed to discover them, but I think we can assume that if General Grant is to direct operations on this frontier he will concentrate a large force on one or more lines, and prudence dictates that we should make such preparations as are in our power. If an aggressive movement can be made in the West it will disconcert their plans and oblige them to conform to ours. But if it cannot, Longstreet should be held in readiness to be thrown rapidly in the valley, if necessary, to counteract any movement in that quarter, in accomplishing which I could unite with him, or he unite with me, should circumstances require it, on the Rapidan. The time is also near at hand when I shall require all the troops belonging to this army. I have delayed calling for General Hoke, who, besides his own brigade, has two regi-

of Inquiry into the matter. Should you think one can be instituted at this time without injury, I request it be ordered. Unless I have been entirely mistaken I think the facts will be found different from what Col O'Neal has supposed & have been stated. I Concur with the Honb^le Mr Phelan in the belief that Col: O'Neal is a most true brave & gallant officer. Still I believed that Cols: Gordon, Morgan & Battle gave promise of making better Brigade Commanders, & therefore recommended them before him. The regt: of Col: O'Neal by orders from the A & I Gen^ls office 12 Feby. '64 has been transferred from this army to that of Gen Polks, I am unable to compare his qualifications with those of the officers of the Alab^a regts: mentioned by Mr Phelan, & therefore cannot say whether he is the best commander that can be selected for

---

ments of another of this army, under the expectation that the object of his visit to North Carolina may yet be accomplished. I have heard nothing on the subject recently, and if our papers are correct in their information, the enemy has thrown reenforcements into that State, and the Neuse is barricaded just above New Berne. There is another brigade of this army, General R. D. Johnston's, at Hanover Junction. I should like as soon as possible to get them both back." The details of the movements which led up to the campaign of 1864 in Virginia are given in notes to Dispatch 92. It is significant, however, and worthy of note here that General Lee at this early stage of the campaign urged the removal from Richmond of "everything not immediately required" and intimated that the successful defence of Richmond was in some degree at least contingent upon movements against the Federals in the South.

a brigade composed of those regts: If he is I
should feel gratified at his promotion.   I enclose
copies of papers showing my action in reference to
matters referred to in Col: O'Neals Complaint.
I also return the papers transmitted by your
Excy. [1]

I have the honour to be with great respect

Your most obt. servt

R. E. LEE

Genl.

---

[1] Enclosures and related papers not found.   For previous
correspondence regarding Colonel O'Neal, see *supra*, No. 49.
As is pointed out in the note to that dispatch, Colonel O'Neal
is said to have been commissioned brigadier-general but was
not assigned to brigade command.   He appears to have been
discontented and to have wished to remove his regiment, the
26th Alabama, from the Army of Northern Virginia.   On Jany.
31, 1864, General Lee wrote to T. J. Foster and others in
reply to a resolution forwarded by them, in which the transfer
of the 26th Alabama to the army in its native State was requested.   General Lee explained the situation of his army at
some length and with admirable courtesy but declined to transfer the regiment "unless one equally good is sent beforehand
to take its place" (O. R., 33, 1133-34).   O'Neal's regiment
was sent to Georgia after this dispatch was written but was
returned to Lee's army when Grant moved against the James
River line.   The case seems to be one of the large number
in which political influence was brought to bear for the
promotion of ambitious officers.   Lee stood firmly against
this at all times and never recommended an officer for promotion who had no other claims.   When O'Neal's commission reached General Lee, it was returned by the latter in
a formal withdrawal of his recommendation.   See No. 124,
infra.

No. 82.

HD QRS. DEPT N. VA.

April 7th '64.

To His Excellency
    JEFFERSON DAVIS
        President of the
            Confederate States.

SIR,

I would beg to call your Excellency's attention to
the following cases, in which sentences of death have
been passed and in which I, having suspended the
execution of the sentences, have forwarded the proceedings with the recommendation that the sentences
be remitted.

I would ask an early consideration of the cases in
as much as in case the recommendations are con-
curred in, I am desirous of having the men returned
to the army in time to take part in the approaching
campaign.

Private James F. Haneycutt Co. A. 4th N. C.
Regt, recommended on account of his extreme youth.

Private James Arnold Co. D. 50th Va. Regt.
recommended on account of his previous character as a soldier, the cheerful discharge of his duty
and gallantry, and of the circumstances developed
on his trial.

Privates David Ramey, I. W. Ramey and S. H.
Bothel of Co. K. and J. W. H. Ramey of G. all of
the 12th S. C. Regiment in consideration of their
former character as soldiers for gallantry and the
faithful discharge of their duties— And in Private

David Rameys case, further in consideration of his refusing to listen to the persuasions of his Uncle and quitting the party of deserters and returning to his duty, his extreme youth and the unanimous recommendation of the court.

Private Cyrus Drum Co. G. 38th N. C. Regt in consideration of the patriotic conduct of his wife, who declaring her reluctance to see him as a deserter, induced him to surrender himself the day after he reached his home.

Private Edmund M. Berry Co. H. 22nd N. C. Regt, In consideration of his character as an attentive, obedient and good soldier; his long service and his gallantry at Seven Pines, Mechanicsville, Gaines Mill, Frasiers Farm Malvern Hill and other battles.

Private S. C. Allred Co L. 22nd N. C. Regt, In consideration of his conspicuous gallantry, his general good conduct his voluntary surrender of himself, and the unanimous recommendation of the Court.

Private Peter Treffenstedt Co E 38th N C Regt. In consideration of his extreme youth, his good character as a soldier, his voluntary return to duty and the unanimous recommendation of the Court.[1]

I am with great respect

Your obt. servt.

R. E. LEE

Genl.

---

[1] These were cases of deserters who had either returned to the army or had been caught and tried. What to do with them and how to show them mercy without damaging discipline was always a problem. In 1863 and again in 1864, President Davis declared an amnesty, under the terms of

No. 83.

[Telegram]

Hd Qrs. Army of Northern Va.

7th April 1864.

Special Orders No $\frac{86}{5}$

So much of the sentences in the following cases as remains unexecuted are remitted, To wit in the case of

1. Private B. F. Coffman Co "G" 52 Va Regt on account of his youth and the mitigating circumstances developed on the trial

2. Private D. C. Courtney Co "C" 9th Va Cavy on account of the mitigating circumstances developed on the trial, and the unanimous recommendation of the Court

3. Private Thomas Y. Ward Co "H" 44—N. C. Regt on account of the mitigating circumstances developed on the trial

4. Private G. G. Fulcher Co "F"—47 Va Regt on account of his previous good character as a soldier, and the unanimous recommendations of his commanding officers

5. Private Albert Osborn Co "A" 22 Ga Regt on account of the resistance he offered to his elder

---

which soldiers who had deserted could return to their regiments without trial or punishment. These acts of leniency had no good effect. Occasionally, and especially during 1864–65, it became necessary to execute such offenders when convicted by courts-martial. In dealing with them, General Lee was personally disposed to mercy but had often to advocate severity in the interests of good order. For a general view of Lee's views on the subject, see his Dispatch of April 13, 1864, *infra*, No. 84.

brother's persuasions to desert and the practical repentance he exhibited after yielding—inducing the party deserting to return to their duty before reaching their homes

6. Pvts. Wm Bracket
Robt Bracket
Joseph Queen
Marada Queen
Henry Buff
James T. Pool
Alex Pool
John Janeey
David W. White

Graham's Battery N. C. Troops In consideration of their previous excellent character and the gallantry they have displayed in action

7. Private John Fisher Co "C" 2—N. C. Regt, on account of his gallantry at the battle of Chancellorsville, his steadfast devotion to the cause and his youthfulness

8. Private W. H. Dorton Co "E" 48 Va Regt, on account of the mitigating circumstances of the case and his previous excellent character as a soldier

9. Private James Dwyer Co "K" 49 Va—Regt, on account of the mitigating circumstances in his case proved subsequent at his trial

10. *Pvts.* Wm. F. Robinson
Jno. W. Robinson

Co "K" 63—N. C. T.

On account of their previous excellent character as soldiers and the mitigating circumstances developed on their trial

11. Private W. H. P. Jones Troop Artillery, on account of the mitigating circumstances developed in his case

12. Pvts. Geo M. Gunn ⎫
    Geo W. Phillips ⎬ Co "G"
    Danl J. Sutton ⎭ 31 Va Inf
    On account of their previous characters as soldiers, and of the high degree of probability which exists that they were misled by officers, to whom it was natural for them to look to for guidance

13. Private C. B. Pryor Co "K" 53—N. G. Regt on account of his previous character as a soldier and the facts developed subsequently to his trial

14. Private Marion Budges, Rives' Battery on account of his youth and the circumstances in his case tending to mislead one of his inexperience

15. Pvts. J. M. Stricklin ⎫ Co "G"
    Joseph Price ⎬ 55 N. C.
    ⎭ Regt
    On account of events which have occurred since their trial

The foregoing will be returned under guard to their respective commands and then restored to duty.[1]

---

[1] No record of these cases appears in the *Official Records.* The men were probably deserters or, as General Lee's last

In returning to their duty, the Genl Comdg, hopes that the above named will avail themselves of the approaching campaign to redeem themselves from the stigma of cowardice, desertion etc. now attached to them and will by their future conduct win for themselves not only forgetfulness of their past crimes but also a reputation of which their children and country may be proud. (End) By comd. Genl R E Lee

W. H. TAYLOR, A. A. G.

No. 84.

H^D Q^{RS} ARMY N. VA.
13th April 1864.

His Excy JEFFERSON DAVIS,
     Presdt. Confed. States,
       Richmond,

MR. PRESIDENT,

I have the honor to acknowledge the receipt of the letter of Col Lee written by your directions, with reference to the case of Privt Jacob Shomore Co. B. 52nd Va. Regt. and requesting my views as to the policy of extending clemency to other offenders now in confinement, or undergoing punishment.[1] With regard to prvt. Shomore, my endorsement expressed the opinion I had formed from reading the application for pardon, and the endorsements of

---

paragraph would indicate, had in some instances been tried by military court for cowardice.

[1] Not found.

Gens. Ewell & Early. I had not seen, nor have I
yet read the record of the case, it being one of these
tried by Gen Ewell's Military court before the late
law requiring these proceedings to be reviewed by
me. My views are based upon those considerations
of policy which experience has satisfied me to be
sound, and which are adverse to leniency, except
in cases showing some reason for mitigation. The
fact that prvt. Shomore had been a good soldier
previous to his desertion, is insisted upon, as it frequently has been in like cases, as a ground of mitigation, and were he alone concerned, I would be
disposed to give weight to it. But I am satisfied
that it would be impolitic and unjust to the rest of
the army to allow previous good conduct alone to
atone for an offence most pernicious to the service,
and most dangerous as an example. In this connection, I will lay before your Excellency some facts
that will assist you in forming your judgment, and
at the same time, present the opinions I have formed
on the subject of punishment in the army. In re-
viewing Court Martial cases, it has been my habit
to give the accused the benefit of all extenuating
circumstances that could be allowed to operate in
their favor without injury to the service. In addition to those parties whose sentences I have remitted
altogether or in part, or whom, when capitally convicted, I have recommended to pardon or commutation of punishment, I have kept a list during the
past winter of certain offenders, whose cases while
they could not be allowed to go unpunished altogether, without injury to the service, had some ex-

tenuating features connected with them. I confirmed the sentences, and all of them have undergone a part of their punishment, but recently I remitted the remainder in the order of which I enclose a copy. [2]

Beyond this, I do not think it prudent to go, unless some reason be presented which will enable me to be lenient without creating a bad precedent, and encouraging others to become offenders. I have arrived at this conclusion from experience. It is certain that a relaxation of the sternness of discipline as a mere act of indulgence, unsupported by good reasons, is followed by an increase of the number of offenders. The escape of one criminal encourages others to hope for like impunity, and that encouragement can be given as well by a repetition of a general act of amnesty or pardon, as by frequent exercise of clemency towards individuals. If the convicted offenders alone were concerned, there would be no objection to giving them another trial, as we should be no worse off if they again deserted than before. But the effect of the example is the chief thing to be considered, and that it is injurious, I have no doubt. Many more men would be lost to the service if a pardon be extended in a large number of cases, than would be restored to it by the immediate effects of that action.

The military executions that took place to such an extent last autumn, had a very beneficial influence, but in my judgment, many of them would have been avoided had the infliction of punishment in such cases uniformly followed the commission of the

---

[2] Doubtless the order printed *supra*, No. 83.

offence. But the failure of courts to convict or sentence to death, the cases in which pardon or commutation of punishment had been granted upon my recommendation, and the instances in which the same indulgence was extended by your Excellency upon grounds made known to you by others, had somewhat relaxed discipline in this respect, and the consequences became immediately apparent in the increased number of desertions. I think that a return to the current policy would inevitably be attended with like results. Desertion and absence without leave are nearly the only offences ever tried by our Courts. They appear to be almost the only vices in the army. Notwithstanding the executions that have recently taken place, I fear that the number of those who have escaped punishment in some one of the ways above mentioned has had a bad effect already. The returns for the month of March show 5474 men absent without leave, and 322 desertions during the month. There have been 62 desertions within the present month specially reported, but the whole number I fear considerably exceeds that some of the large number absent without leave, are probably sick men who have failed to report, and some of the deserters are probably absent without leave, but the number is sufficiently great to show the necessity of adhering to the only policy that will restrain the evil, and which I am sure will be found to be truly merciful in the end.[3] Desertions and

---

[3] The abstracts of field returns printed in the *Official Records* do not generally indicate the number absent without leave, and group under the caption "total number absent"

absence without leave not only weaken the army by the number of offenders not reclaimed, but by the guards that must be kept over those who are arrested. I think therefore that it would not be expedient to pardon & return to duty any of those now under sentence, or release those under charges, except for good cause shown.

I have the honour to be

With great respect

Your obt. servt.

R. E. LEE

Genl.

No. 85.

[Telegram]

Recd at Richmond April 15, 1864.
By telegraph from Orange C. H. 15
    To Gen BRAXTON BRAGG
    Dispatch recd.[1] I think it probably the advance

---

all the wounded, the sick, the furloughed, etc., as well as those technically or actually deserters. Yet the figures bear out General Lee's statement of the difficulties he encountered in keeping the army together as an effective fighting machine. On February 10, 1864 (O. R., 33, 1157), the aggregate present were 39,551; the absent from all causes, 28,870; on February 20 (*ibid.*, 1191), aggregate present 47,871, absent, 37,609; on March 10 (*ibid.*, 1216), aggregate present, 46,141, absent, 32,949; on March 20 (*ibid.*, 1234), aggregate present, 55,090, absent, 43,482; on April 10 (*ibid.*, 1271),—the return nearest the date of this letter,—aggregate present, 61,206, absent, 36,358. The "aggregate present and absent," the theoretical total strength of the army, ranged during this period from 68,421 to 98,572.

[1] Not found.

if made will be North of James River the other feint ascertain troops arriving at Charlottsville. No movement on this Point yet scouts Report 11th and 12th Corps consolidated. Gone to Annapolis[2]

R. E. Lee

41/410
x c
[*Endorsed*]
Orange C. H.   15 April, 64.
    11   R. E. Lee
            Genl
Regards enemy's probable advance
    directions and etc.
R. B. 26
Recd 16 Apl–64

---

[2] *Cf.* Lee to Davis, April 15, 1864, O. R., 33, 1282. Just at this time the Confederate commanders were doubtful of the enemy's intentions. News had reached General Lee from Colonel John S. Mosby and others, as indicated in this dispatch, that a large force had gathered at Annapolis under General Burnside. In addition, it was known that under General Meade on the Rappahannock was a large and rapidly-increasing army. Besides, from the neighborhood of Suffolk came reports that the force there was being augmented by fresh regiments. All this raised the question as to whether the main advance of the enemy would be made from the north, as in 1863, or up the peninsula, as in 1862. General Lee's own idea was that the advance would be from the north of the James, and to meet this he urged the War Department to gather all available troops from nearby States. He wrote (*loc. cit.*): " . . . I think it certain that the enemy is organizing a large army on the Rappahannock, and another at Annapolis, and that the former is intended to move directly on Richmond, while the latter is intended to take it in flank or

No. 86.

ORANGE CO: 19 Apl. '64.

MR PRESIDENT

I have read the letter of Lt. Col H. D. Capers

---

rear. I think we may also reasonably suppose that the Federal troops that have so long besieged Charleston will, with a portion of their iron-clad steamers, be transferred to the James River. . . . I have thought, therefore, that General Johnston might draw something from Mobile during the summer to strengthen his hands, and that General Beauregard with a portion of his troops might move into North Carolina to oppose General Burnside should he resume his old position in that State, or be ready to advance to the James River should that route be taken. . . . We shall have to glean troops from every quarter to oppose the apparent combination of the enemy. If Richmond could be held secure against the attack from the east, I would propose that I draw Longstreet to me and move right against the enemy on the Rappahannock. Should God give us a crowning victory there, all their plans would be dissipated, and their troops now collecting on the waters of the Chesapeake would be recalled to the defence of Washington. But to make this move I must have provisions and forage. I am not yet able to call to me the cavalry or artillery. If I am obliged to retire from this line, either by a flank movement of the enemy or the want of supplies, great injury will befall us. . . . Should you determine it is better to divide this army and fall back toward Richmond I am ready to do so. I, however, see no better plan for the defence of Richmond than that I have proposed." The reference to "troops arriving at Charlottesville" is to the men of Longstreet's corps who were returning to the Army of Northern Virginia from their campaign in Tennessee. Longstreet himself wrote Lee from Charlottesville in a letter which the editors of the *Official Records* think was of April 16, 1864. For General Lee's next view of Grant's plans, see **Lee to Davis, April 18, 1864, O. R., *loc. cit.*, 1290.**

which you did me the honour to transmit to me.[1] The object of the writer is no doubt praiseworthy, but I do not think it would be well to attempt at this time the reestablishment of the Society of the Cincinnati. I think it important to unite as closely as possible the interests of the army with the interests of the citizens. They are one in reality & all for the Country. It would revive I fear the ancient opposition to the order give rise to misconstruction, & furnish themes to the discontented dissatisfied & captious— We want harmony, sympathy & cooperation of all our people. You may recollect before the design of the Cincinnati was to maintain & perpetuate social feelings & relations, & how it was misrepresented. I believe too greatly by the southern states & the politicians of the Jefferson School.[2] We have now but one thing to do; to establish our independence. We have no time for anything else, & nothing of doubtful bearing on this subject should be risked—I have the honour to return to your Excy. the letter of Col: Capers.

With great respect your obt. servt.

R. E. LEE.

His Excy. JEFF^N DAVIS.

---

[1] Not found.

[2] General Lee was historically accurate in stating the opposition of the Jefferson democrats to the Society of the Cincinnati. Jefferson himself viewed it as a danger to a democratic country and expressed himself several times in a most outspoken manner, e. g., in his letter to Washington, April 16, 1784 (Memorial Edition *Jefferson's Writings*, 4, 215 ff.). A further expression of Jefferson's views regarding the society is to be

No. 87.

H^D Q^{RS} A N V$_A$.
22nd April 1864.

His Excy JEFF^N DAVIS
Presdt. C. States Richmond,
MR. PRESIDENT,

I have the honor to acknowledge the receipt of the letter of certain citizens of Winchester to the Secretary of War referred to me by your Excellency. [1]

I have given general instructions to our officers not to molest private citizens who do not take an active part against us, and was under the impression that those for whose arrest that of Messrs. Conrad & Williams was made, were officers of the pretended govt. of Va. [2] I think it necessary and proper to

---

found in his answer to questions addressed to him by M. de Meusnier, etc. (*ibid.*, 17, 80 ff.). Jefferson also notes General Washington's fear that the society might become dangerous, and relates Washington's efforts to have it abolished. See his notes on the fifth volume of Marshall's *Life of Washington* (*loc. cit.*, 17, 401 ff.).

[1] Not found.

[2] Probably Robert Y. Conrad and P. Williams, both of Winchester. Conrad was a distinguished Virginian, a former judge and a leader in the Secession Convention of 1861. Williams was a member of the town council. This appears to be an echo of an incident which occurred during January, 1864. On January 10, one William Dooly was arrested in Winchester by Confederate partisans and carried off, on the ground that he was a Federal sympathizer and spy. On the 16th., Col. R. S. Rodgers, U. S. A., commanding in the vicinity, sent to the mayor of Winchester from Martinsburg to demand the return of Dooly, on pain of holding the mayor

capture all civil officers of the Federal or pretended State Govt., as it is my object to break up the latter by preventing the exercise of its functions.[3] This policy may & doubtless will lead to retaliation on the part of the enemy who will naturally do all in their power to maintain the govt set up under their protection, but this we cannot avoid. I shall repeat

---

responsible for his removal. In reply to the protest of Dr. W. M. Fuller, mayor of Winchester, that Dooly was in the United States service and as such liable to capture, Colonel Rodgers wrote a denial and renewed his threat to arrest as hostages "the most worthy and influential citizens." On January 24, this threat was carried out and Rev. A. H. H. Boyd was arrested in Winchester,—the only able-bodied man of prominence who could be found. The comment of Colonel Rodgers incidentally throws light on the fact that the whole male population was with the army, for in excusing himself for arresting only one citizen, he writes "most of the other citizens of any prominence were either unfortunately absent from [home] or in such a delicate state of health that they were permitted to remain." Mr. Conrad and probably Mr. Williams were later arrested. Upon their protest, Colonel Rodgers offered to release them if they could prove, as they promised to do, that Dooly had in his possession a pass through the Federal lines. The result of the incident does not appear from the published correspondence (see O. R., 33, 393, 400, 401, 409, 1170, 1171).

[3] The "pretended State government" was, it is scarcely necessary to say, the hybrid Pierpont government, so-called, formed in counties of Western Virginia in sympathy with the North. This government assumed the name and dignity of the Commonwealth of Virginia and was recognized by the United States as such. Its seat, after the organization in Wheeling, was at Alexandria. Upon the evacuation of Richmond the executive offices were moved there.

my instructions on this subject to Gen Imboden &
Gen Stuart, & endeavor to put a stop to interference
with citizens except under the conditions above
mentioned.   I return the letter to the Secretary.
Very respy   Your obt servt.-

R. E. LEE
Genl.

No. 88.

[Telegram]

Recd at Richmond Va., Apl. 23, 1864
By telegraph from Orange C. H.
To Genl S. COOPER.
A & I. Genl

Dispatch received.¹ It is impossible for me to
spare Genl Ed. Johnson at this time.²
(signed)   R. E. LEE
General

---

¹ Not found.

² For what purpose is not plain. *Cf.* Lee to Davis, April
28, 1864 (O. R., 33, 1320–21): "I regret I cannot spare General E. Johnson at this time; expecting to go into battle any
day, it would be very hazardous to assign a new commander
to his division.   There is no one in it whom I could recommend for the position.   I could spare Early better at this
time than Johnson, because I might get Gordon or Hoke of
that division in his place."   He adds complimentary references to Johnson's ability and worth.   Johnson's division was
composed of the Stonewall (Walker's), Jones', Steuart's and
Stafford's brigades, Ewell's corps.   For Johnson's biography,
see C. M. H., 3, 611.   He was captured at the Bloody Angle,
May 4, 1864, and was not exchanged until November.

Official copy of Telegram received . . . and respectfully submitted to Genl B. Bragg

JOHN W. RIELY,
A. A. G

[*Endorsed*]
Orange C. H.   23 April, 64.
R. E. LEE
General
Can't spare Genl Johnson.
R B 345
Recd 24   Apl 64

No. 89.

[*Telegram*]

Telegram in cypher.

ORANGE C. H. April 24/64

His Excellency
JEFFERSON DAVIS
Should the enemy remain quiet this week and the
weather good, will it be convenient for you to visit
this army.[1]

(signed) R. E. LEE
Genl

[*Endorsed*]
Genl R E LEE
Orange C. H.
April 24 1864
Telegram in cypher

---

[1] Davis replied on the 26th that he could not come. *Cf.*
No. 90., *infra.* See also, Lee to Davis, April 28, 1864 (O. R.,

No. 90.

H^D-Q^{RS}: 25 Apl. '64.

Mʀ President

The advance of the Army of the Potomac seems to be delayed for some reason. It appears to be prepared for movement but is probably waiting for its cooperative columns. The signal officer on Clarke's Mt: reported in the forenoon of yesterday that a brigade of Cavʸ, with a few ambulances was moving on the Germana ford road.[1] Gen Fitz Lee who has two brigades of Cavʸ in the vicinity of Fredᵍ was notified to attend them, Chambliss' brigade was moved down the plank road to within four miles of the Wilderness tavern,[2] & Genl R. Johnston at the Junction placed on his guard.[3] At night the picket at Germana reported the enemy at Elys ford, but did not know in what force. This

---

33, 1320–21). General Lee probably wished to have a conference with President Davis regarding the general plan of campaign before it opened. This was his custom.

[1] These were the preliminaries for the second Wilderness or Spottsylvania campaign, set by General Grant to begin May 2, 1864. At the time of this letter, orders for the advance had been issued and the delay here mentioned was for reinforcements, better organization and the cooking of rations. For a brief description of these and preceding movements, see note to No. 92, *infra*.

[2] Brigadier-General John R. Chambliss, Jr., whose brigade (9th, 10th and 13th Va. Cavalry) was attached to W. H. F. Lee's division.

[3] Brigadier-General Robert D. Johnston, commanding 5th, 12th, 20th and 23rd N. C. Infantry, Rodes' division, Ewell's (2nd) corps.

mor^g I learn that they had not crossed, but were at the river. Their object is not yet discovered. The delay of the enemy I hope will give us grass sufficient to get our troops together.[4] The Cav^y is halted near Fred^g for the benefit of grazing on the river lands. I have brought the Art^y nearer the front.

I telegraphed to your Excy yesterday to know whether if the enemy remained quiet & the weather favourable this week, it would be convenient for you to visit the Army. It would be very gratifying to the troops & I hope pleasing to your Excy.[5]

With great respect

Your obt servt.

R. E. LEE

Genl.

His Excy JEFF^N DAVIS
Pres: C. States.

No. 91.

[*Telegram*]

Recd at Richmond Apl 30, 1864 at 3 o'clock 45 minutes,

By telegraph from Orange C. H. 3

To His Excy JEFFERSON DAVIS

Burnside's forces with Artillery Wagons Ambulances &C passed through Centerville 28th inst.

---

[4] Lack of forage, it must be remembered, forced General Lee to keep his artillery and cavalry, when possible, at a distance from him.

[5] See *supra,* No. 89 and note.

Its advance reached Manassas that evening the
regular Regiments from Boston, New York and other
points announced having reached Washington on
their way to the front I again recommend troops
be advanced towards the Rappahannock and those
belonging to this army be returned to it[1]

R E LEE

59590

[*Endorsed*]

Genl R E LEE

Orange C H

April 30, 1864

Burnsides forces passed through Centerville on
the 28th inst and etc

---

[1] *Cf.* Lee to Davis, April 30, 1864, O. R., 33, 1331. He
said: " . . . Everything indicates a concerted attack on this
front which renders me the more anxious to get back the
troops belonging to this army, and causes me to suggest, if
possible, that others be moved from points at the south where
they can be spared, to Richmond.   There will no doubt be
a strong demonstration made north and south of the James
River, which Beauregard will be able successfully to resist.
I judge, also, from present indications, that Averell and Sigel
will move against the Virginia and Tennessee Railroad or
Staunton, to resist which Generals Breckenridge and Imboden
should act in concert."   It is significant that before the beginning of this movement, which brought the centre of hostilities
from the Rapidan to the James, General Lee anticipated
practically the full plans of the enemy.   Acting on this telegram, General Bragg in Richmond suggested to General Cooper
orders for the prompt re-enforcement of the army and for the
removal to the Richmond line of available troops.   These
orders were at once carried out: Johnson's brigades from Bristol
and Hagood's from Wilmington were ordered to Richmond,

No. 92.

HᴰQᴿˢ New Verdiersville

4th May 1864.

Mr. President,

I have the honor to acknowledge the receipt of
your letter of the 2nd inst:[1] You will already have

Wise's brigade was recalled from South Carolina and Beauregard was instructed to send Hoke forward unless the latter
intended at once to attack New Berne (see O. R., *loc. cit.*,
1329–30).

[1] Davis' dispatch of May 2 not found. As this correspondence marks the formal opening of the Spottsylvania campaign,
which led to the movement to James River and the investment
of Petersburg,—all of them treated at length and from new
angles in this correspondence,—a brief review of events from
the battle of Gettysburg to this date seems necessary. Following the failure of the offensive movement at Gettysburg
on July 3, General Lee awaited an attack as he had after the
battle of Sharpsburg, and then moved slowly back across the
mountains, through western Maryland and back into Virginia.
His distinguished opponent, General Meade, was severely
criticised by President Lincoln for permitting this withdrawal
but probably realized that his forces were too much shattered
by the hard fighting at Gettysburg to begin active pursuit.
In any event, Lee crossed into Virginia again and resumed his
old position in the valley and on the Rappahannock, announcing, as is stated in this correspondence, that he did not propose to move beyond that line again. General Meade moved
forward slowly and made professions of another advance
against Lee. But when his vanguard met Lee's army in front
of Culpeper Court-House on July 24, Meade drew back. The
so-called "draft-riots" in New York, which came at this time,
put a stop to offensive operations. Until the middle of September, there was no engagement of consequence in Northern

learned that the army of Gen Meade is in motion,
and is crossing the Rapidan on our right, whether
with the intention of attacking, or moving towards
Fredericksburg, I am not able to say.   But it is

Virginia. But on September 13, Meade began a reconnaissance
toward Orange Court-House, withdrew again and showed no
signs of further activity.   On October 9, General Lee took the
offensive,—whether for a feint or for a general engagement is
doubtful,—and crossed the Rapidan which, he had announced,
he expected to keep as his main line.   The sharp engagement
at Bristoe station on October 14, 1863, between Meade's
rear-guard and Lee's van under A. P. Hill, was sufficient to
make both commanders wary.   After a successful movement
on November 7, that resulted in the capture of 1,600 Confederates, Meade overcame his timidity once more, crossed the
river on November 26 and began a flanking movement designed to turn Lee's right.   Vigilance on the part of Stuart
and the prompt advance of Ewell's corps gave Lee time to
draw up his lines and to bring up his artillery.   After vainly
feeling Lee's position at several points, Meade withdrew and
abandoned further action for the winter, except for a futile
movement on February 6.   By this time, preparations for the
spring campaign were already underway in the north.   General U. S. Grant, who had been most successful in the west,
was given the rank of lieutenant-general, under the terms of
an act approved February 29, 1864, and assumed general
control of the field operations.   He at once saw that crushing
numbers were necessary to defeat Lee and as soon as he could
do so, he consolidated all his forces into two great armies,—
one under General W. T. Sherman, to move through Alabama and Georgia, the other under himself to move on Richmond.   He foresaw that the success of these two movements
and their ultimate consolidation would crush out opposition
in the South and end the war.   To co-operate with his main
army in Virginia, he drew in troops from the Carolinas and
prepared for an advance on Richmond from the east, to be

apparent that the long threatened effort to take Richmond has begun, and that the enemy has collected all his available force to accomplish it. The column on the Peninsula if not already moving, will

directed by General Benjamin F. Butler, the tyrant of New Orleans and the most cordially hated man in the armies fighting against the South. The command in the Valley of Virginia, under General Sigel, was also strengthened and was expected to move forward with the ultimate object of striking Richmond from the west, while Butler came from the east and Grant from the north. To oppose an army that aggregated at least 116,000 men, Lee could reckon upon not more than 65,000. General Lee (see No. 80, *supra*) had not been convinced by movements prior to March 30, that Grant would move directly on Richmond. He believed that the first general advance would be in Georgia and that not until that had been successful would there be another movement on Richmond. His general plan was to be ready for any contingency but not to combine the scattered Confederate armies too quickly. Richmond should be prepared for an attack and made ready in every way possible. But until careful observation disclosed the plans of the Federals, a policy of preparation and waiting should be pursued. On March 30, however, General Lee became satisfied that the reinforcement of the army in his front meant that "operations in Virginia" would be "vigorously prosecuted by the enemy" and that, in all probability, Grant would "concentrate a large force on one or more lines." He thought that an "aggressive movement" in the west might disconcert the Federal plans but that, unless this could be done, Longstreet should be "held in readiness to be thrown rapidly in the Valley" where he could meet an attack or could rejoin the main army. The activity of Butler's forces in Eastern Virginia bore out General Lee's belief that Grant would have more than one line, but it caused some discussion as to whether the chief assault on Richmond would be from the east or the north. General

doubtless now cooperate with Gen. Meade, and we
may assume, is as strong as the enemy can make it.
Under these circumstances I regret that there is to
be any further delay in concentrating our own

Lee remained firm in his belief that Grant would lead the
main assault from the Rappahannock (see No. 85 and note
thereto) but urged that Beauregard be drawn north with
such forces as he could gather to meet the advance from
Eastern Virginia.   He thought for the time that this might
enable him to strike a decisive blow, with the help of Longstreet's troops, against Grant and force the enemy back on
their Washington defences.   By April 25, Grant's movement
confirmed him in this opinion and by April 30, he foresaw the
Federal plans precisely as they had been worked out by General
Grant.   His counter-movement was to strengthen his army
to resist the main assault, to draw in Beauregard for the defence of Richmond and to employ the few troops the Confederacy had in Western Virginia to meet the movement up
the valley.   On May 2, from a point of observation on Clarke's
mountain, Lee studied the location of the Federals, announced
with accuracy by what routes they would move and told his
corps commanders to make preparations accordingly.   In
this dispatch, General Lee makes the appeal which is the
dominant note of all his correspondence during the entire
campaign that followed—he must have more troops.   He
makes no excuses, raises no questions and expresses no doubts,
—but he must have more troops.   The rich material in the
De Renne correspondence, on the great "left flank" movement can only be appreciated when studied in close relation
to the published sources. General Lee himself appears to have
filed no full report and was so busy with the direction of his
army that his correspondence, as printed in the *Official Records*, is more fragmentary at this time than during any period
of the war.   Of the published formal reports, the itinerary of
Anderson's corps and those of Generals W. N. Pendleton and
R. S. Ewell are most valuable for precise details.

troops.[2] I fully appreciate the advantages of capturing New Berne, but they will not compensate us for a disaster in Va. or Georgia. Success in resisting the chief armies of the enemy will enable us more easily to recover the country now occupied by him, if indeed he do not voluntarily relinquish it. We are inferior in numbers, and as I have before stated to your Excellency the absence of the troops belonging to this Army weakens it more than by the mere number of men. Unless the force that it will be necessary to leave in North Carolina is able to reduce New Berne,[3] I would recommend that the attempt be postponed, and the troops in N. C. belonging to this army be at once returned to it, and that Gen Beauregard with all the force available for the purpose, be brought without delay to Richmond. Your opportunities of deciding this question are superior to my own, my advice being based upon such lights as I possess. It seems to me that the great efforts of the enemy here and in Georgia have begun, and that the necessity of our concentration at both points is immediate and imperative. I submit my views with great deference to the better judgment of your Excellency, and am satisfied that you will do what the best interests of the country require.

The army was put in motion to-day, and our

---

[2] Longstreet's corps, it must be remembered, had been separated from the Army of Northern Virginia and was just rejoining. Other scattered commands had not yet been recalled or were *en route*.

[3] Against which Hoke was operating with a part of his division detached from Lee's army.

advance already occupies our former position on Mine Run. The enemy's cavalry is reported advancing both towards Fredericksburg and in this direction, evidently with the intention of ascertaining the disposition of our forces.

With great respect
Your obt servt.
R. E. LEE
Genl.

His Excy JEFF^N DAVIS
    Presdt. C. States
    Richmond.

No. 93.

H^DQ^{RS} NEAR SPOTTSYLVANIA C. H.
9th May 1864.

His Excy JEFF^N DAVIS
    Presdt C. States
MR. PRESIDENT,

I was much gratified to learn that the enemy had retired from the Richmond and Petersburg road and that our communications were again open. The subject had occasioned me great uneasiness.[1]

---

[1] The movement to which reference is here made was one that threatened for a time the safety of the Confederate capital and the communications to the south. Advancing up the Peninsula and up the James, Gen. Benj. F. Butler had moved against the Richmond and Petersburg railroad and had sent out a cavalry expedition under General Kautz to destroy the Richmond and Danville railroad, while another column struck the railroad south of Petersburg. Much damage was done and many miles of track were torn up. It

I think that the best way to operate against the force on James River is to attack its communications, if it cannot be driven off by main force. I do not know what can be effected with our gunboats, but am satisfied that some light artillery and sharpshooters operating from the side of the river in our possession, can make the enemy very uneasy about his transportation. The night attack on Gen M^c-Clellan's transports at Harrison's Landing, is represented by him to have caused him embarrassment while his army lay there. His transports were taken down to the broad part of the river and brought up to be unloaded by night. In the narrow part of the stream where the enemy's shipping now lies, one or more batteries of light artillery, and some picked sharpshooters, could do a great deal of damage. They could also operate below on vessels ascending the river. Sharpshooters could be effectively used at night as the enemy would be obliged to use lights in loading and unloading his vessels. I believe that an active and vigilant officer with a good command could alarm the enemy very much for the safety of his communications, and might cause him to withdraw.[2] I thought it probable that the force

---

was not until General Beauregard arrived from the South with material re-enforcements that the lines could be retaken. At the date of this letter, the enemy still held a great part of the railroad. The reports of this movement, including Butler's bragging declaration that he could hold the railroad against the whole of Lee's army, will be found in O. R., 36, 2, 10 ff.,196 ff.

[2] The limitations of the Confederate forces prevented the carrying out of these plans, though the batteries along the

of the enemy south of James River was much exaggerated. I could not see from what source he could obtain the large army he was represented to have, as I believe he nearly exhausted his resources in the case to fill up the Army of the Potomac.

We have succeeded so far in keeping on the front flank of that army, and impeding its progress, without a general engagement, which I will not bring on unless a favorable opportunity offers, or as a last resort. Every attack made upon us has been repelled and considerable damage done to the enemy. With the blessing of God, I trust we shall be able to prevent Gen. Grant from reaching Richmond, and I think this army could render no more effectual service. Some of the prisoners who seem disheartened, say that since the movement began, assurances were given that the army of Gen Grant would be reinforced by forty thousand men from the West. They may have only given this out to encourage the men, but it has occurred to me that if the enemy should not deem his progress satisfactory, he might draw troops from the West. I trust that Gen. Johnston will watch carefully for such a movement.[3]

James River and the Confederate warships, until their destruction, seriously interfered with the movements of Butler and later of Grant.

[3] General Joseph E. Johnston, at this time commanding the army in Tennessee and Alabama, soon to face Sherman in the desperate advance on Atlanta. The engagements to which General Lee here refers as "keeping on the front flank" of Grant's army "and impeding its progress, without a general engagement" included the desperate fighting of May 5 and

We could not successfully resist a larger force than that to which we are opposed, and it is of the first moment that we should have timely information of any increase. I submit these suggestions with great deference to your Excellency, and am confident that nothing in your power will be omitted that can promote our success.

With great respect your obt servt.

R. E. LEE
Genl.

No. 94.

[Telegram]

Telegram Cypher

Hd. Qrs. A. N. V. 14
Via Guineas May 14 [1864]

To Presdt. DAVIS

Supplies can be sent by Petersburg or Danville to

---

6. The Federals had crossed the Rapidan on the night of May 3–4 at Ely's and Germanna Fords and had entered the Wilderness from which, just a year before, Hooker had been driven. In this tangled woodland Lee met Grant on May 5 and again on May 6, throwing him back with heavy losses and reforming his own lines without difficulty in the face of severe odds. On May 9, General Grant started for Spottsylvania Court-House, in the hope of turning Lee's right but found the Confederate behind hastily-constructed but almost impregnable works. On May 12, when Grant assaulted Lee's position, he captured Johnson's division at the Bloody Angle but could not dislodge the army. A week later he moved forward again on his left flank—to find Lee once more behind entrenchments.

Lynchburg and thence by the Orange and Alex.
Roads.[1]   We have three days supply and if more can
be had I trust all will go well.   I earnestly urge that
all cavalry and infantry that can be spared be immediately drawn from S. C. to defend Richmond and
communications[2] & that the Reserves & militia be
at once called out for the purpose of guarding bridges
& roads to this army.

(Signed)   R. E. LEE
by C. MARSHALL
A. D. C.

[*Endorsed*]
    Copy Telegram.
      R. E. LEE
    14 May 64.
      Hd. Qrs.

---

[1] The usual route for supplies from the south would, of
course, have been *via* the Petersburg and Weldon railway to
Petersburg and thence to the capital *via* the Richmond and
Petersburg.   From Richmond they could have been sent *via*
the Richmond, Fredericksburg and Potomac direct to Guinea
Station.   But Butler's movements had made this impossible and, indeed, had torn up a part of the Petersburg and
Weldon as far south as Stony Creek.   The only way open to
the army was a very circuitous one.   Sent to Danville, supplies
would have to go to Burkeville (*via* Richmond and Danville)
to Lynchburg (*via* the Southside) to Gordonsville (*via* Orange
and Alexandria) to Doswell (*via* Virginia Central) to Guinea's
(*via* R. F. & P.).   From Petersburg, since the road to Richmond was closed, supplies would have to go to Lynchburg
(*via* the Southside) and thence as above.

[2] Orders to this effect had already been issued and troops
from South Carolina had reached Petersburg.

No. 95.

[Telegram]

14

Received at Richmond May 14 1864.
By Telegraph from Spottsylvania C. H. 12
Via Gordonsville 12
To His Excellency Prest. DAVIS.

In Butler's official report to Grant May 5th he
states that he has the Eighteenth and Tenth (10)
Army Corps [which] have arrived in his Dept.[1] These
Corps. came from North & South Carolina Georgia
and Florida & constitute most of the Federal Troops
in these States. Cannot we now draw more troops
from these Depts.[2]

R. E. LEE

54 Collect 840
DB.

[Endorsed]
Telegram.   R. E. LEE
12 May 64.

---

[1] See B. F. Butler to U. S. Grant, May 5, 1864, O. R., 36,
2, 430.

[2] Another instance of General Lee's insistence that his army
must be strengthened from the south if it were successfully
to meet Grant.

No. 96.

[Telegram]

Received at Richmond, Va., May 15th. 1864.
From Head Quarters Spottsylvania C. H. 14th.
Via Guineas Station 15th.

His Excellency
President DAVIS

Breckenridge is calling for reinforcements to defend valley.[1] If withdrawn there will be no opposition to Siegel.[2]

Genl. Grant is reopening route by Aquia creek and receiving reinforcements and supplies.

Signed   R. E. LEE

[Endorsed]
Copy Telegram.
R. E. LEE
14 May 1864.
Spotts. C. Ho.

---

[1] Probably in reply to Cooper's letter of May 13, 1864 (O. R., 1, 36, 2, 998) notifying General Lee that he had ordered Breckinridge, unless Lee directed otherwise, to send a brigade to Lynchburg to co-operate with General McCausland in defence of the Virginia and Tennessee railroad.

[2] Franz Sigel, operating in the Valley. One of his columns, under Crook, moved into southwest Virginia, destroyed some supplies and temporarily interrupted communication with Tennessee. Sigel's main force was driven back by troops less than half as numerous and began a retreat.

No. 97.

[Telegram]

10

Received at Richmond May 15 1864 at 11 O'Clock 45 Minutes.

By Telegraph from Spottsylvania C. H 15
Via Guineas Station 15
To His Ex. Prest. DAVIS.

Yesterday afternoon the enemy assaulted a portion of Wilcox's line & was handsomely repulsed. Mahones[1] and Lanes[2] Brigades attacked his left & captured about three hundred prisoners & four stands of colors during the forenoon of to-day. There has been light skirmishing along the lines. The enemy seems to be shifting his position to our right. Another attack was made this afternoon on his left by Wright's[3] & Harrison's[4] Brigades resulting

---

[1] Brigadier-General William Mahone, commanding the 6th, 12th, 16th, 41st and 61st Va. regiments, Anderson's division, Hill's (3rd) corps.

[2] Brigadier-General James H. Lane, commanding the 7th, 18th, 28th, 33rd and 37th N. C. regiments, Wilcox's division, Hill's (3rd) corps.

[3] Brigadier-General Ambrose R. Wright, commanding the 3rd, 22nd, 48th Ga. regiments and 2nd Georgia battalion, Anderson's division, as above.

[4] Doubtless *Harris*,—N. H., who belonged also to Anderson's division and commanded a brigade composed of the 12th, 16th, 19th and 48th Miss. regiments.

in the capture of some prisoners & a stand of colors.[5]

R. E. LEE

84 Col 840
    Ka
[*Endorsed*]
        Telegram.
Genl. R. E. LEE
Spottsylvania C. H. May 15 64.

No. 98.

[*Telegram*]

Received at Richd.   May 18 1864 at 3 O'Clock
        45 A.M. minutes.
By Telegraph from Spottsylvania C. H. 17 to Gen.
    BRAXTON BRAGG.
            Via Guineas 18th.
    Telegram received.[1]   I request that Gen. McLaws
be not ordered to this army, but assigned to duty
elsewhere.[2]

R. E. LEE
Genl.

20 Coll 200.

---

    [5] These brushes are not mentioned in the published reports
of the officers concerned.   They were part of General Grant's
preliminaries to the attempted turning-movement of May 19,
following the unsuccessful but costly efforts of May 12.
    [1] Not found.
    [2] This was Major-General Lafayette McLaws, a native of
Georgia and long a division commander of Longstreet's
corps. (For biography, see C. M. H., 6, 431 ff.)   He had

[*Endorsed*]
    Spottsylvania C. H. May 17 64.
        Gen. R. E. LEE
Requests that McLaws be not sent to him, but
    assigned to some duty elsewhere.
               R. B. 769.
        Recd. May 18 1864.

          No. 99.

      HEAD QURS A. N. VA.
             18th May 1864.
His Excy JEFFERSON DAVIS
    President Confed. States.
MR. PRESIDENT

The position of affairs has undergone no material
change since my telegram to the Secretary of War
last night. The federal army occupies the Valley
of the Ny extending across the road from Spottsylvania C. H. to Fredericksburg. His position is
strongly entrenched, and we cannot attack it with
any prospect of success without great loss of men

---

gone to Tennessee with Longstreet and had some difficulties
with his commander which resulted in his removal from his
command and in court-martial. Longstreet's version of the
affair is to be found in his *From Manassas*, etc. (ed. 1896),
500 ff., 518, 548, etc. General Bragg suggested McLaws'
return to his command (O. R., 36, 2, 955) on May 6, and Cooper
issued the order the next day. At the time of this message,
McLaws was in command at Burkeville but was later sent
to Georgia. No reason has been assigned for General Lee's
wish not to have him with the army. His probable reason
was deference to Longstreet.

which I wish to avoid if possible. The enemy's artillery is superior in weight of metal and range to our own,[1] and my object has been to engage him when in motion and under circumstances that will not cause us to suffer from this disadvantage. I think by this means he has suffered considerably in the several past combats, and that his progress has thus far been arrested. I shall continue to strike him whenever opportunity presents itself, but nothing at present indicates any purpose on his part to advance.[2] Neither the strength of our army nor the condition of our animals will admit, of any extensive movement with a view to draw the enemy from his position.

I think he is now waiting for reinforcements. Scouts report that the 22d corps, composed of invalids, or as they are now termed, veteran reserves, has already arrived, and also the Irish Battalion organized at Washington. The garrisons that have been in the fortifications around the latter place, Baltimore, and in other localities at the north, including some regiments of heavy artillery armed as infantry, have also arrived.

Other reports represent that General Grant has

---

[1] The most accurate estimates are that Grant began this campaign with 274 guns, Lee with 224. The difference of 50 guns was by no means all, however, as Grant's ordnance was superior to that of Lee in range and in ammunition. Lee was only able to hold his own through the admirable service of his field-pieces.

[2] As a matter of fact, Grant began a new movement against Lee's right the next day.

called for additional reinforcements, and been assured
by the Federal Secretary of War that he shall have
all he requires. The volunteers for one hundred days
will be used as garrisons, and all the available troops
in the North will doubtless be sent to the Army of the
Potomac. The importance of this campaign to the
administration of Mr. Lincoln and to General Grant
leaves no doubt that every effort and every sacrifice
will be made to secure its success. A Washington
telegram of the 11th published in a northern paper
of the 13th states that it is reported that the 10th
and 18th Army corps now north of the James will be
called to General Grant, as they are not strong
enough to take Richmond, and too strong to be kept
idle. The recent success of General Beauregard may
induce the fulfilment of this report, if the idea was
not previously entertained.

It is also stated that the troops from General
Sherman's Dept under General Smith, which reinforced Genl Banks for the Red River expedition,
have been ordered back, it may be to join Genl
Sherman or to be brought East. The defensive
position of Genl. Johnston which I doubt not is
justified by his situation, may enable the enemy to
detach a portion of the force opposed to him for
service here. I trust that no effort will be spared to
prevent this, or should it occur, to give timely notice
of it.

From all these sources, General Grant can, and
if permitted will repair the losses of the late battles,
and be as strong as when he began operation.

I deem it my duty to present the actual, and what

I consider the probable situation of affairs to your Excellency, in order that your judgment may be guided in devising the means of opposing the force that is being arrayed against us.[3]   I doubt not that you will be able to suggest the best measures to be taken, and that all that the emergency calls for will be done as far as it is in your power.

With great respect

Your obt servt

R. E. Lee

Genl.

No. 100.

[*Telegram*]

Telegram-Cypher.

Spottsylvania C. H. May 18, via Milford
Recd Richmond May 19, 2 A.M.

To His Ex. Presdt. Davis,

I think Genl Grant is waiting for reinforcements. The 22nd a Corps under Augur and some artillery serving as infantry are arriving.   The Chronicle of the 13th states that the 10 and 18 Corps . . .

---

[3] To be understood, this dispatch must be read in connection with No. 100, written on the same day and much balder in its statement of the precise situation.   Lee insisted here, as during the previous correspondence of this campaign, that he could only hope to cope with Grant by getting reinforcements, not merely to meet the large and regular additions to Grant's army but to recover the heavy battle losses.   The telegram which follows (No. 100) is the first statement he made to Mr. Davis that the alternatives were either a withdrawal to Richmond or the reinforcement of his army.

. . . . . Richmond where they do no good to
Genl Grant. The Forts around Washington and
the Northern cities are being stripped of troops.
The question is whether we shall fight the battle
here or around Richmond. If the troops are obliged
to be retained at Richmond I may be forced back.

(signed) R E LEE

[*Endorsed*]
> Copy
> Telegram
>> Genl LEE
>>> Spotts C. H.
>>> May 18/64
>>> May 19/64

No. 101.

[*Telegram*]

Telegram Cypher.

Recd at Richmond May 18 at 10 o'clock 15 min.
Spottsylvania C. H. May 18, via Guineas
> To His Ex. Presdt. DAVIS
> If the changed circumstances as around
Richmond will permit, I recommend that such troops
as can be spared be sent to me at once. Reports
from our scouts unite in stating that reinforcements
to Genl Grant are arriving. The 22nd Corps in
whole or part has passed through Fredericksburg
and drafted men are arriving from the North[1]

(signed) R E LEE

---

[1] No messages from President Davis to General Lee of this
date appear in the *Official Records*. Lee was beginning to

    Copy
      Telegram
          Genl LEE
             Spotts. C. H. May 18/64
             May 18/64

No. 102.

[*Telegram*]

Telegram in Cypher.

SPOTTSYLVANIA C. H. May 20, 1864.
His Excy. Presdt. DAVIS,

Telegram of 19th received.[1] Am fully alive to importance of concentration and being near base. The latter consideration may impel me to fall back eventually. Will do so at once if deemed best.

---

realize that no substantial reinforcements were to be had. For notice of the troops sent him, see No. 104, *infra*. With the telegrams of this date in the De Renne correspondence, appears one from "Kendrick," the telegraph operator at Guinea's, dated from Milford, to Dr. W. J. Morris, President of the company, as follows:

MILFORD, May 18, 64.
DR. W. J. MORRIS.

Enemy appeared in full view of Guineas this evening and continued to advance. When within few hundred yards of depot I started on hand car with register and magnet. Did not have time to save balance. When about one mile this side we discovered very large fire, supposed to be depot. They tried to cut us off by sending squad of Cavalry around County road, but failed. Do not think they will remain there long. (signed) KENDRICK.

[1] Not found, unless it be dispatch in O. R., 51, 2, 945. It may be noted that Gen. P. G. T. Beauregard, commanding on

My letters gave you my views.[2]   The troops promise[d]
will be advantageous in either event.[3]   I have posted
Breckenridge at Junction to guard communication,
whence he can speedily return to Valley if necessary.[4]
His Infantry numbers twenty-four hundred [5]

(Sgd) R E LEE

Genl

[*Endorsed*]
   Telegram in cipher
     from Genl R E LEE
       Spottsylvania C. H.
        May 20, 1864

No. 103.

[Telegram]
HANOVER JUNCTION, May 22/64
9:30 A.M.

Hon J A SEDDON,
   Secy of War,
      I have arrived at this place with the head of

---

the James, was at this time urging on General Braxton Bragg
and on President Davis the importance of a withdrawal by
General Lee to the Chickahominy line. Davis may have
questioned Lee as to the advisability of a concentration upon
Richmond. See O. R., 36, 2, 1023–25.

[2] *Supra*, Nos. 100 and 101, in which Lee informed the
President that he might be forced back on the capital unless
reinforced.

[3] See dispatch of May 22, *infra*, No. 104.

[4] John C. Breckenridge who had succeeded Major-General
Samuel Jones in command in Western Virginia. The
"junction" referred to is Hanover Junction, for which see
infra, No. 103, Note 1.

[5] *Cf* dispatches of May 22 and 23, *infra*, Nos. 104 and 105.

Ewell's Corps.¹ Longstreet is close up. Hill I
expect to come in on my right but have not heard
from him since I left him last night. I have learned
as yet nothing of the movements of the enemy East
of the Mattaponi²

(Signed) R E Lee
Genl

[*Endorsed*]

    Han Junction 22d May, 64
      R E Lee General
Reports his arrival with Ewell's Corps—Longstreet's close up—Hill to come in on right—Nothing
of the enemy East of the Mattaponi

R B 844
Richd. May

No. 104.

Head Qrs Army W. Va.
5 A.M. 22nd May 1864.
Dickinson's Mill
Telegraph Road

His Excy Jeff Davis
    Richmond
Mʳ President
    I have had the honor to receive this morning your

---

¹ Hanover Junction, now known as Doswell, is the junction
of the Virginia Central (C. & O.) and R. F. & P. railroads.

² Troops and supplies were expected up the Pamunky
River (see No. 113, *infra*) from deep water at West Point on
the York, to support General Grant's army as its left swung
around in that direction. It was also surmised (see No. 104,
infra) that Grant was endeavoring to put the Mattaponi
between his army and Lee.

letters of the 19th[1] & 20th[2] inst: Part of the troops you were so kind as to order to me have joined, viz, Hoke's & Barton's brigades— Corses' & Kemper's reached Milford yesterday evening, but I have not been able as yet to get them to me, I hope to do so to-day.[3] The enemy night before last commenced

---

[1] Not found.

[2] An important communication, printed in O. R., 36, 950 ff. In this letter Mr. Davis reports to General Lee the movement against General Butler's army near Bermuda Hundred, states what troops are with General Beauregard and *en route* to strengthen Lee and then explains the proposals of General Beauregard mentioned in Note 1, on the dispatch of May 20, 1864, *supra*, No. 102. He adds: "My order for the movement of troops, stated above, is not in accordance with that plan. If our armies in Northern Virginia and on the south side of the James River were near enough to each other to combine their operations, we should have therein a palpable advantage, but you, who know the country, its rivers, and the enemy's water transportation, can justly appreciate what would be lost in gaining that advantage. How far the morale of your army would be affected by a retrograde movement no one can judge as well as yourself. It would certainly encourage the enemy, and if he wants time and opportunity to recruit, we would thus have it with absolute security. We should lose the Central railroad and all the supplies, together with the growing crops, in that portion of Northern Virginia. I am willing, as heretofore, to leave the matter to your decision. You are better informed than any other can be of the necessities of your position—at least as well informed as any other of the wants and dangers of the country in your rear, including the railroad and other lines of communication, and I cannot do better than to leave your judgment to reach its own conclusions." In No. 105, *infra*, General Lee answers more in detail.

[3] On May 18, "the brigades of Corse, Kemper, Barton and

to withdraw from his position & to move towards
Bowling Green [4]—The movement was not discovered
until after daylight, & in a wooded country like that
in which we have been operating, where nothing is
known beyond what can be ascertained by feeling,
a day's march can always be gained— The enemy
left in his trenches the usual amount of force generally
visible, & the reports of his movement were so vague
& conflicting that it required some time to shift the
truth.   It appeared however that he was endeavoring
to place the Matapony river between him & our
army, which secured his flank, & by rapid movements
to join his cavalry under Sheridan to attack Richmond— I therefore thought it safest to move to the
Annas to intercept his march, and to be within easy
reach of Richmond.   As soon therefore as his forces
in my front C[d] be disposed of, I withdrew the army
from its position, & with two corps arrived here this
morning— The 3rd corps (Hills) is moving on my
right & I hope by noon to have the whole army behind the Annas.   I should have preferred contesting
the enemy's approach inch by inch; but my solicitude
for Richmond caused me to abandon that plan.
The enemy's whole force with the exception of the
9th corps had left their former positions before
dark yesterday[5]   I have not heard of their infantry

Hoke, with Lightfoot's battalion of artillery" were ordered
from Beauregard's army to re-enforce General Lee (O. R.,
36, 2, 1022).

[4] Caroline County, about three miles from the R. F. and
P. railroad.

[5] *Cf.* Lee to Anderson, May 21, 1864, O. R., 36, 2, 815.

beyond Bowling Green— I have thought it probable
that he might from that point open communication
with Port Royal on the Rappahannock; but I learned
yesterday from a scout returned from the north of
that river, that they had commenced to rebuild the
railroad from Aquia Ck to Fredericksburg— As soon
as I can get more positive information concerning
the movements of the enemy, I will forward it to you[6]

I am with great respect

Your obt servant

R. E. LEE

Genl.

---

[6] On May 19, General Grant took up the flanking movement which had been delayed by Lee's stubborn assault and
began once more to move his left forward. On May 23, he
reached the North Anna and found Lee as formidably entrenched as at any time during the campaign. It is significant
that Lee was not at this time certain of the line Grant would
take in moving on Richmond. The Confederate commander,
it would appear (see No. 105), thought that Grant would adhere
to the line of the Richmond, Fredericksburg and Potomac
Railroad and would not continue as previously by his left
flank. General Lee had not abandoned his policy of attacking
Grant on the march, but he realized the growing danger to
Richmond and apparently anticipated that close defence for
which he had already warned Mr. Davis to prepare the capital.
The rivers "Anna" mentioned by General Lee are the North
and South Anna, small streams but important for military
purposes. The North Anna is the dividing line between
Spottsylvania and Caroline counties on the north and Louisa
and Hanover on the south. The South Anna flows through
Louisa and Hanover and courses east to join the North Anna
near Hanover and to form the Pamunkey, one of the two
streams that unite to form the York.

No. 105.

HEAD QUARTERS A. N. VA.

23rd May 1864.

His Excy JEFFN DAVIS
President Confed: States
Richmond Va.

MR. PRESIDENT

Your letter of the 19th inst giving me a general account of the condition of military affairs has been received.[1] This army is now lying south of the North Anna. I have moved General Breckinridge's command in front of Hanover Court House to guard the main route from Richmond.[2] I will add to it Col: B. T. Johnson's,[3] which I think will be sufficient to check any movement in that direction if made. At present all my information indicates that the movement of General Grant's army is in the direction of Milford Station,[4] and General Hampton who is in front of that place is of the opinion that it will march upon Hanover Junction by that route. If that is its course, I think it is for the purpose of adhering to the railroad which, as I informed you yesterday, I hear is being repaired north of the

---

[1] See the substance of this letter in Note 2, No. 104, *supra*.

[2] *Cf.* Lee to Breckinridge, May 21, 1864: "Remain at Junction. Defend the position. Get up all your transportation and be prepared to move. Fitz Lee is following cavalry (O. R., 36, 3, 810).

[3] Colonel, later Brigadier-General Bradley T. Johnson, commanding the Maryland line,—2nd Maryland Infantry, 1st Maryland Cavalry, 1st, 2nd and 4th Maryland Artillery.

[4] On the Fredericksburg railroad, a few miles above Hanover Junction.

Rappahannock.[5] During its reconstruction, General Grant will have time to recruit and reorganize his army, which as far as I am able to judge, has been very much shaken. I think it is on that account that he interposed the Mattapony between us. Whatever route he pursues I am in a position to move against him, and shall endeavor to engage him while in motion. I shall also be near enough Richmond I think, to combine the operations of this army with that under General Beauregard and shall be as ready to reinforce him if occasion requires, as to receive his assistance. As far as I can understand, General Butler is in a position from which he can only be driven by assault, and which I have no doubt, has been made as strong as possible. Whether it would be proper or advantageous to attack it, General Beauregard can determine, but if not, no more troops are necessary there than to retain the enemy in his entrenchments. On the contrary General Grants army will be in the field, strengthened by all available troops from the north, and it seems to me our best policy to unite upon it and endeavor to crush it. I should be very glad to have the aid of General Beauregard in such a blow, and if it is possible to combine, I think it will succeed. The courage of this army was never better, and I fear no injury to it from any retrograde movement that may be dictated by sound military policy,[6] I do not think it would be well to permit the enemy to approach the Chickahominy,

[5] That is to say, north of Fredericksburg.

[6] Davis, in his letter of May 20, had raised some question as to the effect of a "retrograde" movement on the army.

if it can be prevented, and do not see why we could not combine against him after he has crossed the Pamunky as on the Chickahominy.[7] His difficulties will be increased as he advances, and ours diminished,

---

[7] The situation, briefly stated, was this: General Beauregard with a small army was defending Petersburg and was watching General Butler. He believed that General Lee could achieve the best results by assuming the defensive on the inner, or Chickahominy line, in front of Richmond, while sufficient troops from Lee's army were sent him to destroy Butler. In this way, Beauregard believed that the Federals south of the James could be kept from effecting a junction with Grant and that General Lee, thereby, would have a much simpler task. He anticipated, of course, that after he had struck Butler he could move with practically his whole force to assist General Lee. In the dispatch here printed, General Lee explains his reasons for opposing Beauregard's plan. Butler, he thought, though "bottled up," was in a position from which he could only be driven by a costly assault. On the other hand, the Federals south of the James could be kept where they were by a comparatively small force. The rest of Beauregard's men could cooperate in what was really the one task before them—meeting and defeating Grant. Lee was furthermore opposed to fighting on the close line of the Chickahominy, preferring to remain in the open where he might have opportunity of carrying out his favorite plan and of striking Grant while moving. In this hope Lee was defeated. Grant's next move, which could not be disclosed until too late to prevent it, was to slide his left flank once more and to take position on the Chickahominy. Here he was kept at bay until the desperate encounter at Cold Harbor showed the Federal chieftain the wasteful futility of attempting to turn Lee. The movement across the James, which Lee speedily foresaw, was the next step in the campaign. It should be noted here that at no time during his career did General Lee's military genius shine more brightly than in

and I think it would be a great disadvantage to us
to uncover our railroads to the west, and injurious
to open to him more country than we can avoid.[8]
I am with great respect
Your obt Servt
R. E. LEE
Genl.

No. 106.

[Telegram]

TAYLORSVILLE May 25, 1864
To Genl BRAGG.
I see no advantage in transferring Echols from his
present Brigade, to Command that of McClausland.
Dissatisfaction already existing, would I think be
increased. A Commander will have to be appointed
or assigned for McClausland's Brigade, or it can be
left in Command of the Senior Colonel B. H. Jones[1]
(Signed) R. E. LEE
Genl

---

the disposition of his small army to meet Grant on the advance
from the Rapidan. Try as he would, Grant could not move
forward but that he found Lee safely entrenched ahead of
him, inviting an assault.

[8] This consideration was by no means a small one, as the
Virginia Central Railroad, which could not have been held
had troops been sent to reinforce Beauregard, was the main
channel for communication with the Valley of Virginia.

[1] John Echols (1823-1896) was a native Virginian, a former
student of the Virginia Military Institute and a lawyer of
prominence before the war. He served as colonel of the
27th Virginia and was promoted for gallantry to the rank of

"Official Copy"
Respectfully submitted to His Excellency
The President
FRANK PARKER
Maj. & A. D. C.
[*Endorsed*]
Telegram
Genl LEE to Genl BRAGG
Taylorsville
May 25/64.
May 26/64

No. 107.

HEAD QURS. ARMY NO. VA.
4¾ A.M. 25th May 1864.

His Excy JEFFERSON DAVIS
Presdt Confed. States
Richmond, Va.
MR. PRESIDENT
I have the honor to enclose a dispatch of the 16th
inst from Lieut Genl Grant to Major Genl Burnside,
captured on the person of the A. A. A. G. 1st Brigade,
1st Division 9th Army Corps giving an account of

---

brigadier-general in April, 1862. During most of the war
he served in Western Virginia where his personal influence,
not less than his tested ability, made him extremely valuable.
After the surrender of Lee's army in April, 1865, Echols
pressed forward and accompanied Mr. Davis on his retreat
to Georgia. John McClausland (born 1837) was a graduate
of the Virginia Military Institute and an instructor there at
the outbreak of the war. He organized the famous "Rockbridge

certain successes of the Federal arms, and of the amount of reinforcements sent to the Army of the Potomac.[1] I understand that all the forts and posts have been stripped of their garrisons. Norfolk, Fort Monroe, Washington &c are left with but small guards, and every available man has been brought to the front. This makes it necessary for us to do likewise, and I have no doubt that your Excellency will do all in your power to meet the present emergency. If Genl Beauregard is in condition to unite with me in any operation against Genl. Grant, I should like to know it, and at what point a combination of the troops could be made most advantageously to him.[2]

Artillery" and later was a recruiting officer in Western Virginia where he raised and was commissioned colonel of the 36th Virginia. At this time he still ranked colonel but had been engaged in numerous sharp fights in Western Virginia where he served during most of the war. At the battle of Cloyd's farm and during Early's raid into Maryland, he was conspicuous.

[1] Doubtless Grant to Burnside, May 16, 1864, O. R., 36, 2, 825: "I have official notice that up to yesterday 24,700 men had sailed and were ready to sail from Washington to reenforce this army. This number is exclusive of about 3,000 for the garrison of Belle Plain. Butler had carried the outer works at Fort Darling, Sheridan has cut both railroads; had whipped Stuart's cavalry, and had carried the outer works at Richmond, besides whipping the infantry sent out to drive him away; thinks he could have gone into the city, but not knowing our positions, nor those of Butler, did not know that he could stay; therefore went in pursuance of his orders. . . ."

[2] Cf. Beauregard to Davis, May 21, 1864. In this letter Beauregard expresses the belief that with 10,000 men he could "hold in check and neutralize" Butler's army. His

We have been obliged to withdraw from the banks of the North Anna, in consequence of the ground being favorable to the enemy, and the stage of the water such that he can cross at any point.

Our lines cover Hanover Junction, extending up the river to Anderson's ford, and thence south to Little River. The enemy yesterday moved around us in all directions, examining our position, and entrenching as he came, until he reached the Central Road above Verdon.[3] I presume he has destroyed all within his reach. In the evening he fell back towards the North Anna.

> With great respect
> Your Obt. Servt.,
> R. E. LEE
> Genl.

---

own force Beauregard estimated to be: infantry, 13,000, artillery, 850, cavalry, 680, total, 14,530. He wrote: "With regard to re-enforcing General Lee, I shall be most happy to do so whenever you shall judge proper to order it" (O. R., 36, 3, 818-19). This statement was in answer to a request as to what he might do to carry out the plan proposed by Lee. It is to Beauregard's credit that he yielded to the judgment of the President, General Lee, General Bragg and Secretary Seddon in this matter. It is equally to his credit that he did not fail to caution the executive of dangers on his own line. When he dared do so, he spared Hoke. As will be apparent from the dispatches covering the period June 14-17, Beauregard's forces probably saved Richmond at a time when the absence of a single other brigade from his little army would at the least have meant the capture of Petersburg and the isolation of Richmond.

[3] A way-station on the Virginia Central Railroad, a few miles west of Hanover Junction.

No. 108.

[Telegram]

Hd. Qrs. Atlees
10¾ a.m. 28 May 64.

General Braxton Bragg
   Richmond, Va.

I have just learned that Genl. Glary from causes unknown to me burned Meadow bridge last night. Please cause it to be re-established as soon as practicable. Troops will assist in the re-construction. Timber suitable for the purpose should be sent as there is none just there. Meanwhile a pontoon bridge should be laid. It is important to this army.

Please have a telegraph operator sent to Atlees.[1]

R. E. Lee

Offl.
   W. H. Taylor
      A. A. G.

[Endorsed]

Hd. Qrs. Atlees 28 May 64. R. E. Lee Genl. Requests that Meadow Bridge be immediately reestablished. R. B. 945 Telegraph operator Ashland. Recd. 28 May 3: 2 p.m.

---

[1] " Genl. Glary" is evidently a mistake in transmission, as there was no officer by that name in the Confederate army. Meadow Bridge was highly important at this time. It crossed the Chickahominy River a short distance from the railroad and was the only bridge on the Bridge Road. The nearest was at the point where the Mechanicsville Turnpike crossed the river. Appended to this dispatch is a telegram from W. H.

No. 109.

HEAD QURS. 28th May 1864.
Near Hughes Shop on the
road to Atlees.

His Excy JEFFERSON DAVIS
    President Confed States
MR. PRESIDENT

Information I received yesterday at noon led me
to believe that the enemy was proceeding from near
Hanover Town by Hawes'[1] Shop towards the Mechanicsville Road, and induced me to take position
on the ridge between the Totopotomey and Beaver
Dam Creeks, so as to intercept his march to Richmond. On reaching this point I could only learn
that cavalry had been seen as far as Hawes' Shop,
and that a column of infantry was seen from Hanover
Court House passing down what is called the River
Road, which I understand to be the road from Hanover Ct. House to Hanover Town. The want of
information leads me to doubt whether the enemy is
pursuing the route just described, or whether, now
that he finds the road open by Ashland, he may not
prefer to take it. This causes me to pause for a

Taylor, General Lee's adjutant-general, in which the Super-
intendent of the South Telegraph Company is requested to
send an operator to Atlee's, where General Lee's headquarters
were established that day. Atlee's is located on the Virginia
Central Railroad, about one mile beyond the Chickahominy.

[1] The name is Haw and the store is written "Haw's" on
the maps. Haw's store is located just north of the Totopotomoy, opposite Salem Church.

while, but should he proceed on the road to Mechanicsville, the army will be placed on the Totopotomey
Ridge.

Should he on the other hand take the Telegraph
Road,[2] I shall try to intercept him as near Ashland as
I can. In either event I shall endeavor to engage
him as soon as possible, and will be near enough to
Richmond for General Beauregard[3] to unite with me
if practicable. Should any field nearer to Richmond
be more convenient to him and he will designate it,
I will endeavor to deliver battle there.

I am with great respect

Your obt. servt.

R. E. LEE

Genl.

---

[2] The significance of this dispatch lies, of course, in the dis-
closure that General Lee was not at this time certain whether
Grant would move on Richmond from the north or northeast.
The position which General Lee had taken was between two
small streams, one of which, the Totopotomoy, ran almost
east and west, and the other, Beaver Dam Creek, ran west and
east until it turned south and joined the Chickahominy.
Grant was moving as fast as he could to take position on the
Chickahominy and, in consequence, passed around General
Lee's right, which necessitated only a simple turn to place
Lee in the familiar positions around Cold Harbor. There
General Grant met the most severe repulse of the campaign.
Had Grant followed the Telegraph Road, mentioned by Gen-
eral Lee, his course would have been more to the west.

[3] General Beauregard's main line was along the "neck"
between the James and Appomattox where Butler had been
"bottled up." He could cross the river at Drewry's Bluff and
advance over the field of Seven Pines or he could entrain to
Richmond and march to Lee's line. When Hoke was sent

No. 110.

[*Telegram*]

Received at Richmond May 29, 1864.
By telegraph from Hd Qrs A. N. Va.

To Genl B. BRAGG

Via Atlees I telegraphed Genl
Beauregard this morning that I would be happy to
see him here to-day. I can not say where I will be
tomorrow[1]

R. E. LEE

244/80 R

[*Endorsed*]
Atlees
May 29, 1864.
RO. E. LEE Genl
Reports that he has telegraphed Genl Beauregard
that he would be happy to see him today—can't say
where I will be tomorrow   R B 958
Recd May 29 64.

---

from Beauregard to Lee, he went by train to Richmond and
marched out on the Mechanicsville turnpike. See No. 115,
infra.

[1] On May 28, President Davis sent to General Beauregard
by special messenger a copy of General Lee's letter of the
same date, with verbal instructions (Davis to Beauregard,
O. R., 51, 2, 966; Beauregard to Davis, O. R., 36, 3, 849).
Both Lee and Beauregard sent telegrams regarding the meeting between them, which was held the next day. See No.
111.

No. 111.

[Telegram]

ATLEES, May 29, 1864.
9 o'clock P.M.

His Excellency
JEFFERSON DAVIS

In conference with Genl Beauregard he states that he has only twelve thousand Infantry and can spare none.[1] If Genl Grant advances tomorrow I will engage him with my present force

(Signed) R E LEE
General

[Endorsed]
Copy Telegram
Genl R E LEE
ATLEES May 29, 1864

---

[1] This was the position Beauregard had previously taken and had been communicated by him to President Davis several times. On the date of this dispatch Beauregard wrote the President: "My force is so small at present that to divide for the purpose of reinforcing Lee would jeopardize the safety of the part left to guide my lines and would greatly endanger Richmond itself" (O. R., 36, 3, 849). This put an end to the proposal to move a part of Beauregard's army across the James to cooperate with Lee and determined the latter to meet Grant if he attacked. It is of course possible that had Beauregard joined Lee, a decisive blow might have been struck Grant. But on the whole, the decision reached was wise for the time and fortunate for the future. Small as was Beauregard's little army it held Grant's advance on June 14–16. The dispatch of troops from Butler to Grant at this time temporarily changed the situation and enabled Beauregard to loan Lee a part of his command for temporary service. See *infra*, No. 114, especially Note 3.

No. 112.

[Telegram]

Received at Richd. May 30 1864.
By telegraph from Atlees 30.   To Gen. B. BRAGG.
7.30 A.M.   I was informed that two (2) Georgia
Battalions the 11th. & 12th. were under orders for
this army.   Only the 12th. has reported.   Will the
11th. or any other Georgia Battalion or Regiment
be sent here?¹

R. E. LEE
Genl.

34/680

[Endorsed]
Atlees
   May 30 '64.
      R. E. LEE
         Genl.
Reports that he has been informed that 2 Geo.
Batts, the 11th. & 12th. were under orders for this
army.   Only 12th. has reported.   Will 11th. or any
other Geo. Batt. or Regt. be sent here?
R. B. 960.
   Recd. May 30 1864.

---

¹ The 12th Georgia battalion of heavy artillery had been
ordered from Savannah on May 15, 1864 (O. R., 36, 2, 1011),
had passed Wilmington with 480 men on May 20 (*ibid.*, 3,
808), and had been ordered to General Lee on May 21 (*ibid.*,
813). The "11th," not mentioned during the campaign,
may be the "18th" which was brought from Georgia at the
same time (aggregate strength 250–300) but had been sent

No. 113.

[Telegram]

Received at Richd. May 30 1864.
By telegraph from Head Quarters 30.
To Gen B. BRAGG via Stones Farm.

3.15 P.M. Scout from lower Pamunky reports that Genl. Custer and Junior officers of enemy's Cavalry near Old Church state that Butler's fleet will be at West Point today. This may be the fleet reported going down the James yesterday and is probably conveying Smith's Corps to Grant.[1] The idea is general amongst them that Butler is to reinforce them. One steamer was at White House yesterday & was communicated with by officer & detachment from Grant's army. Scout left vicinity of White House at 8 this morning at that time had heard nothing of appearance of fleet. Citizens reported Boats at Brick House.

R. E. LEE
Genl.

102/2040 Chg.

---

to the Mattoax bridge to relieve a detachment of the 28th Va. (*loc. cit.*, 813). The 46th, 47th and 56th Georgia regiments had also been ordered from the south to join Lee (*ibid.*, 2, 1011).

[1] See *supra*, No. 103. Troops dispatched from Butler to Grant could go down the James River by steamer, up the York to West Point and thence up the Pamunkey to White House, at the head of navigation. They would then be within a short march of the Federals. On May 26, in obedience to orders, General Butler notified General Grant that he would send 17,000 men by this route. See O. R., 36, 3, 234, 235, 278, etc.

[*Endorsed*]
    Stones Farm
      May 30. 1864.
        R. E. LEE
        Genl.

Scouts from lower Pamunky reports that Genl. Custer & Jr. officers of enemy's Cav. near Old Church state that Butler's fleet will be at West Point to-day. May be the fleet reported going down the James yesterday and is probably conveying Smith's Corps to Grant. Steamer at White House yesterday & was communicated with by officer and detachment from Grant's Army. Scouts left vicinity of White House at 8 this A.M. At that time heard nothing of appearance of fleet. Citizens report Boats at Brick House.

    R. B. 994   Recd. May 31. 64.

No. 114.

          H^DQ^{RS} ARMY N. VA.
             30th May 1864.

His Excy JEFF^N DAVIS
    Presdt. C. States,
MR PRESIDENT,

As I informed you by telegraph,[1] my conference with Gen. Beauregard resulted in the conclusion on his part, that we cannot spare any troops to reinforce this army. He thinks the enemy in his front superior to him in numbers. Of this I am unable to judge, but suppose of course that with his means of

---

[1] See *supra*, No. 111.

information, his opinion is correct. I think it very important to strengthen this army as much as possible, and it has occurred to me that the presence of the two armies north and south of James River, may render it possible to spare with safety some of the troops in Richmond or its defences.[2] It is immaterial to what State the troops may belong, as I can place them in brigades from the same, and even if they be few in numbers, they will add something to our strength. I submit this proposition to your judgment and hope you may be able to find means to increase our numbers without endangering the safety of Richmond. I think it important that troops enough should be retained to man the works at Drewry's & Chapin's Bluffs and to support the batteries around the city, in order to guard against a sudden attack by cavalry or otherwise. If this army is unable to resist Grant the troops under Gen. Beauregard and in the city will be unable to defend it.[3]

Very respectfully
Your obt. servt
R. E. LEE
Genl.

---

[2] Major-General Ransom, commanding the department of Richmond reported his strength on May 31 as follows: effective total present, 5,746, aggregate present, 6,986, aggregate present and absent, 9,989.

[3] At 7:30 P.M., General Lee telegraphed Mr. Davis that "Genl. Beauregard says the [War] Department must determine what troops to send for him. He gives it all necessary information. The result of this delay will be disaster. But-

No. 115.

[Telegram]

Received at Richd.   May 31, 1864.
By telegraph from Atlees Station 31   To Gen BRAX-
TON BRAGG

O. K.   5 A.M.   Best route for Hoke when arrived
at Richmond is to march to Mechanicsville and halt
there[1]

R E LEE

16/320
 F

---

ler's troops (Smith's corps) will be with Grant tomorrow.
Hoke's division at least should be with me by eight tomorrow"
(O. R., 36, 3, 850).   The same evening General Beauregard
wired that he considered his instructions sufficient to warrant
him in sending Hoke to Lee.   At almost the same time the
War Department ordered the transfer (*ibid.*, 857).   This
correspondence regarding the transfer of troops from Beauregard must not be interpreted as a clash between that
officer and Lee.   Both felt, and with good reason, that their
position was critical and that to weaken the one or not to
reinforce the other would mean disaster.

[1] See dispatch of May 30 (No. 114, *supra*) and Note 3 thereon.
Hoke's division (return of May 21) was composed of Martin's,
Hagood's, Clingman's and Colquitt's brigades, with Read's
battalion of artillery.   The aggregate present strength was
7,656 (O. R., 36, 3, 817).   The troops were seasoned and were
much needed by General Lee who now saw that Grant intended
to make at least one more assault on his line before concluding
his "left flank" movement.   The prompt transfer of Hoke
was another proof of the speed with which the Confederate
War Department moved under pressure.   A very interesting
monograph might be written on the employment of railroad
transportation in the war between the States.

[*Endorsed*]
> Atlees Station May 31, 1864.
> R E LEE,
> Genl.

Reports best route for Hoke when he arrives in Richmond, is to march to Mechanicsville and halt there

R B 988

Recd 31 May.

No. 116.

H⁰Q COLEMANS
8 P.M. I June 64.

His Excy Presd^t DAVIS
MR. PRESIDENT

Your note of to-day in reference to Genl Echols[1] just received— If Genl. Echols is too unwell for duty there is no objection to his returning to Western Va—He should make application in the proper way —Col Patton[2] is already, I think, in command of his brigade.[3]

> I am with high respect
> Your obt servt
> R. E. LEE
> Genl.

---

[1] Brigadier-General John Echols, who had seen service in Western Virginia and had joined Lee with the rest of Breckinridge's command. See No. 106, *supra*, Note I.

[2] George S. Patton, who, on June I, 1864, signs himself "commanding brigade" (O. R., 36, 3, 864).

[3] In the correspondence of this date appears the following message from Beauregard to Lee:

No. 117.

H^DQ^{RS} Near Gaines Mill

1 P.M. June 3rd 1864.

His Excy Jeff^N Davis
    Presdt. C. States
Mr. President

Your letter of 4 P.M. yesterday is just received.[1] My letter to the Hon. Secretary of War of 5 A.M. this morning,[2] will have informed your Excy of the events of yesterday & the day before and your aid Col Johnson conveyed to you those of to-day. The right of your line extends to Turkey Hill, which is the last hill on this side of the Chickahominy, and covers McClellan's Br: [idge]   I do not know how the report of the advance of the enemy's cavalry to that point originated.   It is not correct.   I sent Gen. Fitz Lee with his divⁿ over the Chickahominy

---

Near Chester, Va. June 1st, 1864 7 P.M.
General Robert E. Lee,
    Shady Grove Church, Va.

Prisoners and deserters report Gilmore, with two divisions, about 8,000 men, still in my front.   One of his Divisions with Smith's Corps, say 16,000 men in all, have gone to White house, probably to join Grant—I have left here one Division, which can be moved to North Side of James River soon as balance of Gilmore's Corps shall have been withdrawn, or Government shall have determined to abandon line of Communications from Petersburg to Richmond.

(Signed) G. T. Beauregard.

[1] Not found.

[2] Not found, Lee to Seddon, June 2, 1864, 8 P.M., gives details of the operations of June 1 and 2.

to Bottom's Br. [idge] yesterday.   He reports this morning that he has the river strongly guarded to that point, with pickets over to the James.

So far every attack of the enemy has been repulsed. His assaults began early this morning, and continued until about 9 o'clock.   The only impression made on our line was at a salient of Gen Breckenridge's position, where the enemy broke through and captured front of a battalion.   He was immediately driven out with severe loss by Gen Finnegan's brigade & the Md. Battalion, and the line restored.[3]

---

[1] Later assaults are reported in Lee to Seddon, June 3, 1864, 8:45 P.M.: "Repeated attacks were made upon General Anderson's position, chiefly against his right, under General Kershaw.   They were met with great steadiness and repulsed in every instance.   The attack extended to our extreme left, under General Early with like results.   Later in the day it was twice renewed against General Heth, who occupies Early's left, but was repulsed with loss.   General Hampton encountered the enemy's cavalry near Haw's Shop, and a part of General W. H. F. Lee's division drove them from their intrenchments. . . .   Our loss to-day has been small, and our success, under the blessing of God, all that we could expect" (O. R., 36, 3, 869).   The battle which General Lee thus modestly reports was Grant's famous frontal assault on Lee's line, commonly called the Battle of Cold Harbor, though the engagement of June 1 has an equal right to that name.   From the North Anna, Grant had advanced towards the Chickahominy (*supra*, No. 109, Note 2) and had renewed his head-on attacks.   The assaults repulsed on the third were the most vigorous and hazardous that Grant had ever made and they cost him at least 3,000 men.   So certain was death in the advance that numbers of his officers refused to carry out his orders for further assaults.   The result of this fight, more

I am gratified to learn of the efforts made by yours Excy to bring out troops. I think it very important that those men engaged in preparing ammunition should remain, as your Excy has directed.

Gen Hoke reports that the troops in his front are said to belong to Butler's forces, and it is said that prisoners have been captured from the 18th corps. I hope that Gen Beauregard will be able to find out the strength of the enemy in his front, and that he can spare additional reinforcements for this army at once.[4] No time should be lost if reinforcements can be had.

Very respy your obt servt.

R. E. LEE
Genl.

---

than anything else, prompted Grant to move his army across the James. (See his statement, O. R., 36, 1, 22.)

[4] While sure that Butler had sent heavy reinforcements to Grant, estimated to be 16,000 (see Note 3, Dispatch of June 1, 1864, *supra*, No. 116), Beauregard was still uncertain of Butler's strength and on June 2, he telegraphed General Lee that 8,000 were still in his front, against whom he had "one division, which can be moved to North Side of James River as soon as balance of Gilmore's corps shall have been withdrawn, or Government shall have determined to abandon line of communication from Petersburg to Richmond." On June 2, Lee wired that it would be "disadvantageous" to abandon the Petersburg line but asked: "Can you not leave sufficient guard and move with balance of your command to north side of James River and take command of right wing of army?" (O. R., 36, 3, 864.) To this Beauregard replied (in a telegram included in the De Renne papers but printed in Freeman, *Calendar of Confederate Papers*, 59) that he had ordered a reconnaissance of his front and had sent Ransom's brigade

No. 118.

HD. QRS. A. N. VA.
5th. June 1864.

His Excl. President DAVIS,
    Richmond
MR. PRESIDENT:

I enclose two dispatches just recd.   I can only send Gen. Breckenridge with his command if you think proper.   If he is to go, transportation should be at once prepared for him.[1]

R. E. LEE
Genl.

---

to Bottom's bridge.   "I am willing," he added, "to do anything for our success, but cannot leave my department without orders from the War Department."   Later in the day in telegrams (included in this collection, but already printed, one in O. R., *loc. cit.*, 868, the other in Freeman, *op. cit.*, 59) Beauregard announced that the reconnaissance showed it would be dangerous to send away Ransom's brigade.   "We must elect at present between Bottom's bridge and railroad communication between Petersburg and Richmond," he wrote.   At 9 P.M., General Bragg ordered Ransom's brigade across the river, to re-enforce General Lee, as here requested. This order, however, Beauregard did not execute until the next day, owing to certain activities in his front.   In a formal letter to Bragg he explained his position in detail and the dangers which would threaten the Confederate capital by the reduction of his force (see O. R., *loc. cit.*, 871–72).   It is worthy of note that this letter together with the messages in the *Calendar of Confederate Papers* fill out and make plain correspondence for these critical days which is scarcely intelligible from the *Official Records*.

[1] The dispatches not found, but see **Lee to Davis, June 6, 1864,** *infra*, Nos. 119 and 120.

[*Endorsed*]
> Hd. Quarters A. N. Va.
> June 5th. 64
> R. E. LEE Genl.

Can only send Breckenridge with his command. If to go transportation should be furnished at once.

> R. B. 1048.
> Recd. June 5th.

No. 119.

> HEAD QRS A. N VA.
> on the field
> 7½ A.M. June 6 '64.

His Excellency
> JEFFERSON DAVIS
> President Conf. States

MR. PRESIDENT

I think some good officer should be sent into the Valley at once to take command there and collect all the forces regulars, locals & reserves, & endeavour to drive the enemy out— I do not know Gen Vaughan who seems to be now in command[1]— Gen. Echols has gone home sick and I think from the nature of his disease is incapacitated for field service though a most excellent officer[2]— Gen Breckenridge

---

[1] George C. Vaughn of Tennessee who had previously served in the Valley of Virginia and had been captured in 1863 at Vicksburg. He had been brigadier-general since September 20, 1862, and later in 1864 was returned to service in Tennessee (C. M. H., 8, 339–41).

[2] Echols, though a man of powerful physique, had been wounded in 1862 and had not fully recovered.

is at present disabled by the fall of his horse & has gone to Richmond.[3] From the representations made to me I think he will be well in a day or two— I recommend that he be sent out to the Valley to take command & do what is practicable in rousing the inhabitants & defending the country. Other persons of influence in that country should be sent on the same mission. Gen W. E. Jones wrote to me before reaching Staunton that he had with him 4000 infantry & dismounted cavalry, 1000 mounted men & plenty of artillery following—Gen Imboden who was at that time below Staunton wrote to me that he had 3000 men— I was in hopes their united forces would have defeated Gen. Hunter. The only assistance I can get from this army as I wrote you last night would be to send back Wharton's & Echols' brigades numbering now about 2100 muskets —They are now in reserve & I have ordered them to be provisioned for two days—[4] I have also sent into Richmond

---

[1] This, it is scarcely necessary to state, was John C. Breckinridge of Kentucky, candidate for the Presidency in 1860 and later Secretary of War in Mr. Davis' Cabinet.

[2] *Cf.* O. R., 36, 2, 863, 870. Breckinridge was ordered to Western Virginia within the next few days. The exact date does not appear in the *Official Records*. The advance which these troops were sent to check was that of General David Hunter who had succeeded the incompetent Sigel in the Valley of Virginia. On June 6, the date of this dispatch, Hunter won a victory at Piedmont and two days later, having joined Averill and Crook at Staunton, turned to the east and marched toward Lynchburg. He arrived in front of the Hill City on June 16 but was met by the troops sent from Lee's army and was repulsed. Early, in the meantime, with 12,000 men from

to ascertain whether they could be transported by rail to Staunton & in what time.   These are elements necessary to a proper decision in the case.   It is apparent that if Grant cannot be successfully resisted here we cannot hold the Valley— If he is defeated it can be recovered— But unless a sufficient force can be had in that country to restrain the movements of the enemy, he will do us great evil & in that event I think it would be better to restore to Gen. Breckinridge the troops drawn from him.   The enemy is now moving in my front— He is withdrawing from our left but I have not yet been able to discover what is his purpose or intention.   I fear he may have, during the night thrown a force across the Chickahominy below as Prisoners taken in front of Longstreets & Ewell's corps day before yesterday stated that they belonged to Gilmore's corps & that the whole of that corps had united with Gen Grant & that Gilmore was here in person— That there was nothing left at Bermuda Hundred except negro troops & some cavalry— Their statements must always be taken with hesitation, but the officers, who examined them say that they were apparently telling what they believed to be true.

I am very respectfully
Your obt servt
R. E. LEE
Genl.

Ewell's corps, moved westward and led Hunter to begin a retreat which did not end until the Federals reached the Ohio! Sheridan, sent from Grant to succor Hunter, did not find him

No. 120.

HEAD QURS GAINES MILLS
3 P.M. 6 June 1864.

His Excy JEFF DAVIS
President
Richmond Va.

MR. PRESIDENT

I have rec^d your note in answer to mine by Col Venable[2] Genl. Wharton has his command already to move with provisions for two days, ammunition &c.[3] I am awaiting information for which you have written & which I hope will decide the question of his going or not satisfactorily— G[1] Breckenridge I think ought to go at all events if able— He can do a great deal personally in rallying the troops & people— Genl Wharton may have time to get there to assist in beating Hunter & then return to us— I agree with you in thinking that we require here every man we can get— Genl Grant is withdrawing from his right & extending to his left towards the Chickahominy— G[1] Early with Ewells corps is advancing down our front to try to attack the enemy in flank, but reports

---

and clashed with Wade Hampton and Fitz Lee at Trevilian's station on June 11. Early did not rejoin Lee but began his advance up the Valley, to which reference will later be made.

[1] Not found.

[2] Colonel Charles S. Venable, aide-de-camp to General Lee and later professor in the University of Virginia.

[3] Gabriel C. Wharton, brigade commander in Breckinridge's division, who had seen service in Western Virginia and Kentucky. He was soon returned to the Valley and aided in Early's raid on Washington (C. M. H., 3, 684-85),

that in consequence of the nature of the country &
the labyrinth of fortifications made by the enemy
it is almost impossible to get along— I shall make
every effort to strike at him, but fear that his usual
precautions will prevent unless I undertake to assault
his fortifications which I desire to avoid if possible.[4]

I am with high respect

Your obt servt.

R. E. Lee

Genl.

---

[4] General Grant, it is scarcely necessary to note, was moving
toward the James in order to cross that stream and attack
Richmond from the South. It may, however, be of interest
to quote Grant's own statement of his purpose: "From the
proximity of the enemy to his defences around Richmond
it was impossible by any flank movement to interpose between him and the city. I was still in a condition to either
move by the left flank and invest Richmond from the north
side or to continue my move by his right flank to the south
side of the James. While the former might have been better
as a covering for Washington, yet a full survey of all the ground
satisfied me that it would be impracticable to hold a line
north and east of Richmond that would protect the Fredericksburg railroad—a long, vulnerable line which would exhaust
much of our strength to guard, and that would have to be
protected to supply the army and would leave open to the
enemy all his lines of communication on the south side of the
James. My idea, from the start, had been to beat Lee's
army north of Richmond if possible; then, after destroying
his lines of communication north of the James River, to transfer the army to the south side and besiege Lee in Richmond
or follow him South if he should retreat. After the battle of
the Wilderness it was evident that the enemy deemed it of
the first importance to run no risks with the army he then had.
He acted purely on the defensive behind breastworks, or

No. 121.

H^D Q^{RS} ARMY N VA.
9th June 1864.

His Excy JEFF DAVIS
President C. States

MR. PRESIDENT,

In my report to the Hon Secty of War yesterday evening,[1] I stated that Gen Sheridan with a large force of cavalry had crossed the Pamunky in the afternoon of the 7th at New Castle Ferry, and encamped that night about Dunkirk and Aylett's on the Matapony. He was accompanied by artillery, wagons, ambulances, and beef cattle. I have received no definite information as to his purpose,

---

feebly on the offensive immediately in front of them, and where in case of repulse he would easily retire behind them. Without a greater sacrifice of life than I was willing to make, all could not be accomplished that I had designed north of Richmond. I therefore determined to continue to hold substantially the ground we then occupied, taking advantage of any favorable circumstances that might present themselves, until the cavalry could be sent to Charlottesville and Gordonsville to effectually break up the railroad connection between Richmond and the Shenandoah Valley and Lynchburg; and when the cavalry got well off to move the army to the south side of the James River, by the enemy's right flank, where I felt I could cut off all his sources of supply except by the canal" (O. R., 36, 1, 22). The first step in his removal from his position in front of Cold Harbor, in order to cross the James, was for Grant to extend his left below Lee's right on the Chickahominy, to cross that stream and to make for the James. He was beginning preparations for this movement at the date of this letter.

[1] O. R., 36, 3, 879.

but conjecture that his object is to cooperate with Gen Hunter, and endeavor to reach the James, breaking the railroads &c as he passes, and probably to descend on the south side of that river.[2]   I think it necessary to be on our guard and make every arrangement in our power to thwart his purpose and protect our communications and country.   I have directed Gens. Hampton and Fitz Lee with their divisions to proceed in the direction of Hanover Junction, and thence, if the information they receive justifies it, along the Central R. R., keeping the enemy on their right, and shape their course according to his.   The pause in the operations of Gen. Grant induces me to believe that he is awaiting the effect of movements in some other quarter to make us change our position, and renders the suggestion I make with reference to the intention and destination of Gen Sheridan more probable.   It was stated by a prisoner captured yesterday belonging to Gen. Sheridan's command, that they had heard that Gen Morgan was in Pa. and that they were going in pursuit.   I mention this improbable story as you may know whether there is any truth in the statement with reference to Gen Morgan.   A negro servant belonging to our army who had been captured by the enemy, made his escape from Gen Sheridan yesterday at 10 A.M. near Mangonick Church, and was under the impression that they would encamp that night at Bowling Green.   Three prisoners brought in to

---

[2] Except in so far as the return on the south side of the James was concerned, this forecast was in precise accord with General Grant's plans.

Gen Hampton confirm in part the statement of the servant.

An extract from the Philadelphia Inquirer published in our papers reports that the army of the N West under Gen Pope was on its way to reinforce that of the Potomac, and a gentleman from the Valley says that a force of two or three thousand men, believed to be under Gen Pope was moving to join Gen Hunter, and should have reached Staunton by this time.[3] There may be therefore some probability in the story. I do not know whence reinforcements can be drawn to our armies unless Gen Kirby Smith can cross a part of his force to join Gen. Johnston and enable him to assume the offensive.

Very respectfully

Your obt servt

R. E. LEE

Genl.

No. 122.

[Telegram]

Dated Mechanicsville June 9 1864.

4.45 P.M.

Rec'd at Richmond 6 O'Clock 30 Mins. P.M.

To Genl. BRAGG.

Your dispatch of one O'Clock just received. Have ordered Ransom's Brigade[1] to march by route

---

[3] See *supra*, No. 119, Note 4. Hunter had reached Staunton the previous day. For Grant's ideas as to the possible outcome of Sheridan's raid to look for Hunter, see his report, O. R., 35, 1, 24.

[1] Ransom's brigade, it will be remembered, had been sent

it came to Gen. Beauregard.   If not necessary please countermand order.

R. E. Lee

[*Endorsed*]

Mechanicsville June 9th.

R. E. Lee Genl.

Has received Dispatch of 1 O'Clock to-day.   Has ordered Ransom's Brigade to cross James River by route it came, to report to Beauregard.   Asks to be countermanded if not necessary.

R. B. 1110

Recd. Had. Qrs.   A. C. S. June 9th

No. 123.

[*Telegram*]

Dated Mechanicsville Road 9 J Received at Richmond June 9 1864 9 O'Clock P.M. To General Bragg.

I have received & acknowledged all your dispatches either by telegraph or courier. [1]

R. E. Lee

D. H.   Genl.

(Recd. 9:10 P.M. June 9)

---

to General Lee by Beauregard on June 4.   Their return at this time was demanded by the advance of a column toward Petersburg.   This attack was met and repulsed the same day (O. R., 1, 36, 3, 884–85).

[1] There is no evidence in this correspondence that General Lee resented the temporary supervision of General Bragg who at this time was acting as military adviser to the President and had practically supplanted the Secretary of War.   During the time of Bragg's stay in Richmond, Lee, as previously, sent important communications direct to President Davis.

[*Endorsed*]
Hd. Qs. A. N. VA.   June 9th. 64 9 P.M.
R. E. Lee
Genl.
Has recd. & acknowledged all dispatches.
R. B. 1102
Recd. Hd. Qrs. A. C. S. June 9th. 64.

No. 124.

HEAD QURS. ARMY No. VA.
11 June 1864.

Hon. JAMES A. SEDDON
Secretary of War
Richmond, Va.

SIR:

I enclose a recommendation of Colonel Morgan[1] of Alabama for Rodes Brigade.   From all that I can learn of Colonel Morgan and from Genl. Ewell's and Gen'l Rodes' opinion expressed in this recommendation I think his appointment is the best which can be made.   I enclose also the commission sent to Col. O'Neal which I respectfully return for the consideration of the Department.   Since my first letter to his Excellency the President I have seen Colonel O'Neal and made more particular inquiries into his capacity to command the brigade and I cannot recommend him to the command.   I therefore recommend the speedy appointment of Col. Morgan,

---

[1] John Tyler Morgan of Alabama.   See No. 51, *supra*.

as this brigade under a competent officer will accomplish much.[2]

> With great respect
> Your obt. Servt.
> (sgd.) R. E. LEE
> General.

An official copy
> W. H. TAYLOR
> A. A. G.

[*Endorsed*]
Head Qurs A. N. V.   11 June 1864.

> R. E. LEE
> General.

Recalling his recommendation of Col. E. A. O'Neal for the position of Brig. Genl., and returning the commission sent to him &c. Recommends the speedy appointment of Col. Morgan.

No. 125.

> HᵈQᴿˢ A N Vᴀ
> 12:10 P.M.   14th June 1864.

His Excy JEFFᴺ DAVIS
> Presdt. C. States

MR. PRESIDENT

I have just received your note of 11½ P.M. yesterday,[1] I regret very much that I did not see you yesterday afternoon, and especially after your having taken so long a ride. If the movement of Early meets with your approval, I am sure it is

---

[2] See Nos. 51 and 81, *supra*.
[1] Not found.

the best that can be made, though I know how difficult it is with my limited knowledge to perceive
what is best.

I think the enemy must be preparing to move
South of James River. Our scouts and pickets
yesterday stated that Gen Grant's whole army was
in motion for the fords of the Chickahominy from
Long Bridge down, from which I inferred that he
was making his way to the James River as his new
base.[2] I cannot however learn positively that more

---

[2] This dispatch and those following, to No. 137, inclusive,
relate to the movement which carried the immediate scene of
hostilities from the James to the Appomattox and inaugurated
the siege of Petersburg. As General Grant's own statement
makes plain (No. 120, *supra*, Note 4) the repulse of his attacks
at Cold Harbor convinced him that Richmond could only be
taken from the north by costly assaults. His frank confession
that he was unwilling to pay such a price deserves to be taken
at its face value. At the same time, it is not improbable that
the behavior of his troops at Cold Harbor and the unwillingness of his lieutenants to order the final attack convinced him
that the men would not face the certain death that awaited
them. As some other course had to be pursued, the most
natural one was to move his base from the north to the south
side of the James where he could be in communication with his
gunboats and could receive without danger supplies and ammunition sent him from Washington. The possibility of such a
move on McClellan's part had been discussed by General Lee
in 1862 and was the rational step in the circumstances. It is
not probable that the movement would have attracted the
attention of historians but for several striking passages in
General Lee's telegrams that indicate ignorance of Grant's
change of base. These passages are three in number and are
all in telegrams to Beauregard under date of June 16. Lee
wrote: "I do not know the position of Grant's army and can-

than a small part of his Army has crossed the Chickahominy. Our contest last evening, as far as I am
able to judge was with a heavy force of cavalry and
the 5th corps of his army. They were driven back
until dark as I informed you, by a part of Hill's

---

not strip north bank of James River" (10:30 A.M.); "have not
heard of Grant's crossing James River" (3 P.M.) and "has
Grant been seen crossing James River?" (4 P.M., O. R., 51, 2,
1078). These have been construed to mean that Lee had
been duped and that Grant had achieved a remarkable coup.
Some have gone so far as to say that in this, as in no single
manœuvre of the war, Grant had the better of his great adversary. A careful reading of dispatches in print prior to
the appearance of this collection should have kept critical
writers from such errors, though it might not have explained
Lee's dispatches satisfactorily. The advance guard of the
Army of the Potomac reached Wilcox's Landing on James
River on the night of June 13 (O. R., 36, 1, 23) and commenced
crossing on the morning of June 14. A pontoon bridge was
completed by midnight of the 14th, which enabled the whole
army to move over rapidly. As General Lee wrote President
Davis during the progress of the campaign from the Rapidan
to the James, the nature of the country rendered it easy for
Grant to get a day's start of him in any movement he planned.
This Grant did on June 13–14 but he did no more. At 9 P.M.,
June 14, Lee reported that troops were at Wilcox's Landing,
while Beauregard had already announced to the War Department, at 3:15 P.M., that steamers were coming up the river
and that pontoons could be seen (O. R., 40, 2, 653). Hoke's
division was forthwith ordered to re-enforce Beauregard (*ibid.*,
654). The next morning, June 15, at 9:30 A.M., Beauregard
reported that musketry and artillery fire had been heard on
the Southside, and he forwarded statements of prisoners that
an advance was being made on Petersburg (*ibid.*, 655). Even
earlier, at 7:45 A.M., Beauregard had forwarded to General
Lee, who did not receive it, the statement of a prisoner who

corps. Presuming that this force was either the
advance of his Army, or the cover behind which it
would move to James River, I prepared to attack it
again this morning, but it disappeared from before
us during the night, and as far as we can judge from

---

said that "he belongs to Hancock's corps (Second), and that
it crossed day before yesterday and last night from Harrison's
Landing" (O. R., 51, 2, 1078). At the head of Pickett's
division, Lee reached Drewry's Bluff, on the south side of the
James at 9:40 A.M., June 16, and immediately wired General
Beauregard to advise him of conditions (O. R., 40, 3, 659).
Beauregard followed with a request for information (O. R.,
51, 2, 1078). Then was exchanged the correspondence already
quoted on which has been based the claim that General Lee
was ignorant of Grant's movement across the river. A careful scrutiny of Lee's statements, in the light of his known acquaintance with the whereabouts of Grant's advance on June
14, would seem sufficient to refute the contention that he had
been deceived. No man of his ability could have failed to
understand the significance of Grant's movement to the river,
especially as Lee had discussed, two years before, the possibility of precisely such action on the part of McClellan. It
would seem altogether reasonable, in the circumstances, to
interpret his questions to Beauregard as answers to the latter's
request for troops: Was Beauregard certain, when he asked
for more men, that Grant had really crossed the river. Was
Beauregard advised as to the exact location not of the advance
or of troops that might have come up the James, but of
Grant's *army*? But if the *Official Records* cannot directly prove
that Lee was not deceived by Grant's movement, the dispatches here printed settle the question beyond a doubt.
This dispatch of itself, written while the movement of Grant's
army was in progress, makes it perfectly plain that Lee expected Grant to cross the river. Three hours later (No. 126)
he was certain that Grant was at least in a position to cross the
river and he had dispatched Hoke for a like change of base

the statements of prisoners, it has gone to Harrison's landing. The force of cavalry here was pressed forward early this morning, but as yet no satisfactory information has been obtained. It may be Gen Grant's intention to place his army within the forti-

whenever conditions warranted it. He confirmed this statement a little later (4 o'clock) and added that Grant had broken up his base at the White House (No. 127). The next afternoon, still lacking definite information, he determined further to reinforce Beauregard (No. 128) and to move to the exterior line of Richmond defences where he would be ready for developments on either side of the river. That he did not send more troops to Beauregard was due to the latter's statement that with his original command, including Ransom's brigade, he believed he could hold Butler at bay and defend Petersburg. Lee also ordered a pontoon bridge thrown across the James for the movement of the entire army to face Grant if conditions called for it (No. 129). At 12:45 on the 15th, he was of opinion that Grant's plans did not "appear to be settled" as cavalry was active on the north side of the James, but he prepared for all eventualities (No. 130). On the morning of June 16, when he crossed the river, he promptly ordered troops to retake the lines which had been occupied by the enemy on Beauregard's withdrawal to defend Petersburg. He was only uncertain as to whether the troops facing Beauregard in front of Petersburg were of Grant's army or of the forces that had originally confronted Beauregard (No. 134). The latter's brilliant defence of Petersburg and the strength of the forces in his front confirmed General Lee in his belief that the greater part of Grant's army had crossed the river and he advised General Hampton on June 17 (hour not given in the dispatch). It must be remembered, finally, that the removal of troops from the White House to join the army on the James had further involved the issue and rendered it somewhat uncertain, on June 16, whether the new forces in front of Beauregard were a part of Grant's army from across

fications around Harrison's landing, which I believe
still stand, and where by the aid of his gunboats, he
could offer a strong defence.   I do not think it would
be advantageous to attack him in that position.
He could then either refresh it or transfer it to the
other side of the River without our being able to
molest it, unless our ironclads are stronger than his.
It is reported by some of our scouts that a portion
of his troops marched to the White House, and from
information derived from citizens, were there embarked.[3]   I thought it probable that these might
have been their discharged men, especially as a
scout reported under date of the 9th inst: that transports loaded with troops have been going up the
Potomac for three days and nights, passing above
Alexandria.   On the night of the 8th, upwards of
thirty steamers went up, supposed to be filled with
troops, no doubt many of these were wounded and
sick men.   Still I apprehend that he may be sending
troops up the James River with the view of getting
possession of Petersburg before we can reinforce it.
We ought therefore to be extremely watchful &

---

the river or were troops who had come up the James by transports. We may conclude with absolute certainty that General
Lee anticipated the movement across the James, prepared
for it and was no more uncertain as to the precise time of
crossing than the nature of the ground and the limitations on
his sources of information made inevitable. Viewed in its
true light, the transfer of Grant's army across the river was
met as promptly and as forcefully as the weakness of Lee's
forces permitted.

[3] To pass down the York and up the James to rejoin Grant.

guarded. Unless I hear something satisfactory by evening, I shall move Hoke's division back to the vicinity of the Ponton Bridge across James River in order that he may cross if necessary. The rest of the army can follow should circumstances require it.

The victories of Forest and Hampton are very grateful at this time, and show that we are not forsaken by a gracious Providence. We have only to do our whole duty, and everything will be well. A scout in Prince William reports that the enemy are rebuilding the bridges on the O & A R. R.[4] adjacent to Alexandria. This may be with the view of opening the Manassas Gap R R to communicate with the Valley, their tenure of which I trust will not be permanent.

Most respectfully
Your obt servt
R. E. LEE
Genl.

No. 126.

H^DQ^{RS} AN VA.
3¾ P.M.   14th June 1864.

His Excy JEFF^N DAVIS
    President C. States
MR. PRESIDENT

As far as I can judge from the information I have received, Gen. Grant has moved his army to James River in the vicinity of Westover. A portion of it I am told moved to Wilcox's landing, a

---

[4] The Orange and Alexandria, now a part of the Southern railway.

short distance below. I see no indications of his attacking me on this side of the River, though of course I cannot know positively. As his facilities for crossing the River and taking possession of Petersburg are great, and as I think it will more probably be his plan, I have sent Gen Hoke with his command to a point above Drewry's Bluff in easy distance of the first Pontoon Bridge above that place. He will execute any orders You may send to him there.[1] I cannot judge now whether he should move at once to the other side of the River, but think it prudent that he should be in position to do so when required. From my present information Gen. Grant crossed his army at several points below Long Bridge,[2] and moved directly towards James River, sending a force in this direction to guard the roads so as to make it impracticable for us to reach him.

Very respectfully
Your obt servt
R. E. LEE
Genl.

---

[1] See Bragg to Beauregard, June 14, 1864 (O. R., 1, 40, 2, 653), Hoke to Beauregard, June 14, 1864 (*ibid.*, 654). Beauregard, on June 7, had requested the return of this and of Ransom's division, with these significant words: "Should Grant have left Lee's front, he doubtless intends operations along James River, probably on south side. Petersburg being nearly defenseless would be captured before it could be re-enforced." Two days later Beauregard enlarged on the prospect of Grant's crossing the river and outlined a plan of defence (O. R., 36, 878–879, 886).

[2] On the Chickahominy, beyond the outer defences of Richmond.

No. 127.

HEAD QU*s. A N VA
June 14th 1864.   4 P.M.

Gen BRAXTON BRAGG
    Comg. Armies C. States
GEN.

I have directed Gen Hoke's command to proceed this afternoon to the vicinity of the first pontoon bridge above Drewry's Bluff—[1] I have deemed it prudent that he should be within reach of Petersburg. For as far as I am able to judge of the movements of the Army of Gen Grant I think it probable that he will cross James River. He has moved his Army across Long Bridge & the bridges below that point to James River apparently striking for Harrison's & Wilcox's landing.[2] He shows no indication of operating on this side & has broken up his depot at the White House.[3]

        I am with great respect
           Your obt servt.
              R. E. LEE
                Genl.

---

[1] Drewry's Bluff, with the famous Fort Darling, was at the southwestern end of the Richmond defences, across James River and was defended with strong works against an attack from the south or west. It effectually blocked a movement up the James River against Richmond.

[2] On the James almost directly east of Petersburg.

[3] On the Pamunkey, one of the most important lines of water-communication for an attack on Richmond from the

No. 128.

H^DQ^{RS} ARMY N VA.

12:20 P.M.   15th June 1864.

GENERAL,

Your letter of 8.45 A.M. enclosing various dispatches from Gen Beauregard, is just received.[1] I directed Gen Hoke this morning, unless he should receive contrary orders from you, to cross the James River and report to Gen. Beauregard. I had a visit this morning from Col [Samuel R.] Paul aid de camp of Gen Beauregard, who stated among other things

---

east. With the correspondence for June 14. is filed in the De Renne collection the following dispatch from General Lee's son, G. W. C. Lee, to President Davis:

Dated Bottoms Bridge   13 June 1864.
      Recd at Richmond   June 13, 1864.
To His Excellency the President
   I learn that Maj-Genl Elzy and staff are in Richmond
   Cannot he be temporarily assigned to his former command.
He can take charge at once, some one is very much needed

G   W   C   LEE
Col. & A D C

[1] Not found. Between the time of this and the previous letter to General Bragg, important developments had taken place. Smith's corps of Grant's army, one of the first across the James, had moved towards Petersburg on the night of the 14–15 and was preparing to assault. Fortunately for the Confederates, however, Smith delayed doing so and did not advance on the poorly-manned works until about sundown (see Grant's report, O. R., 36, 1, 25). Smith's attack was met with valor by Wise's brigade. With the arrival of Federal

that the General was of opinion that if he had his original force, he would be able to hold his present lines in front of Gen Butler and at Petersburg. He is however particularly anxious to have Ransom's brigade, which I believe is now at Chafin's Bluff, and I doubt whether he will be satisfied or consider himself strong enough until he is ordered to him.[2] I think therefore it had better be done. If Gracie's brigade cannot be returned to that place, perhaps the locals under Gen Custis Lee might be able to hold it. But as long as this army remains in its front, I will endeavor to make it safe. I had determined to move this army back near the exterior line of defences near Richmond, but from the movements of the enemy's cavalry this morning, and reports that have reached me, I do not wish to draw too far back. Unless therefore I am better satisfied, I shall remain where I am to-day, as the enemy's plans do not seem to be settled.[3]

---

re-enforcements, General Beauregard was forced to abandon his line at Bermuda Hundred Neck and to rush all his troops to Petersburg.

[2] General Lee could not be certain at this time whether Grant's whole army, the vanguard or troops that had come up the James were moving against Beauregard and could not accordingly afford to strip the Richmond defences. His first accurate information of the nature of the Federal troops before Petersburg came in a dispatch from Beauregard dated 11:45 A.M. (O. R., 40, 2, 656).

[3] At 6:00 P.M. General Lee telegraphed more in detail that the enemy's cavalry had been seen that morning on the Salem Church Road and at Malvern Hill, and that it had been driven down the river road.

I am much grieved to hear of the death of Lt.
Gen. Polk.[4]

> Very respectfully
> Your obt servt
> R. E. LEE
> Genl

General BRAGG
&c &c

No. 129.

HᴰQᴿˢ ARMY N VA.
12½ P.M.   15th June 1864.

GENERAL,

I directed Col Stevens[1] this morning to throw a
ponton bridge across the river at Chafin's Bluff, for
which he thought he had, or could obtain sufficient material I do not think it would be well to remove the
Ponton Bridge now at Drewry's Bluff, and if we can
only maintain one across that part of the river, that
at Drewry's would be more generally advantageous.

A bridge below Chafin's Bluff would be more
exposed to the enemy's gunboats and would prevent
free access of our own to the batteries at Chafin's.[2]

> Very respy
> Your obt servt

General BRAGG   R. E. LEE
&c &c   Genl.

---

[4] Leonidas Polk, Protestant Episcopal bishop of Louisiana
and Lieut.-Gen. P. A. C. S., killed near Marietta, Georgia,
June 14, 1864.

[1] Colonel Walter H. Stevens, chief engineer, Army of
Northern Virginia.

[2] The James River at Drewry's Bluff makes a sharp turn

No. 130.

H^DQ^RS ARMY N VA.
12¾ P.M.   15th June 1864.

His Excellency JEFF^N DAVIS
    President C. States,
        Richmond
MR. PRESIDENT,

As I informed you last evening I had intended
to move the troops nearer the exterior lines of
defences around Richmond, but from the movements of the enemy's cavalry and the reports that
have reached me this morning, his plans do not
appear to be settled.   Unless therefore I hear something more satisfactory, they will remain where they
are.[1]   Should I move my camp, it will be somewhere
on Cornelius Creek in the cleanest wood I can find
near the New Market Road or Osborne Turnpike.[2]

Most respy
    Your obt servt
        R. E. LEE
            Genl.

---

almost east.   At the point where it turns southeast again is
Chafin's Bluff.   Below the latter point, the Confederates had
no works except those for the protection of the fort.

[1] The presence of cavalry on the north side of the river,
(see No. 128, *supra*) had raised some question in General
Lee's mind as to how much of Grant's army had crossed,
although he knew that the movement was in progress.   It
would manifestly have been foolish to leave the Richmond
defences open to a cavalry raid or to a strong column on the
north side of the river.

[2] Cornelius Creek ran southwesterly into the James River

No. 131.

RIDLEY'S SHOP
CHARLES CITY ROAD
6:50 P.M.   15th June. [1864]

MR. PRESIDENT,

Your note of 1:20 P.M. to-day has just been received.[1] As soon as I heard of the enemy's crossing the Chickahominy at Long Bridge I moved Heth's division across the river[2] to White Oak Swamp bridge, and prepared the other troops for motion. Our skirmishers at daylight were moved forward, and finding no enemy in front of our lines for between one and two miles were recalled, and the army moved over the Chickahominy. Gen Heth's divn holds the White Oak Swamp bridge, the rest of Hill's corps is at Ridley's Shop[3] at the intersection of the Long Bridge and Charles City roads. Longstreet's corps is to his right on the Long Bridge Road, and Hoke's division at the intersection of the Darby Town and Long Bridge roads. Our cavalry occupy the Willis Church road and Malvern Hill.[4] The only enemy we have yet seen is that that has come up from the Long Bridge, and is opposed to Gen Heth

---

just above Drewry's Bluff. The Osborne turnpike and the New Market road paralleled the James at this point and crossed the creek about a mile apart. Substantial works were located at this point, about five miles from Richmond.

[1] Not found.   [2] That is, the Chickahominy.

[3] Given on the maps as "B Shop,"—blacksmith's shop. In rural Virginia the "shop" is traditionally a smithy.

[4] The forces north of the James were thus lying in a northeast-southwest line pointing toward the river at Dutch Gap.

at White Oak Swamp bridge and extends to this point We have driven him from this position down the Long Bridge Road, but I have not yet heard that White Oak Swamp Bridge is uncovered Gen Early was in motion this morning at 3 o'clock & by daylight was clear of our camps. He proceeded on the mountain road direct to Charlottesville, and arrangements have been made to give him 15 days supplies. If you think it better to recall him, please send a trusty messenger to overtake him to-night I do not know that the necessity for his presence to-day is greater than it was yesterday. His troops would make us more secure here, but success in the Valley would relieve our difficulties that at present press heavily upon us.[5] As I write, Wilcox's division is pressing the enemy down the Long Bridge Road.

Most respectfully
Your obt servt.
R. E. LEE
Genl.

No. 132.

H^{D}Q^{RS} 7:50 P.M.
RIDDLE'S SHOP 15th June. [1864]

MR. PRESIDENT,

I omitted to mention in my note just written the importance of warning our papers not to allude even

---

[5] After being dispatched to meet and drive back Hunter, Early was instructed to move down the Valley, to cross the Potomac and to threaten Washington. This movement, it was hoped, would relieve the Valley and might possibly lessen the pressure on Richmond.

by implication to the movements of our troops. I have just learned that the correspondent of the Inquirer[1] is aware of Gen. Early's movements but had written to his paper not to publish it. As secrecy is an important element of Gen. Early's expedition, I beg that your Excellency will cause notice to be sent to all the newspapers not to allude to any movement, by insinuation or otherwise. Of course it will not do to particularize that movement, as it may not be known I think it would be well to charge the Telegraph operators not to forward a dispatch referring in any way to Army movements.[2]

Very respy
Your obt servt
R. E. LEE
Gl.

---

[1] The Richmond *Inquirer*, the ante-bellum "democratic Bible of the South," founded by Thomas Ritchie, edited by him, continued by his nephews and edited for a time by O. Jennings Wise, son of Governor Henry A. Wise of Virginia. Ritchie's biography has been written by C. M. Ambler (Richmond, 1913).

[2] The frequent references in General Lee's dispatches to the intelligences procured from the New York and Philadelphia papers will show how valuable to either side were the newspapers of the other. The Richmond press was as diligently sought after by the Federals as were the Northern papers by the Confederates. The Richmond press, at this time, was conservative with the exception of the *Examiner*, edited by the radical John M. Daniel, an earnest opponent of the administration. The Federals appear, however, to have used the *Dispatch* most frequently to study Confederate movements. *Cf.* Lee to Davis, July 1, 1864, *infra.*

No. 133.

8:20 P.M. 15 June '64.

Mᴿ PRESIDENT

I have just recᵈ your note of to-day—¹ I directed Ransoms brigade this afternoon, if no contrary orders had been recᵈ—, to report to Genl. Beauregard,² & replaced it for the night by one of Longstreet's—Genl G. W. C. Lee will repair to Chafins tomorrow at 3 A.M. with a portion of his command, leaving the Va: reserves to support the batteries at Bottoms bridge—

I am much grieved at the death of Genl Polk. I am unable to recommend a successor—As much as I esteem & admire Genl Pendleton, I could not select him to command a corps in this army. I do not mean to say by that he is not competent, but from what I have seen of him, I do not know that he is—³ I can spare him, if in your good judgment, you decide he is the best available. I know nothing of the character of those officers you designate. As far as I do know some, I should think they would

---

¹ Not found.

² Cooper ordered the brigade forward from Chaffin's to Beauregard in all haste (O. R., 40, 2, 658).

³ The reference is to Brig.-Genl. W. N. Pendleton, chief of artillery, A. N. Va. Nothing could better illustrate General Lee's absolute candor than this frank unwillingness to recommend Pendleton. The latter, a minister of the Protestant Episcopal Church, was one of General Lee's personal friends and later was his rector at Lexington. Yet because he had no proof of Pendleton's qualifications for the higher place General Lee would not recommend him.

not answer. Major Genl Stewart I do not know—⁴
I regret I am unable to aid you, for I know the
importance of selecting a proper officer.

Only the enemys Cav^y, opposed us today & they
were driven back on all the roads— If Genl Johnston
would like Genl Ewell⁵ I would spare him. My own
opinion is that Genl E s health is unequal to his
duties, but he does not agree with me— Johnston
knows & likes him, & I do the same.

Most truly & respy yours
R. E. LEE
Genl.

His Excy JEFF^N DAVIS
President.

No. 134.
HEAD QURS A. N. VA.
DREWRY BLUFF 7½ P.M.
16th June 1864

His Excy JEFF^N DAVIS
President Confed: States
MR. PRESIDENT,

I received this morning at 2 A.M. a dispatch from
Genl. Beauregard, stating that he had abandoned

---

⁴ Alexander P. Stewart of Tennessee, familiarly known to
his men as "old straight," a West Pointer of the class of 1842
and room-mate of John Pope and J. E. B. Stuart. His military record was excellent and his achievements at Murfreesboro, Chickamauga and elsewhere had won him praise. He
was given the promotion and was commissioned lieutenant-
general, June 23, 1864 (C. M. H., 1, 693–95).

⁵ Lieutenant-General Richard S. Ewell, one of Lee's corps
commanders and an able fighter. General Ewell's health

his line on Bermuda Neck and would concentrate all his force on Petersburg. He also said that his skirmishers and pickets would be withdrawn at daylight. [1] I immediately ordered General Pickett's division to proceed across James River and occupy the lines, directing Genl. Anderson to move another division to the River and proceed in person to Bermuda and take direction of affairs. I requested Genl. Beauregard not to withdraw his skirmishers and pickets until the arrival of those troops, though I feared from the lateness of the hour that he would not receive my message in time. Genl. Anderson's troops were in the vicinity of Malvern Hill, and it was 9 o'clock A.M. to-day before the division crossed the river at Drewry's Bluff. One brigade with Genl's Anderson & Pickett at its head preceded the division more than an hour; but before it could reach the lines, they had been occupied by the enemy, who advanced a force as far as the Petersburg Turnpike. On learning this condition of affairs, I ordered over a second division to the support of the first, and a third to the vicinity of the bridge. The enemy was easily driven back, and General Anderson soon regained our second line of entrenchments. At last accounts the enemy in force occupied our first line,

---

had been so much impaired by hardship and wounds that he could not share actively in the campaign. He was assigned, shortly after the date of this, to the command of the Richmond defences and did not rejoin General Lee until the evacuation of Richmond. For fuller details see *infra*, No. 139, note 8.

[1] Doubtless Beauregard to Lee, June 15, 1864, 11:15 P.M. (O. R., 40, 2, 657).

extending from Howlett's house on the river by Ware
Bottom Church, from which I fear it will be difficult
and costly to dislodge him.   I have not learned from
Genl Beauregard what force is opposed to him in
Petersburg, or received any definite account of operations there, nor have I been able to learn whether
any portion of Grant's Army is opposed to him.
Taking advantage of his occupation of the Bluff at
Howlett's house the enemy brought up five vessels
and prepared to sink them in Trent's Reach.   Two
had been sunk with Torpedoes in their bows when
the officer who reported it to Captain Pegram left.
I suppose the object is to prevent our gunboats from
descending the river.

A dispatch just received from General Beauregard
states that he countermanded the order for the withdrawal of his pickets and skirmishers, and that they
occupied our second line at 10¼ A M to-day, but
that they were afterwards forced to retire upon
Petersburg.[2]

I am with great respect
Your obt servt
R. E. Lee
Genl.

---

[2] Not found.   The movement here reported was one of the
greatest importance to the army and, indeed, to the Confederate cause.   When Beauregard was forced to abandon
the Bermuda Hundred line, in his efforts to save Petersburg,
he thereby opened the mouth of the "bottle" in which Butler
had been sealed, and thus enabled the Federal commander to
advance his lines and to recapture the railroad from which
he had been driven in May.   This meant the practical sever

No. 135.

HEAD QRS DREWRY'S BLUFF
16 June 1864.

His Excy JEFF^N DAVIS
President Richmond

MR. PRESIDENT

For some few days back we have been only able to get sufficient corn for our animals from day to day— Any accident to the railroads would cut short our supplies. I directed Col Corley[1] to make this representation to the Qr Mr Genl to-day: he has returned & says Genl Lawton[2] is doing everything he can, but cannot provide more than about 2000 bushels per day. We require 3200 bushels daily for all our

---

ance of the Confederate line of communications between Richmond and Petersburg and the isolation of Beauregard's command. Realizing the importance of this line, Lee took the offensive and regained it. In the meantime, Beauregard with a small force had been fighting the Federals in front of Petersburg with splendid courage. From June 15 to June 18, Beauregard's little force held at bay a Federal army thrice its size and prevented the capture of Petersburg. Not until Lee's army had driven back Butler and had passed beyond him to Beauregard, was Petersburg safe. General Beauregard has never been given the credit he deserved for his masterly defence of Petersburg at a time when the fall of that city would have meant the separation of Lee from his lines of communication with the South.

[1] Colonel James L. Corley, quartermaster-general, Army of Northern Virginia.

[2] Brigadier-General A. R. Lawton, previously mentioned, quartermaster-general of the Confederate States army and formerly brigade commander in Lee's army.

animals— I think it is clear that the railroads are not working energetically & unless some improvement is made, I do not know what will become of us— I am therefore obliged to appeal to your Excellency as reluctant as I am to trespass upon your time & attention.   I beg that every exertion may be made, not only to supply our daily wants, but to lay up something for future use— Our existence depends upon every ones exerting themselves at this time to the utmost—[3]

I am with great respect
Your obt servt.
R. E. LEE
Genl.

No. 136.

[Telegram]

(Copy)   HEAD QRS ARMY N. VA.
June 17th 1864.

Hon. J. A. SEDDON,
Secy. of War,
SIR,

Genl. Beauregard telegraphs that last night the enemy assaulted his lines twice and were repulsed,

---

[3] This dispatch, it will be observed, is somewhat more blunt in its phrases than most of those from General Lee's pen. His request was doomed to be repeated again and again during the remaining months of the war and went unheeded far more frequently than it was granted.   The days of starvation were already upon the army.

leaving 400 prisoners, including eleven commissioned officers, in our hands.[1] To-day the enemy carried a weak point in his lines. Our troops assaulted and carried our original lines near Bermuda Hundreds with slight loss on our part.[2]

Very respectfully

Your obdt servt

(Signed) R E LEE

Genl

Respectfully submitted for the information of the President.

JAMES A. SEDDON

Secretary of War.

June 18/64.

[*Endorsed*]

Copy   Telegram to Sec War
     Genl LEE   Hd Qrs A N V June 17, 64
June 18/64

---

[1] This information was already in the hands of the War Department. See Beauregard to Bragg, June 16, 1864, 9:45 P.M.(O. R., 40, 2, 660).

[2] *Cf.* Lee to Davis, June 17, 1864, 10:30 A.M., in which these movements are explained more in detail (O. R., *loc. cit.*, 661–62). The operations of June 17 practically restored the Confederate army to the strategic positions it had occupied south of the James before Grant moved his base. Within a few days the lines were drawn around Petersburg and were not materially changed until that city was evacuated.

No. 137.

Confidential.

HEAD Q^rs A N Va.,
June 18th 1864.

His Excellency
JEFFERSON DAVIS
President Confed. States

Mr PRESIDENT

From information received last night it is pretty certain that Grant's whole force has crossed to the South Side of the James River— Wilson's division of cavalry crossed yesterday. I have ordered all the troops over towards Petersburg leaving the outer defences of Richmond in charge of Gen G. W. C. Lee to whom I have ordered Col. Gary's command and several light batteries to report— Gen Wm F. Lee I have ordered to Petersburg with Barringer's N. C. brigade[1] leaving Chambliss[2] to cooperate with Hampton if practicable in striking at Sheridan who is apparently making for the White House. If he cannot cooperate with Hampton I have ordered him to follow Gen. W^m F Lee to Petersburg.[3]   Gen Hampton will continue to watch Sheridan and endeavour to strike at him but if the latter escapes & takes transport at the White House Hampton is

---

[1] Rufus Barringer, of North Carolina, commanding the 1st, 2nd, 3rd and 5th N. C. cavalry.

[2] John R. Chambliss of Virginia, in command of W. H. F. Lee's old cavalry brigade.

[3] *Cf.* R. E. Lee to W. H. F. Lee, June 17, 1864 (O. R., 40, 2, 663).

ordered to move as rapidly as possible for Petersburg.[4]
The enemy having transferred Wilsons division of
Cavy to the S. Side obliges me to call over Genl
W. F. Lee—[5]

        Most respy your obt servt

                R. E. LEE

I go to Petersburg
  REL

No. 138.

HEAD QURS ARMY NO. VA.
    NEAR PETERSBURG VA.
        June 19th 1864.

His Excellency JEFFERSON DAVIS
    President Confed. States
MR. PRESIDENT
   I have received your letter of the 18th[1] I was
able to leave with General G. W. C. Lee only the

---

[4] *Cf.* Lee to Wade Hampton, June 18, 1864: "If Sheridan
escapes and gets to his transports at the White House you
must lose no time in moving your entire command to our right
near Petersburg. Keep yourself thoroughly advised of his
movements and intentions as far as practicable" (O. R., 40,
2, 667). Correspondence with the cavalry officers is frequent
in the *Official Records*, for this time (*loc. cit.*).

[5] These were the troops whose activities on the north side
of the river, after Grant's main army had crossed, raised
whatever doubts there may have been in General Lee's mind
as to the extent to which Grant had transferred his forces to
the south side of the river. Richmond's northern defences
were now left in the hands of the local forces, composed largely
of department clerks, with small details from the main army.

[1] Not found.

forces which belong to Richmond. I placed at his disposal two battalions of artillery under Colonel Carter in addition to what he originally had, which I thought might be advantageously employed in connection with [M. M?] Gary's cavalry and such infantry support as General Lee could furnish, in operating on the James River against any parties that might be landed, or in embarrassing its navigation. I wished him to display as much force as possible, and to be active and vigilant in warding off any threatened blow. His[2] force is not more than sufficient for this purpose, but if we can get early intelligence, and especially maintain the road from Petersburg to Richmond in running order, I think we shall be able to meet any attack the enemy may make upon the latter place. Night before last he apparently reduced the force on his lines in front of Bermuda Hundred, and from the reports received during the night, matters seemed to be so threatening in Petersburg, that I directed General Anderson to

---

[2] *Cf.* R. E. Lee to G. W. C. Lee, June 21, 1864: " . . . You must judge of the essential points to hold in order to thwart the enemy in his approach to Richmond. Whatever operations you may decide upon I advise that you use all your available force for the purpose. I should hope your force with Carter's artillery could drive the enemy back." The combination of fatherly exhortation and military command in this correspondence with General Custis Lee is striking. Custis Lee, the great commander's oldest son, had for some time been with the President in Richmond and showed, perhaps, some misgivings when thus summoned into the field. His conduct, however, was such as to eiicit "the highest praise" (see O. R., 40, 2, 674).

march at once with Kershaw's and Field's divisions, Pickett's division being left to guard our lines from Howlett's to Ashton Creek. I halted one division of Hill's on the north side of the Appomattox, in supporting distance of both places. General Beauregard had felt constrained to contract his lines on the east side of Petersburg before my arrival, and I found his troops in their new position. I am unable to judge of the comparative strength of the two lines, but as far as I can see, the only disadvantage is the proximity of the new line to the city.[3] No attack has been made by the enemy since my arrival, though sharp skirmishing and cannonading has been kept up. My greatest apprehension at present is the maintenance of our communications south. It will be difficult, and I fear impracticable to preserve it uninterrupted. The enemy's left now rests on the Jerusalem road, and I fear it would be impossible to arrest a sudden attack aimed at a distant point. In addition, the enemy's cavalry, in spite of all our efforts, can burn the bridges over the Nottoway and its branches, the Meherrin & even the South side road is very much exposed, and our only dependence

---

[3] The new line was described by Beauregard as follows: "General Hoke's line, commencing at the river and in advance of Taylor's Creek, will follow the ditch behind the race-course, afterward crossing the creek and joining General Johnson's left toward the Baxter road. General Johnson's line will cross the Baxter road nearly at right angles, thence running to the Jerusalem plank road, and from that point following the original lines" (O. R., *loc. cit.*, 666). This became a part of the main line during the siege of Petersburg.

seems to me to be on the Danville. Every effort
should be made to secure to that road sufficient rolling
stock by transferring that of other roads, and to
accumulate supplies of all kinds in Richmond in anti-
cipation of temporary interruptions. When roads
are broken every aid should be given to the companies
to enable them to restore them immediately. Dupli-
cate timbers for all the bridges should be prepared
in safe places to be used in an emergency, and every
other arrangement made to keep the roads in running
order.[4]

Most respectfully and truly yours

R. E. LEE

Genl.

No. 139.

PETERSBURG 21 June '64.

Mʀ PRESIDENT

I have recᵈ your letter of the 20ᵗʰ Inst: enclosing
one from the Pres: of the Petersburg & Richmond
R.R.[1] It is stated the road will be in operation this

---

[4] *Cf.* Lee to Seddon, June 21, 1864 (O. R., *loc. cit.*, 671-72)
in which Lee urges that the Danville, Piedmont and Southside railroads "be well stocked with the rolling-stock and
materials not so essential to us" and also that these roads be
guarded. For this purpose, he suggested the appointment
of a competent brigadier-general to assume charge of the 3,000
reserves whom General Pickett had for the work.

[1] Not found.

mor⁸ ²—Genl Grant will concentrate all the troops
here he can raise, from every section of the U. S. I
saw it stated some days since in one of their papers.
That A. T. Smith's corps, which had returned from
the Red River, had embarked at Vicksburg in a
number of transports & ascended the Missᵖⁱ— I
have not heard of it since. Its destination may
have been Memphis. I hope Early will be able to
demolish Hunter,³ but I doubt whether Hampton
will be able to injure Sheridan. His force is small
in comparison with the enemy's & he seems to be
looking to reinforcements more than to what he can
accomplish himself.⁴ I hope your Excʸ will put no
reliance in what I can do individually, for I feel that
will be very little. The enemy has a strong position,
& is able to deal us more injury than from any other
point he has ever taken. Still we must try & defeat
them. I fear he will not attack us but advance by
regular approaches. He is so situated that I cannot

---

² Lee, at midnight, June 16, notified the President of the
Richmond and Petersburg railroad that Butler had burned
"about one-half mile of the railroad below Walthall Junction"
and urged him to repair the track "as soon as it is practicable"
(O. R., 4ᴏ, 2, 660).

³ Hunter escaped; Early promptly moved up the
Valley.

⁴ Hampton, it will be recalled, was moving against Sheridan,
whose cavalry still remained on the north side of the James.
For Hampton's view of his situation, see his letters to Bragg
(June 20, 1864; O. R., loc. cit., 669–670). For Lee's con-
gratulations to Hampton upon the success of his movement,
see O. R., 36, 3, p. 903.

attack him.[5] The battery at Howlett's will open to-day at 12 M— The Navy & G. W. C. Lee cooperating as far as they can—I very much regret to learn that my reply to your confidential note has not reached you— It was sent the night I recᵈ it by the messenger (one of Genl Bragg's I think) who brought your note.[6] I stated that notwithstanding my esteem & admiration for Genl. Pendleton—his truthfulness, sincerity & devotion to the country, I had never thought of recommdᵍ him for the command of a corps in this army. You must not understand that I think him incapable for such a command, but I had never seen anything that caused me to select him, & therefore was unable to recommend him. I can spare him if you think he is the best available. I do not know the officers in Genl J's army whom you enumerate. Genl Stuart may be the best.[7] Genl Johnston had a high opinion of Genl Ewell & I can bear testimony to his soldierly qualities. But I think his health & nervous system has been shaken by his great injury & though active & attentive that

[5] This is the first reference in this correspondence to the probable outcome of the campaign,—the first time Lee admitted that he could not expect victory. It is needless to point out that the strategy he here anticipated on the part of General Grant is that which the Federal commander pursued until the capture at Petersburg. Beaten or driven back in every assault, he advanced to victory "by regular approaches."

[6] The note from Davis not found; Lee's reply (June 15, 1864, 8: 20 P.M) is printed *supra*, no. 133.

[7] A. P. Stewart, see note to dispatch of June 15, 1864, 8: 20 P M

he cannot without breaking himself down undergo
the arduous duties of a Corps Commd[r] I can spare
him if Genl Johnston desires.[8]   I should think he

---

[8] Lieut.-General R. S. Ewell, long commander of the Second
(Jackson's) Corps.   At Groveton, Va., in the engagement of
August 28, 1862, Ewell was so severely wounded that his leg
had to be amputated.   Continuing in the service he was, on
May 19, 1864, badly injured when his horse was shot.   Thereafter he was disabled for field duty (C. M. H., 1, 677-78).
Ewell protested on June 1, 1864, against invalidism.   He wrote
(O. R., 36, 3, 863): "The opinion of my medical attendant,
Dr. McGuire, and that of myself, is that I am as able for duty
today as at any time since the campaign commenced.   I am
unwilling to be idle in this crisis, and, with the permission of
the commanding general, I would prefer to remain with this
army until circumstances may admit of my being replaced in
command of my corps."   On June 4, however, General Lee
thought it necessary for General Ewell's health to give him
rest and consequently placed Early in command of the corps
(*ibid.*, 873).   Writing of General Ewell on June 12 (*ibid.*,
897-98) General Lee, in typical phrases said: "During the
late movements of the army, the condition of General Ewell's
health rendered it proper that he should be relieved temporarily from the command of his corps.   Although now restored
to his usual health, I think the labor and exposure to which he
would be inevitably exposed would at this time again incapaci-
tate him for field service.   The general, who has all the feelings
of a good soldier, differs from me in this opinion, and is not
only willing but anxious to resume his command.   I, however,
think in the present emergency it would jeopardize his life;
and should his strength fail, it would prove disadvantageous
to the service.   I, therefore, propose that he be placed on some
duty attended with less labor and exposure."   And he recommends Ewell for the place to which he was immediately appointed,—that of commander of the Richmond defences.
Here Ewell remained until he joined his old chieftain on the

would require a commander at once as I understand
Genl Loring is the Senior present.⁹

Praying that you may enjoy all health & happiness.

I remain most resp^y & truly

R. E. LEE

Genl.

His Excy JEFF^N DAVIS
Pres: C. States.

No. 140.

[Telegram]

Received at Richmond, June 21, 1864.

By telegraph from Petersburg 21

To His Excellency, JEFFN. DAVIS,

I left Lt. Col. Williams¹ engineer, in charge of
battery at Howletts. He should have been there.
I will order an officer there to-night.

24/480   R. E. LEE

[Endorsed]

Telegram

Genl. LEE

Petersburg

June 21/64.

June 22/64.

---

retreat toward Appomattox. He was captured before the
surrender.

⁹ W. W. Loring of Florida, a native of North Carolina,
major-general, P. A. C. S. Loring is especially remembered
for his services in Egypt after the war.

¹ Lieut.-Col. John A. Williams, engineer corps.

No. 141.

[Telegram]

Received at Rd. June 25, 1864.
By Telegraph from Hancock's 25   To Genl. HAMPTON
7 A.M.   Care Genl. BRAGG.

For want of cavalry our Railroad communications south have been cut.   If you cannot engage Sheridan to advantage he can be watched with a smaller force. Send to me Chambliss Brigade and any other Brigade which can be spared.[1]

R. E. LEE.
39/780   HANCOCKS June 25th. 64.   VV.

[Endorsed]

For want of Cavalry our R. R. communications South are cut.   If you cannot engage Sheridan with advantage Send me Chambliss Brig. & any other Brigades that can be spared.

R. B. 1296.
Sent to Genl Custis Lee to be forwarded to Genl. Hampton.

Recd. June 25th. 64.

---

[1] General Hampton's report of his operations prior to the receipt of this telegram will be found in O. R., 36, 1, 1095ff; his movements after this date are recorded in his report in O. R., 40, 1, 807ff.   The operations described were really the first offensive action taken by Grant after he had brought his troops into works before Petersburg.   On June 21 Grant had dispatched the 2nd and 6th corps to the south to assail General Lee's right flank below Petersburg.   This advance

No. 142.

H^{D}Q^{RS} A N V$_A$.
26th June 1864.

His Excy J$_{EFF}$^{N} D$_{AVIS}$
  Presd^t C. States
M$_R$ P$_{RESIDENT}$,
  I have had the honor to receive today your
letter of the 24th enclosing, me some letters said
to have been written by Maj. Ward.[1] I hope the
accounts he gives of the sufferings of the citizens
of Northern Neck and the South Side of the Rappahannock are exaggerated, though I fear there is much
truth in his statements, and can imagine that great
atrocities have been perpetrated upon our unfor-

---

was promptly met and driven back by three brigades of Hill's
corps, directed by General Lee himself, who happened to be on
that part of the line at the time. The attack was renewed by
the Sixth Corps on June 22, with the support of Wilson's
cavalry—that troublesome body which had hung on Lee
north of the James. The cavalrymen reached the railroad
at Reams' Station, nine miles south of Petersburg, and after
tearing up a part of the track, moved on toward the Southside
railroad. W. H. F. Lee went in pursuit, struck the cavalry
on June 23 and turned it aside. At the Staunton River, the
Federals met local defence troops and once more were turned.
In the meantime, Hampton, who had been engaged with
Sheridan at Trevilians, hurried after the Federals, as did
infantry detached from the main army. Wilson was forced
to leave his plunder, including more than a thousand captured
slaves, and was compelled to return to the main line of the
Federals.
  [1] Not found.

tunate fellow citizens. I know of no way to afford them relief, except by their own energy and strength. If they will organize themselves under proper leaders, they can so punish these marauding bands as to drive them from the country. It would be better for them to send away or destroy their property, horses, provisions &c than to retain them to invite the inroads of the enemy. I will write to Col Mosby to see if he can operate in that country, though I think it would be very hazardous to him as he would certainly be betrayed by the negroes and traders of the country, and his retreat could be easily cut off.[2]

If officers could be selected of proper energy and boldness, it would tend greatly to the proper organization of the people, but I do not know how to select them.

The writer of the letter referred to me, seems to look for help more to persons foreign to the country than to those resided in it. I think if that is the feeling of the Community, there is no remedy for their sufferings. They must come out and defend themselves, and take the consequences of their action.

Very respectfully
Your obt servt
R. E. Lee
Gen

---

[2] A part of Mosby's command was, however, later dispatched to the Northern Neck, a section which was isolated from the Confederate forces and easily overrun by marauding Federals who used the rivers.

No. 143.

[Telegram]

Received at Richmd.   June 27th 1864.
By Telegraph from Head Quarters A. N. Va.

Near Petersburg 28

To Gen. B. BRAGG

Col. Gorgas reports four thirty pounder Parrotts and two ten inch mortars in defence around Richmond.[1] I desire to be sent to me immediately two thirty pounder Parrotts & the two ten inch Mortars unless wanted there.[2]

R. E. LEE

377/40 Col.

[Endorsed]
Hd. Qrs. A. N. Va.
Near Petersburg.
June 28TH. 1864.

R. E. LEE
Genl.

Desires two thirty pounder Parrotts & two ten inch Mortars sent to him immediately.
Copy referred to Col. Gorgas for compliance.

R. B. 1320.
Recd. June 28th. 64.

---

[1] Not found.

[2] To this apparently Gorgas replied with a telegram that appears in the De Renne collection: "I am informed that one 30 prd. and one 4.62 rifle were brought back from Chester. Are these the guns referred to?   The guns are now in charge of Lt.-Col. Pemberton." (June 27.)   See No. 144.

No. 144.

[*Telegram*]

DUNN'S HOUSE, June 27th. 64.

GENL. B. BRAGG

Please return the two thirty pounder Parrotts
that were removed from here unless they are needed
at Richmond.[1]

(Sd) R. E. LEE
Genl.

No. 145.

[*Telegram*]

Received at Richmond June 29th. 1864.
By telegraph from Hd. Qurs. A. N. Va.
Near Petersburg 29.

To Gen. BRAXTON BRAGG:

The matter of Cutherells detail as Clerk was
referred to his Commanding officers as soon as your
letter was received. Cutherell is performing duty
at Brigade Hd. Qurs. His absence will probably
necessitate additional detail. The papers have not
been returned here owing no doubt to active
operations.

R. E. LEE.

48/960

[*Endorsed*]

Hd. Qrs. A. N. Va. June 29th. 64.

R. E. LEE
Genl.

---

[1] See *supra*, No. 143.

Catherill's detail as clerk was referred to his commanding officers as soon as your letter was recd. Papers have not yet been returned owing no doubt to active operations.

R. B. 1331
Answered by letter.
Recd. June 29th. 64.

No. 146.

H^D Q^{RS} A N V^A
30 June 1864.

His Excellency JEFF^N DAVIS
Presd^t C. States

M^R. PRESIDENT

I have the honor to enclose to your Excellency two letters received from Gen Whiting, one of which you will perceive, contains matters that he desires to be brought to your attention.[1]   I think Gen Whiting exaggerates the difficulties and dangers of his position.   So far as the report to which he alludes of Gen Smith's corps being intended to operate against Wilmington, is concerned, I believe that if such a destination was publicly assigned to it, the object was to cover the real purpose.   I believe that Gen Smith's command, when it went to the White House, and when it returned to James River, pursued the course intended for it.

I do not know, even if the enemy designs to attack Wilmington, how assistance can be given to Gen Whiting from this quarter, or from any other, unless

---

[1] Not found.

he can draw some of the reserves of N. Carolina to his support. Nor do I see under the circumstances, what benefit can result from repeated publications of the weakness and necessities of his position by Gen Whiting. It increases the risk of the enemy becoming acquainted with his weakness, and may induce an attack. I think it would be well to call Gen. Whiting's attention to this consideration, and inform him that he must endeavor to strengthen himself as much as possible, and in case of attack, make the best defence he can. Dwelling upon possible dangers and looking for assistance that cannot be given, is not a good preparation on his part for defence.[2]

> With great respect
> Your obt servt
> R. E. LEE
> Genl.

---

[2] Major-General William Henry Chase Whiting had a somewhat tragic career. At this time he held an important post in charge of the defences of the Cape Fear River. Born at Biloxi, Miss., in 1824, of Northern parents, he was educated at Georgetown and at the United States Military Institute, from which he was graduated at the head of the class of 1845. He served in the army until the outbreak of the war when he was commissioned major of engineers and assigned to Charleston. Later transferred to North Carolina, he aided in the construction of coast defences there and joined Johnston in Virginia in time to participate in the battle of First Manassas. He was promoted on the field by President Davis to the rank of brigadier-general and was assigned to the brigade previously commanded by General Bee. He participated in the spring campaign of 1862. Later in the same year he was returned to the command of the defences on the Cape Fear River and was kept there during the rest of the war, except for brief ser-

No. 147.

H^D Q^{RS} ARMY N VA
1st July 1864.

His Excy J^N DAVIS
Presdt. C. States

MR. PRESIDENT,

I have the honor to communicate to you the following items of Northern news taken from the Philadelphia Inquirer of the 29th ult: which you may find interesting.

Staunton's dispatch to Gen Dix announces Sherman's failure on the 27th June with a loss of 2500 including one Brigadier and a number of field officers.[1]

The defeat of Gregg by Gen Hampton at Nance's

---

vice in Virginia with Beauregard. His conduct with the latter raised some suspicions as to the temperance of his habits and undoubtedly clouded a career that gave great promise. Throughout volumes 36 and 40, part 3, of the *Official Records* will be found insistent appeals for more troops to defend a position which General Whiting believed to be hourly threatened. It was in answer to these that General Lee suggested the quiet reprimand proposed in this dispatch. Whiting was to "make the best defence" he could: none could be expected to do more. When relieved of command on the Cape Fear in the winter of 1865, General Whiting continued as a volunteer and shared the savage defence of Fort Fisher. From wounds received at this time, he died in captivity, March 10, 1865 (C. M. H., 4, 352ff.).

[1] The battle of Kenesaw Mountain, one of the bloodiest engagements in Sherman's advance on Atlanta. Joseph E. Johnston, the Confederate leader, confronted with superior forces, had withdrawn in the face of Sherman's advance but had paused at Kenesaw Mountain, had fortified himself strongly and had invited an attack. Sherman made it in

shop is admitted. Gregg is said to have been severely handled. The Federal loss in killed and wounded in the affair of Gen Mahone is said to have been severe, and they admit that 2000 prisoners were captured Gen Hunter claims to have been victorious in every fight, and only retired because his powder was exhausted.

There is no indication of any knowledge on their part of the movement of our troops in the Valley. The $300 commutation clause in the draft act has been repealed by a vote of 72 to 79 in the lower house. An amendment was made to the law giving all cities, towns, counties &c sixty days to fill up their quotas by volunteering. The President may call for any number of men to serve for one, two, or three years, and a bounty of $200 is allowed volunteers or substitutes for one year, $300 to those for two years, and $400 to those for three. If the quota be not filled in sixty days, the President may order a draft for one year, and no payment of commutation will be allowed Bounties as above are given to substitutes of drafted men, and the editor supposes to drafted men held for service also.

The executives of each state may recruit in any of the rebel states.

much the same fashion as Grant assaulted the works at Cold Harbor on June 3 of the same year. Sherman reported an aggregate loss of "nearly 3,000, while we inflicted comparatively little loss on the enemy, who lay behind his well-formed breastworks." For this campaign,—one of the most brilliant withdrawals in military history,—General Johnston never received the credit he deserved. His removal came at a time when he was best in a position to turn on Sherman.

The bill as amended was sent back to the Senate and referred to the Military Committee. It passed the House on the 28th June.

With reference to the markets the following remarks occur. "Usually a sudden jump in gold sends up actively all prices at the Broker's Board, but at present there is too much fear that the advance may be so startling as to render necessary quotations of greenbacks at their rate in gold, instead of the latter at its price greenbacks, which would bring the standard of operations at once down to a specie basis. Most fortunate would it be for the country and the community in general if this revolution should soon take place, for millions would be saved that will hereafter disappear in the culminating crash unless some such disposition of affairs does transpire We hope for the best, but the merchants, brokers and capitalists are inclined to take in every sail and await the revelations for the future. Gold opened at 230, an advance of 8 per cent, and thus steadily advanced to 238, which was the closing quotation, an advance of 28 pr cent over the closing quotation of yesterday. The violent fluctuation cannot fail to cause apprehension for the future."[2]

The paper contains quotations of gold in New York as high as 245. Produce of all kinds also advanced.

Very respy.

Your obt servt

R. R. LEE

Genl.

---

[2] Gold, it must be remembered, attained its highest premium, 286, in Northern quotations during this month.

No. 148.

H^D Q^{RS} A N V_A.
2nd July 1864.

His Excellency JEFF^N DAVIS
   Presd^t C. States
MR. PRESIDENT,

As far as my judgment and experience enable me to decide, I am convinced that the cavalry service will be benefitted by having one officer to control its operations, and to be held responsible for its condition. Since the death of Gen Stuart,[1] I have placed each division under the charge of its division commander, and when two or more have operated together, have directed the superior officer to assume command. The disadvantage of this arrangement in my opinion is that he neither feels nor exercises that authority which is required by the responsibility of his position. It is taken up one day and laid aside the next, and is not as effective as if exercised by one who is permanently and solely responsible. You know the high opinion I entertain of Gen Hampton, and my appreciation of his character and services. In his late expedition he has displayed both energy and good conduct,[2] and although I have feared that he might not have that

---

[1] The famous J. E. B. Stuart ("Jeb" Stuart), major-general, P. A. C. S., mortally wounded at Yellow Tavern, Virginia, May 11, 1864.

[2] Though Lee, in his dispatch of June 21, *supra*, had been doubtful of Hampton's success.

activity and endurance so necessary in a cavalry commander, and so eminently possessed by Gen Stuart, yet should you be unable to assign Anyone to the command of the cavalry in this army whom you deem possessed of higher qualifications, I request authority to place him in the command.[3] If this be done, it will necessitate appointing a commander for his division, and will hereafter recommend to you some person for that position.

With high respect

Your obt servt

R. E. LEE

Genl.

No. 149.

CAMP PETERSBURG 3 July '64.

MR PRESIDENT

I had the honour to receive last ev^g by the hands of Col: Wood[1] your letter of the 2nd Inst:[2] & to learn from him the arrangements made to release the prisoners—I think under the blessing of a merciful

---

[3] Hampton was assigned to command the cavalry corps on Aug. 11, 1864 (S. O. No. 189, A. N. Va., 1864, Par. VII, O. R., 42, 2, 1171) but was not commissioned as lieutenant-general until February, 1865. General Stuart, it will be recalled, though a "corps" commander, never held the rank of lieutenant-general.

[1] Colonel John Taylor Wood, grandson of Zachary Taylor and President Davis' nephew by his first marriage.

[2] Not found.

Providence they will be successful & result in great good. If any human agency can insure success I think it will be accomplished by Col. Wood to whom I would be willing to trust the operations on land as well as sea. I think we cannot with safety attempt any communication with the prisoners. The first indications of relief must be borne to them by the guns of the captured gunboats— Neither in my opinion would it be safe to throw across the Potomac any party. Their advance to the river even would be dangerous Their transit would certainly be discovered. Col: Wood will send a boat to Cherrystone to cut the telegraph wire to Old Point, if possible cut the wire from the point to Washington before the attack. If this can be done a great advantage will be gained. It would be very desirable to send with him some officer known to the prisoners, to organize inspire confidence & put them quickly in motion. I hope the officers there can do this— separating the Cav^y, art^y & Inf^y & officer them according to the arm of service. The only officer here whom I could recommend for the duty is Genl Hoke. If he was now taken from his division in the present emergency I would not know what to do with it. I am afraid it would be lost to us. As the next best arrangement I can make I send to-day an officer to Gen Early to inform him that an effort will be made to release the prisoners about the 12 Inst: & if successful he will certainly know it through Northern Sources. In that event, if circumstances will permit he must send down a brigade of Cav^y with Genls Gordon & Lewis to command & lead around

Washington the prisoners &c—I think this is all that can be done. The rest must be left to the operators.[3] No corps has left Genl Grant. Men whose time has expired & the sick are constantly descending the river. But convalescents & 100 day men are returning in equal quantities as far as I can judge by the boats reported The 9th corps which is reported to have left I know is here. Indeed all the corps are located along the lines— The day after the engagement with the battery on James river a single turreted monitor is reported to have passed Fort Boykin towed by a gunboat & accomp[d] by another down the river, & up to the 1st Inst: had not returned. The enemy was unusually quiet last night & this mor[g] [4]—With great respect

Your obt servt
R. E. Lee
Genl.

His Excy Jeff[N] Davis
Pres: C. States.

---

[3] The reference here is to a bold project, conceived at this time, by which Wood and a company of like daring spirits proposed to capture a number of Federal gunboats in the Chesapeake and to use them in conjunction with a land raid by General Early to liberate the Confederate prisoners at Point Lookout. Needless to say, the plan did not succeed. See Nos. 152 and 155 and O. R., series 2, 7, 458.

[4] Along the lines which had now been permanently drawn for the siege of Petersburg. Shortly after this date, General Lee began to forward daily reports of actions and casualties on the front.

No. 150.

[Hd.-Qrs. A. N. Va., July 4–6 (?) 1864][1]
Mʀ President
I send you a Herald[2] of the 2nd Inst: brought in
to-day by a deserter— It contains some items of
interest— The resignation of Mʳ Chase[3], appointment of Mʳ Fessenden,[4] repeal of the gold bill &cˢ[5]—
As our papers seem to take it for granted that Burnside's corps has gone to Washington, which if true,
I do not know[6] I refer you to the letter in which it
is stated that Genls Grant Meade & Butler met at his
quarters on the 28th Tuesday last— We took three
prisoners from his corps on the 27th— He may have
gone since & it is very difficult for me to get correct
information here.   I think though he is on the

---

[1] Without date, but evidently early in July, 1864, because
of the reference to Chase's resignation which was presented
June 30, 1864.

[2] Doubtless the New York *Herald*, then famous for its war
news.

[3] Salmon P. Chase, Secretary of the Treasury. A brief
but accurate account of the reasons for his resignation will be found in Hosmer, *Outcome of the Civil War*,
157ff.

[4] William Pitt Fessenden, chairman of the U. S. Senate
Finance Committee, who succeeded Mr. Chase as Secretary
of the Treasury.

[5] *Cf.* Hosmer, *op. cit.*, p. 131.

[6] Burnside was still in Lee's front and was to have a part in
the next important event,—the battle of the Crater. The
6th Corps (Wright's) was ordered to Washington July 9, 1864
(O. R., 40, 3, 106). *Cf. infra*, No. 153.

lines—They do not appear to have any information of
Earlys movements.[7]

With great esteem
Your obt servt
R. E. LEE

His Excy JEFF^N DAVIS
Pres: C. States.

No. 151.

H^DQ^{RS} ARMY N VA.
5th July 1864.

His Excellency JEFF^N DAVIS
Presdt C. States
Mr. President,

The subject of recruiting and keeping up our
cavalry force, has occupied much of my thoughts,
especially since the opening of the present campaign.   The enemy is numerically superior to us
in this arm, and possesses greater facilities for recruiting his horses and keeping them in serviceable condition.   In the several engagements that have taken
place between the cavalry of the two armies, I think
great loss has been inflicted upon him, but it has been
attended with a diminution of our force which we
were less able to bear.   Could I sweep his cavalry
from the field, or preserve a fair proportion between
its numbers and our own, I should feel that our

---

[7] Great pains had been taken to conceal Early's movements
as the strength of his force was limited and its ability to
achieve a success was, in consequence, contingent upon its
ooorot oporation.

present situation was in a measure secure. But in
view of the disparity that exists, and the difficulty
of increasing or even maintaining our force, I cannot
but entertain serious apprehensions about the safety
of our southern communications. Should we be
unable to preserve them, I need not point out the
consequences. I do not know from what quarter
reinforcements can be had. There is one regt.
of Georgia Cavalry under Col Anderson which I
believe is desirous of joining this army. The War
Department can best decide whether it can be spared
but if it can be, I beg that it may be ordered to me
without delay. You will know whether any can be
drawn from Gen Johnston's Dept. That which is in
Western Va is needed there and I am aware of no
other source of supply. I think that horses might
be obtained from Texas, as we have now access to
the Mississippi at various points. Those horses would
make very serviceable animals for cavalry, and could
be brought across the river by swimming, as cattle are
higher up the stream and on the Missouri river if only
a few can be obtained in this way, it would be of
great assistance. It has also occurred to me that
horses at least for artillery service could be obtained
on the Northern and Western borders of Va. by the
system of exchange which is now being successfully
carried on for subsistence. If good agents were
selected and sent to the Western and Northwestern
parts of the State, with authority to exchange cotton
and tobacco for horses, the facilities for carrying on
the traffic would be greater than that in articles of
more difficult transportation, and at the present

prices of those commodities in the North, the profits would be a great temptation, and insure the success of the experiment.[1] I think if anything is to be done, now is our most favorable opportunity. I hope your Excellency will be able to devise some means of obtaining an increase of our supply of horses, and recruiting our cavalry, as upon that in a great measure I believe, depends the issue of the campaign in Va.

Very respectfully
Your obt servt
R E LEE
Genl.

No. 152.

CAMP PETERSB^G 5 July '64.

MR PRESIDENT

Your letter of the 4th Inst: was delivered to me this mor^g by Col: Wood.[2] He with the gentlemen accomp^g him are on the road to Stony Creek depot, 28 miles by the road they have to march where they will take the cars to Weldon. I procured horses for two & an ambulance for the other two & the baggage. I sent directions to Genl Whiting[3] to

---

[1] This form of trade, though repeatedly prohibited by law, was at this time a regular means of procuring limited quantities of supplies. It was a tradition in the Confederate army that a Federal soldier would "sell the shirt off his back" for tobacco.

[2] Not found.

[3] Commanding at Wilmington, from which point, as this dispatch makes plain, the proposed expedition against Point Lookout was to start.

provide them with two 20 p^d Parrotts if possible &
to furnish every other facility in his power to expedite
their movements— I hope they will sail on Saturday.
I have gone over all the points of the expedition with
Cols: Wood & Lee,[4] & we can now only trust to their
energy & judgment & the blessing of a merciful
Providence. The arrangement made with Genl.
Early is the best I can suggest   He is to send a help-
ing hand after he hears of the success of the expedition, & I think there is no danger of his precipitating
matters. I do not see how the attention of the
Potomac flotilla can be attracted to a remote point,
unless Early's movements may call them to Washington. This would be the best diversion, & in the
best quarter. Every thing I think has been done
that can be; & we have good ground to hope for
the success of the enterprize.[5]

Most respy. your obt servt

R. E. LEE
Genl.

His Excy JEFF^N DAVIS
Pres: C. States.

No. 153.

H^{D}Q^{RS}: 6 July '64.

MR. PRESIDENT

As I have felt some anxiety as to the position of the
9th[1] corps from the various reports concerning it, I

---

[4] John Taylor Wood and G. W. C. Lee.

[5] See *supra*, No. 149 and *infra* No. 155.

[1] See *supra*, No. 150.

directed that the pickets along our lines should be
directed to capture a prisoner along their front.
Genl Hill has just come in to report that one from
the 2nd corps was brought in to him last night.   He
was a New Yorker, sharp & shrewd, from whom but
little could be gained.   But he had on his person a
diary kept by himself & brought up to the 5th Inst.
It was there recorded under date of the 4th Inst.
that he had with a Comrade that day passed through
the 9th & 5th corps visiting certain friends &c—
This would seem to be good evidence—that the
9th corps is present before Petersburg.[2]

With great respect your obt servt.

R. E. LEE
Genl.

His Excy. JEFF^N DAVIS.

No. 154.

[*Telegram*]

Received at Richmond July 7 1864.
By Telegraph from Hd. Qrs. near Petersburg 7
To G^ENL. B. BRAGG

How did you ascertain that Grant was crossing
forces from City Point to Bermuda Hundreds[1] Scouts
report that Garrison at Yorktown been advanced to
Williamsburg.[2]

25/500 Co.   R. E. LEE

---

[2] It was—about 18,000 effectives.

[1] The answer would probably have been, from the report of
signal-officer J. F. Moore.   See the report, O. R., 40, 3, 747.

[2] *Cf.* W. T. Robins to T. O. Chestney, *ibid.*, 749.

[*Endorsed*]
    Hd. Qrs. near Petersburg July 7th.
               R. E. LEE
                 Genl.
    Inquires how Genl. Bragg learned that Grant was crossing troops from City Point to Bermuda Hundreds. Scouts report the garrison of Yorktown advanced to Williamsburg.
               R. B. 1368.
Recd. at Hd. Qrs.
    A. C. S. July 7, 64.

No. 155.

[*Telegram*]

Received at Richmond, Va. July 8 1864.
                     at 7.25 P.M.
            Hd. Qrs. near Petersburg.
His Excellency
    J. DAVIS
    Telegram received. The expedition is spoken of all through the army, information having been brought from Richmond. I will inform the leaders and let them judge.[1]
           (Signed) R. E. LEE
[*Endorsed*]
    Genl. R. E. LEE
    Hd. Qrs. Near Petersburg
        July 8 1864.
        Telegram in cypher.
        Rccd. July 8 1864.

---

[1] *Cf.* Nos. 149 and 152 *supra*. See also Davis to Lee, July 8, 1864. In this, Davis, avoiding specific reference to the

No. 156.

Mʀ PRESIDENT

I have the honour to send you a N. Y. Herald of the 8ᵗʰ containing some items of interest. You will see the people in the U. S. are mystified about our forces on the Potomac— The expedition will have the effect I think at least of teaching them they must keep some of their troops at home & that they cannot denude their frontier with impunity— It seems also to have put them in bad temper as well as bad humor[1]

Point Lookout expedition, notified Lee that G. W. C. Lee had not been enabled to start from Wilmington as he had hoped because of delay in getting arms. He added: "In this town I hear the expedition is spoken of on the street. Shall it proceed under change of circumstances and possibility of notice being given to the enemy? If not, stop it as you deem best" (O. R., 40, 3, 749). The letter here printed is General Lee's response. R. E. Lee's letters to G. W. C. Lee and J. T. Wood do not appear in the O. R. but from other references there (loc. cit., 753, 757, 761) it appears that the publicity which had been given the proposed expedition and the delay in procuring arms prompted the President to direct its abandonment. A brief account of the part which General Early was expected to play in the movement will be found in the narrative of Col. (later General) Bradley T. Johnson, who commanded the cavalry at the time (C. M. H., 2, 125 ff.). In his well-known diary, under date of July 9, 1864, J. B. Jones reports a rumor in Richmond that the expedition against Point Lookout had succeeded (Rebel War Clerk's Dairy, 2, 246).

[1] Early had pressed up the Valley, had crossed the Potomac and had created wild excitement in the North. The Sixth Corps, as has been noted, had already been dispatched from

—Gold you will see has gone as high as 271 & closed at 266¾—¹² Provisions &c are rising— I see also they are moving the prisoners from Pt— Look out—³

I trust that you & your family are in good health & wish you every happiness—

Very respy your obt servt

R. E. LEE

His Excy JEFFⁿ DAVIS

No. 157.

HEAD QRS   A N VA.

July 12th 1864.

His Excy JEFFERSON DAVIS
   President C. States
      Richmond
MR. PRESIDENT

Letters which I have received from Gen. Holmes¹ do not represent affairs in North Carolina in a favourable condition— I do not know what position he

---

Grant's army to defend the Federal capital, and the Nineteenth Corps, just arrived at Old Point from Louisiana, had also been rushed to Washington.   On July 8, Early had defeated Lew Wallace at Monocacy and had moved straight on Washington.   He reached the outer works on July 11, but not in time to take the city.

² Before the end of the month it went to 286, as previously noted.

³ Which would have been threatened had Early not been turned back.   For other reasons that prompted the removal, see O. R. series 2, 7, index heading *Point Lookout.*

¹ Lieut.-Genl Theophilus H. Holmes of North Carolina, commanding Confederate forces in Weldon and vicinity.

holds in the State or what is his command— If
his health and strength qualify him for the duty I
should think it would be well to give him supreme
control of the reserves of the State— From his account their organization proceeds slowly perhaps
necessarily so, but every stimulant should be given
to hasten it— If Gen. Holmes is incapacitated for
these duties I recommend that some officer be sent
there who is qualified— From all that I can learn he
does not expect to obtain more than twenty five
hundred of the Junior Reserves for service in Eastern
Carolina & the maintenance of the railroads in that
section.   He represents affairs in the Western part
of the state to be in a critical position.   Col. Palmer
commands in that district and Gen Holmes thinks he
ought to be ordered to report to him— I do not know
Col. Palmer nor do I see any actual necessity for his
being under Gen. Holmes' command provided Col
P. has control over the reserves in that section of the
State & is able to repress the deserters and disloyal
who are represented to be banding together to resist
authority.[2] The Governor would be more efficacious
than any one also in repressing this spirit of insubord-
ination and in enforcing law and order. If Col.
Palmer's is independent the reserves of the Western
section should be reported directly to him— Now,

[2] By S. O. 170, Par. XLIX, A. & I. G. O., July 20, 1864, Col.
J. B. Palmer was directed to report to Brig.-Genl J. G. Martin
who assumed command "of the reserves of the District of
Western North Carolina" (O. R., 40, 3, 788). On the 18th
(*ibid.*, 781) General Holmes was ordered to resume command
of the "North Carolina Reserve Corps."

I understand, they are reported to Gen. Holmes who assigns them to Col. Palmer.[3]

I am with great respect

Your obt servt.

R. E. LEE

No. 158.

[*Telegram*]

Received at Richmond, Va. July 12 1864.

at 8.45 P.M.

Hd. Qrs. Near Petersburg 12

His Excy JEFFN. DAVIS
Prest. C. S.

Telegram of to-day received. I regret the fact stated. It is a bad time to release [relieve] the commander of an army situated as that of Tenne. We may lose Atlanta and the army too. Hood is a bold fighter. I am doubtful as to other qualities necessary.[1]

(Signed) R. E. LEE

[*Endorsed*]

Genl. R. E. LEE

Hd. Qrs. Army N. Va.

July 12 1864.

Telegram in cypher.

Recd. July 12 1864.

---

[3] This letter is one of many in the long and complex correspondence regarding the exact status of the North Carolina troops, over whom Gov. Zebulon B. Vance exercised an authority which conflicted often with that of the Confederate Government. President Davis was frequently at his wit's end to know how to avoid difficulty with the testy chief executive of the State.

[1] Amplified more fully in No. 159, *infra, q. v.*

No. 159.

CAMP 12 July '64.

9½ P.M.

Mᴿ. PRESIDENT

I send you a paper of the 10th Inst. containing Mʳ Secry. Stanton's bulletin to Gen. Dix, acknowledging a defeat of Genl Wallace at Monocacy by Genl. Early.[1] I have also recᵈ a dispatch from Genl Fitz Lee this evᵍ reporting that he met Gen. Gregg with his division advancing towards Reams station, charged him with three of his regts: & drove him back, capturing some 30 men & two officers— His loss small. The enemy's not known He thinks he was moving against the R. R. We have only had it in operation two days, but have got through several trains of Corn & provisions.

I am distressed at the intelligence conveyed in your telegram of today. It is a grievous thing to change commander of an army situated as is that of the Tennessee. Still if necessary it ought to be done. I know nothing of the necessity. I had hoped that Johnston was strong enough to deliver battle. We must risk much to save Alabama, Mobile & communication with the Trans Missᵖⁱ— It would be better to concentrate all the Cavʸ in Missᵖⁱ & Tenn: on Shermans communications— If Johnston abandons Atlanta I suppose he will fall back on Augusta— This loses us Missᵖⁱ & communication with Trans

---

[1] Not found, but *cf.* Halleck to Grant, July 9, 1864 (O. R., 40, 3, 93), and Lincoln to Grant, July 10, 1864 (*ibid.*, 121) in which the defeat of Genl. Lew Wallace is acknowledged.

Miss^pi— We had better therefore hazard that communication to retain the Country. Hood is a good fighter very industrious on the battle field, careless off & I have had no opportunity of judging of his action, when the whole responsibility rested upon him. I have a high opinion of his gallantry, earnestness & zeal. Genl Hardee has more experience in managing an army.[2]

May God give you wisdom to decide in this momentous matter.

Truly & respy   Yours

R. E. Lee

His Excy Jeff^n Davis
Pres: C. States—

P.S.   To-day we could get no papers from the enemy, from which I inferred there was some good news they wished to withold. The one sent was captured. You must excuse its condition.

R. E. Lee

---

[2] So far as the editor has been able to ascertain this letter and the telegram of the same date printed above (No. 158) are the only references General Lee ever made in writing to the removal of General Joseph E. Johnston from the army in front of Atlanta and the substitution of John B. Hood as commander. And these, too, seem all the more remarkable in their frankness. General Johnston, it will be recalled, was never esteemed by President Davis, and his conduct of the Atlanta campaign increased the President's distrust of Johnston's ability. On the 18th, Johnston was relieved of command,—a step for which, perhaps, President Davis has been more criticised than for any other. It cannot be said from the letter and telegram here printed that General Lee encouraged

No. 160.

H^D Q^{RS} ARMY N VA.

21st July 1864.

His Excy JEFF^N DAVIS
     President C. States
MR. PRESIDENT,

Since we began to use the Weldon R R,[1] we have been endeavouring to accumulate a reserve of corn at this place, in case the road should be again cut. But since we have brought away the supplies that accumulated at Weldon, Gaston & Wilmington during the interruption of traffic on the road, it has been found that we cannot get more than sufficient for daily consumption, and sometimes not enough for that, thus making it necessary, to entrench upon the small reserve of four or five days that we have on hand. The reason of this state of things is that corn is not brought in sufficient quantities from the south to Weldon, Gaston & Wilmington, the points with which the Weldon R. R. communicates. I hope it is

---

or approved the change. Aside from his frank statement that he was doubtful of Hood's qualities as commander of an army, and aside from his quiet recommendation of General Hardee, the whole tone of the letter seems, to the editor at least, to caution President Davis against a hasty change. The most that he can say is the stoical "if necessary it ought to be done." Lee, it is needless to say, had a very high opinion of General Johnston's military qualities.

[1] The Petersburg and Weldon, now the Atlantic Coast Line, the most direct route at the time from Richmond and Petersburg to the Carolinas.

being brought by the Danville² & Piedmont³ roads
to Richmond and that it is being accumulated there
in sufficient quantities to serve the army in case of
a renewal of the interruption of our roads. But I
think that if possible, it should be brought from the
south by the Weldon road also, as it is capable of
aiding in the required accumulation, and we cannot
tell how soon it may be needed. Commissary stores
exceeding our wants are now coming to this point &
being forwarded to Richmond, but I think it would be
advisable to make arrangements to place a sufficient
supply of corn at the points above indicated to enable
us to draw from them to the extent of the capacity
of the road, without at the same time relaxing in any
degree the efforts to bring it to Richmond by the
Danville Road. I dislike to add to the troubles and
labors of your Excellency, but deem this subject
sufficiently important to be brought directly to your
attention.⁴

With great respect
Your obt servt
R. E. Lee
Genl.

---

² The line from Richmond to Danville, long known as the
"Richmond and Danville" and now a part of the Southern
system.

³ The Piedmont was a weak and uncertain line from Danville into North Carolina, subject to frequent washouts and
interruptions.

⁴ Lee's insistence upon this point was not without reason.
Already the army defending Petersburg was on extremely short
rations and, on several occasions, was on the point of starva-

No. 161.

[Telegram]

Received at Richmond, Va. July 28th. 1864.
By Telegraph from Dunn's Hill July 28th. 64.
HON. SECY. OF WAR.
Genl. Early reports that the enemy has retired
across the Potomac at Williamsport burning over
seventy wagons & abandoning twelve caisons. Our
troops occupy Martinsburg.[1]

(Signed) R. E. LEE
Genl.

Respectfully to Genl. B. BRAGG

H. L. CLAY
A. A. G.

[Endorsed]
   Dunn's Hill July 28/64.
   R. E. LEE
   General.
   Telegram to Secty. War.
   Genl. Early reports enemy has retired across
Potomac at Williamsport, burning over 70 wagons
& abandoning 12 caisons. Our troops occupy
Martinsburg.

R. B. 1522
Recd. Hd. Qrs. A. C. S. July 29/64.

---

tion. Many commands that left the Petersburg defences on
March 31, 1865, received no rations, other than a small amount
of parched corn, until after they surrendered at Appomattox.

   [1] The reports and correspondence for this campaign will be
found in O. R., 37, parts 1 and 2. General Early, falling back

No. 162.

HEAD Q^RS A N VA
Aug. 9th 1864.

His Excellency
    JEFFERSON DAVIS
        Presdt Confederate States
MR. PRESIDENT

The soap ration for this Army has become a serious question— Since leaving Orange C. H. the Commissary Lt Col. Cole has only been able to make three issues of three days rations each. The great want of cleanliness which is a necessary consequence of these very limited issues is now producing sickness among the men in the trenches, and must effect their self respect & morale. The importance of the subject and the general complaints which have arisen must be my excuse for troubling you with the matter— An offer of 24000 pounds at $3.75/100 has been made to the Commissary of the Army but the Commissary General declined to authorize the purchase at that price.— He speaks of the purchase of several lots at a smaller price $2.50/100 per pound but holds out no definite prospect of sending an adequate supply— such is the condition of the troops & their immediate necessities in regard to soap are so great that I hope the purchase of the 24000 pounds at even the

---

on the valley of Virginia, employed this respite in tearing up the line of the Baltimore and Ohio railroad and dispatched McCausland's brigade on the famous raid to Chambersburg. An excellent account of the campaign is that in C. M. H., 3, chap. xxix.

advanced price of $3.75/100 will be authorized &
that contracts will be entered into at once for the
future regular and adequate supply of the soap
ration to the troops[1]— Their health, comfort &
respectability cannot otherwise be secured.

With great respect your obt servt

R. E. LEE
Genl.

No. 163.

H^D Q^RS A N V_A.
22nd Aug: 1864.

His Excy JEFF^N DAVIS
    Presdt C States,
MR PRESIDENT,

The enemy availed himself of the withdrawal of
troops from Petersburg to the north side of James
River, to take a position on the Weldon R. R.
He was twice attacked on his first approach to the
road, and worsted both times, but the attacking
force was too small to drive him off. Before the
troops could be brought back from north of James
River, he had strengthened his position so much, that
the effort made yesterday to dislodge him was
unsuccessful, and it was apparent that it could not

---

[1] The schedule of impressment prices for May and June,
1864, quotes soap at $2.00 the pound (O. R., 42, 1152), but the
schedule for Oct. 1864–Jany. 1865 fixed the price at $1.00 the
pound. The lack of a soap ration was every whit as "serious"
a question as General Lee explained. Itch had been added to
the other burdens of the army.

be accomplished even with additional troops, without a greater sacrifice of life than we can afford to make, or than the advantages of success would compensate for. As I informed your Excellency when we first reached Petersburg, I was doubtful of your ability to hold the Weldon road so as to use it. The proximity of the enemy and his superiority of numbers rendered it possible for him to break the road at any time, and even if we could drive him from the position he now holds, we could not prevent him from returning to it or to some other point, as our strength is inadequate to guard the whole road. These considerations induced me to abandon the prosecution of the effort to dislodge the enemy.[1]

---

[1] Following the raid by Wilson's cavalry and the Second and Sixth Corps, on June 21, Grant settled down to the formal investment of Petersburg. As steadily as possible, he advanced his lines opposite those held by the Confederates and was able, with persistence, to take positions in some instances not more than one hundred yards from the Confederate front. This fact probably suggested to Grant the possibility of mining the Confederate works. The method by which this was accomplished and the disastrous results to his army that followed are familiar to all readers. No new light on the battle of the Crater, which followed the explosion of the mine, is to be found in the De Renne collection. The details, therefore, need not be dwelt upon here. The next development in the campaign was the dispatch of Sheridan on his infamous raid through the Valley of Virginia,—one of the darkest blots on the military fame of Grant. As the Confederate commander sent Fitz Lee's division of cavalry and Kershaw's division of infantry after Sheridan, Grant decided to make a feint on Richmond "to prevent his [Lee's] sending his troops away, and, if possible, to draw back those sent." On August 13, accordingly, he sent

I think it is his purpose to endeavor to compel the evacuation of our present position by cutting off our supplies, and that he will not renew the attempt to drive us away by force. His late demonstration on the north side of the James was designed I think in part, to cause the withdrawal of troops from here to favor his movement against the road, but also to endeavor if possible to force his way to Richmond.[2] Being foiled in the attempt, he has brought back all

---

two corps and one division north of the James and made a feebly futile attack on the Confederate lines. As Lee moved a part of his army across the river before he was aware that Grant's forces had been driven back, the Federals decided to make a new assault on the Petersburg and Weldon railroad. This is the movement mentioned in this dispatch and stated in detail in O. R., 42, 1, index caption, *Weldon railroad.* The Fifth Federal Corps under Warren advanced quickly and with spirit, and struck the railroad at the Globe tavern. Here more than 1,000 of Warren's men were captured by a flank movement by Heth's division. On August 19, A. P. Hill, with two divisions, assailed Warren's left while Mahone's division fell on his right. After a bloody action, Warren retired to temporary works which he was able to hold against Hill. Two days later Grant sent more troops to tear up the railroad beyond the point where Warren had struck it. But the new forces, vigorously assailed by Hill and by the Confederate cavalry, broke under fire and fled precipitately. Grant accomplished his main purpose, in that he destroyed an important link in the railroad, but he paid for it at heavy cost. Lee, in the same way, lost veterans whom he could not replace.

[2] Grant, as we have seen, maintained that his movement on the north side of the James was merely a feint. On September 29, however, he did more serious work on the north side by his assault on Fort Harrison.

the troops engaged in it, except those at Dutch Gap, and it is possible that they too will be withdrawn to this side of the James.[3] It behooves us to do everything in our power to thwart his new plan of reducing us by starvation, and all our energies should be directed to using to its utmost capacity our remaining line of communication with the south. The best officers of the Q M Dept should be selected to superintend the transportation of supplies by the Danville road and its Piedmont connections and all the roads south of it.

I shall do all in my power to procure some supplies by the Weldon road, bringing them by rail to Stony Creek, and thence by wagons. One train has already been sent out, and others are prepared to go. I think by energy and intelligence on the part of those charged with the duty, we will be able to maintain ourselves until the corn crop in Va comes to our relief, which it will begin to do to some extent in about a month. It should be our effort to provide not only for current wants but if practicable, to accumulate a surplus to provide against those occasional interruptions of the roads which the enemy's policy justifies us in anticipating. I think this can be done with proper effort, and by the full use of all the rolling stock we can accumulate.

Our supply of corn is exhausted to-day, the small reserve accumulated in Richmond having been used. I am informed that all the corn that was brought from

---

[3] The Federals were already back on the south side of the James.

the south was transported to this place and Richmond, but the supply was not sufficient to enable the Q M department to accumulate a larger reserve. If this be true, it is desirable that steps be at once taken to increase the quantity brought over the southern roads, and if practicable, corn should be brought into Wilmington until our crop becomes available.

I trust that your Excellency will see that the most vigorous and intelligent efforts be made to keep up our supplies, and that all officers concerned in the work, be required to give their unremitting personal attention to their duty.[4]

With great respect
Your obt servt
R. E. LEE
Genl.

No. 164.

HᴰQ^{ʀs} ARMY N VA.
9th Sept 1864.

His Excy JEFF^N DAVIS
    Presdt. C. States
MR. PRESIDENT,

In connection with the subject of bringing into the field all able bodied men, to which I recently called your Excellency's attention, I beg leave to submit a few additional considerations.

---

[4] The substance of this letter, addressed on the same day to the War Department, will be found in O. R., 42, 2, 1194. For Davis' reply, see *ibid.*, 1197.

The duties of the Bureau of Conscription and of the Department superintending the enrollment of Reserves might in my opinion be consolidated in each state with advantage. The duties of both might be performed by one. A large number of able-bodied men and officers fit for and liable to do field duty, are now employed by the conscript Bureau. I think those men and officers should be sent to the field, and their places supplied by an adequate number of Reserves. The latter I think would be more efficient, at least if we look at the motives that may be supposed to influence them. The detailed conscript engaged in enrolling duty is interested in continuing the necessity for his own detail, which would cease as soon as all able-bodied men in his district have been brought out. The Reserves on the other hand would know that just in proportion as our regular armies are strengthened, will the necessity of a call upon their own class be diminished. They would therefore more naturally exert themselves to increase those armies. I therefore respectfully advise that but one force be employed to enroll conscripts and reserves in that it be taken from the latter class and the disabled men, all able-bodied men and officers now employed by the Bureau being at once sent to the army. In selecting officers for the business of conscription and enrollment, I earnestly recommend that some be employed at their own homes. The influence their action will have in determining all questions of detail and exemption renders the propriety of this suggestion apparent. I also advise that no enrolling officer be permitted to grant a furlough pending an application for discharge or detail. Let it be their business to send men to the field who are physically able & of the right age. We may safely trust the men so sent to establish their own claims to exemption or detail.

I think that care should be taken to have an adequate force of reserves in each district, for the duties above referred to, but not more than are actually necessary. I would also recommend that inquiry be made whether any advisory boards employ able-bodied men as clerks. [1]

Very respectfully
Your obt servt
R. E. LEE
Genl.

---

[1] "Detailed men" and "reserves" represented two distinct classes,—the former those who were fortunate enough to be "detailed" for service in executive departments, at prisons, etc., the latter those past conscript age, boys under sixteen, etc. Though the "detail" evil never became in the South the scandal it was in the North, it was a constant source of irritation to the soldiers and of concern to the military commanders. To General Lee, who saw his small army dissolving, while no recruits except boys under sixteen, conscripts and old men were coming to the colors, the necessity of keeping able-bodied men from details was imperative. With the correspondence of this date there appears in the De Renne collection the following:

Extract of letter from Brig Gen John Echols commd^g Dept E. Tennessee to Gen. R. E. Lee, dated Sept. 5th, 1864.

. . . "East Tenn is in a terrible condition from the large numbers of guerillas, and bush-whackers, deserters from both armies who infest the whole country. Murders are of almost daily occurrence and atrocities of all kinds are perpetrated. The public roads are all unsafe and an officer cannot

No. 165.

H^D Q^{RS} ARMY N VA.

10th Sept 1864.

General BRAXTON BRAGG,

Comd^g Armies C. S.[1]

Richmond,

GENERAL,

I have the honor to acknowledge the receipt of your letter of the 7th inst., and the accompanying report of the result of an inspection of the conscript

---

travel without a strong escort. The country of south western Va. is fast getting into the same condition. There we have strong organized bands of deserters from the eastern armies who are defying authority and levying contributions upon the citizens. I have already directed the most active measures to be taken against them where they are most troublesome, and am employing the Reserves in this duty. But this state of things cannot be entirely remedied, and men properly brought into the service, and kept in when sent forward, unless we have a more rigid and faithful enforcement of the law and military regulations by the officers of the conscript Department. I am satisfied that the conscript laws are not rigidly and thoroughly enforced in south western Va. or we should have more men in the commands drawn from that section. I hope that the commd^g Genl may find the time and opportunity to press this subject upon the attention of the authorities. I think that the public interests would be promoted by an entire change in the conscript agents in this portion of Virginia, which cannot be too soon attended to."

Official

CHARLES MARSHALL

Lt Col & A. D. C. [Cf. O. R., 43, 2, 864 ff.]

[1] Strictly speaking, Bragg was not "comdg Armies C. S." No commission to that effect had ever been given him or, in all probability, would ever have been approved by the Con-

service in Georgia.² The facts presented by the last named document are not calculated to give much encouragement. The very small number of men sent to the field by the Conscript law had already attracted my attention, and I have made some suggestions to the President which I thought calculated to make the law more effectual in its operation.³ Among them I advised that none but reserves and disabled soldiers should be employed to collect conscripts, and that all able bodied men and officers now detailed on that duty, who are of the proper age, be sent to the field. The reserves I think will be likely to do the work more thoroughly, as they will know that the increase of the regular armies diminishes the probability of a call upon their own class. I also advised the enrolling officers be not allowed to grant furloughs to conscripts pending the application of the latter for exemption or detail. I think it a sound principle that the enrolling & conscript officers should be restricted entirely to the duty of putting men in the field. I think we may safely leave it to the conscripts themselves to make out their claims to relief from active service. As the system of exemptions and details is now conducted, I do not expect any material increase of our strength. I was informed by Gen Kemper⁴ that in this state

federate Congress. Bragg's temporary position as military adviser to the President corresponded to that of Halleck, Federal Chief of Staff.

² Not found. Many references to the conscription service in Georgia occur in O. R., series 4, 3.

³ *Supra*, No. 165.

⁴ Brigadier-General James L. Kemper, distinguished at

alone there were no less than forty thousand exempts, details and applications for detail yet undecided. Of the applicants I suppose the greater part have furloughs Another point that I regard as very essential to the thorough enforcement of the law, is that no officer be put on enrolling duty at his own home. I recommended to the President to have an inspection made of the conscription service with a view to obtain accurate information as to its working. To me it now seems a very imperfect system of recruiting our armies. It is possible that nothing better can be done, but it is certain that in no department of the service are energy, intelligence and practical ability more vitally important to our success. I think the Department should be filled by the best capacity and the greatest vigor and industry that can be obtained, and should be confined to the single duty of putting men in the army. Very respectfully your obt servt.   R. E. LEE

Genl.

No. 166.

[*Telegram*]

(Copy)

DUNN'S HILL, Sept. 24/64.

Hon. J. A. SEDDON, Secy. War.

Genl. Echols[1] reports that on 22d. Genl. Vaughan attacked the enemy at Blue Springs, Tenn. and drove

---

Gettysburg but at this time incapacitated for field service and commanding the Virginia reserves. Kemper's estimate is undoubtedly high.

[1] Brigadier-General John Echols, frequently mentioned in

them seven miles into their entrenchments at Bull's Gap, killing and wounding several and taking some prisoners. Our troops behaved well.

(Signed) R. E. LEE

[*Endorsed*]

R. B. 1934.

R. E. LEE
Genl.

Dunn's Hill, Sept 24th. 64.

Telegram to Secty. of War. Genl. Echols reports Genl. Vaughan attacked enemy on 22d. and drove him to his entrenchments   Our troops behaved well.

Recd. Hd. Qrs. A. C. S. Sept. 24/64.

No. 167.

[*Telegram*]

Recd. at Richmond Octo. 4/64.   10 A. M.

CHAFFIN'S BLUFF Octo. 4. 64.

Hon. J. A. SEDDON
Sec. of War.

Genl. Breckenridge reports that the Enemy attacked Saltville[1] on the 2nd. inst. and received a bloody repulse. They retired during the night in confusion apparently in the direction of Sandy River,

---

this correspondence, was at this time in command of forces in Southwest Virginia which often joined with the commands in East Tennessee for mountain movements. Brigadier-General G. C. Vaughn, mentioned here, was generally the officer who co-operated with Echols.

[1] Smyth County, Southwest Virginia, where the "salt works"—most valuable to the South—were located

leaving most of their dead and wounded in our hands.
He is pursuing them.   All our troops behaved well.[2]

(Signed) R. E. LEE
Official Copy   General.
    John W. Riely,
        Asst. Adjt. Genl.
           Res. sub. to Genl. Bragg.
A. & I. G. O.
Octo. 4. 64.

[*Endorsed*]
    R. B. 1988
      R. E. LEE
      Genl.
        Chaffin's Bluff Octo. 4/64.
Genl. Breckenridge reports enemy attacked Saltville on 2nd. & were repulsed. He is pursuing. Our
troops behaved well.
    Recd. Hd. Qrs. A. C. S. Octo. 4. 64.

No. 168.
[Telegram]

Received at Richmond, Va. 9.18 P.M. Oct. 7th 1864.
    By Telegraph from Chaffin's Bluff Oct. 7/64.
Hon. J. A. SEDDON
    Secy. War.
Major Boyle [1] reports a small party of Enemy's

---

[2] General Lee was extremely anxious for Breckinridge to
rout the enemy and to join Early in order that General Kershaw
and his command, then with Early, might return to the army
at Petersburg. *Cf.* Lee to Breckinridge, Oct. 5, 1864 (O. R.,
43, 2, 885).

[1] Major Cornelius Boyle, probably at this time provost-
marshal at Gordonsville.

Cavalry partially destroyed Rapidan Bridge on the
6th., escaped before they could be arrested.[2]

(Signed) R. E. LEE

Respectfully referred to Gen Bragg.

JOHN W. RIELY

A. A. G.

[*Endorsed*]

R. E. LEE

Genl.

Chaffin's Bluff Octo. 7/64.

Telegram to Secty. of War, announcing partial
destruction of the Rapidan Bridge by Enemy's
Cavalry.

Recd. Hd. Qrs. A. C. S. Octo. 8/64.

No. 169.

[*Telegram*]

CHAFFIN'S BLUFF, Oct. 19/64.

Hon. J. A. SEDDON

Secretary of War.

Genl. Breckenridge reports that his scouts on
the night of the 16th. burned the railroad bridge over
Mossy Creek.[1] Before daylight on the 18th. the

---

[2] *Cf.* Seddon to Lee, Oct. 6, 1864, with report of an advance
from the Rapidan (O. R., 43, 2, 886). The movement was
insignificant.

[1] In Jefferson County, Tennessee, through which ran the
East Tennessee and Virginia railroad. Bull's Gap was the
point at which this railroad crossed Bays Mountains and
was, in consequence, a strategic position of importance.

enemy hurriedly evacuated Bull's Gap retreating towards Knoxville, and Genl. Vaughan pursuing.

(Signed) R. E. Lee

Respectfully submitted for the information of the President.

JAMES A. SEDDON
Secretary of War.

Oct. 20/64.

[*Endorsed*]
Copy Telegram
Genl. LEE to Sec. War.
Chaffin's
Oct. 19/64
Operations in E. Tenn.
Oct. 20/64.

No. 170.

CHAFFINS 25 Oct. '64.

Mʀ PRESIDENT

Mʳ Stringfellow has just handed me your note enclosing one from Mʳ Stewart— Mʳ S. said upon your advice he had come to consult me upon a project he had in view, especially as to its morality.— I gave him opinion as far as I understood it & thought from what he said he had not determined to undertake it, but that it would depend upon an interview he would have with you I know so little of Mʳ S. that is his capacity for such an undertaking as he intimated rather than explained that when Mʳ Stringfellow first came to me I told him, as I have written to

Genl Fitz Lee, that I could give him no advice or recommendation as to his course— He must make up his own opinion as to what he should do— Col: E. G. Lee has just called on me on the same subject, having been referred to me by Mr Stewart— As Mr S. told me, what I very well knew, that his project must be kept a profound secret, I could neither explain it to Mr Stringfellow or Col: Lee even as far as he had unfolded it to me— In fact I have not a high opinion of Mr Stewarts Discretion, & could not advise any one to join him in his enterprize. I had inferred that his companions were to be taken from Canada, until I got a note from Genl Fitz Lee, asking if he must send some half dozen of his men to M^r S— To take a party of men from here seems to me to ensure failure & I could not recommend it. I supposed he would make up his mind as to what he would do & arrange his party in his own way.— I have had nothing to do with it— I return Mr Stewarts letter

With great respect

Your obt servt

R. E. LEE

His Exc^y JEFF^N DAVIS
Pres: C. States

P.S—Upon reperusal of your note I perceive you ask my advice— I do not think Mr Stuart by his habits life &c qualified for the undertaking he proposes— It was on this account that I could not advise others to join him. He may be an entirely different man from what I suppose him & the best fitted for the business, but I do not know it— I know nothing of the means or information at his disposal & can form no opinion as to his probable success.[1]

R. E. LEE

No. 171.

PETERSBURG 2 Nov '64.

Mʳ PRESIDENT

I had the honour to receive last evᵍ your letter of the 31st[2]— I am sorry to hear that Genl Laws anticipates injustice at the hands of Genl Longstreet— I do not, & think that Genl Laws has nothing to do but his whole duty, & he need fear nothing— I know of no objection to making the transfer of his brigade to Hokes division, provided the change is acceptable to the brigades themselves— It is neither right or politic to consult the wishes of the Commʳ alone.[3]

---

[1] None of the correspondence referred to can be found in the *Official Records*. The proposed expedition, which did not become a reality, was probably somewhat like that which cost John Y. Beall his life, or else it was aimed at the destruction of railroads, posts, etc., in the North. General Lee apparently neither approved the undertaking nor the organizer.

[2] Not found.

[3] The officer to whom reference is here made is Brigadier-General Evander M. Law (not Laws) commanding in Field's division, Longstreet's (First) corps, a brigade composed of the 4th, 15th, 44th, 47th and 48th Alabama regiments. His record was good during the campaigns of 1862, but when he was sent to Tennessee with General Longstreet, he had numerous difficulties with that officer. At length resigning, he again incurred the wrath of Longstreet by journeying to Richmond and (Longstreet alleged) by suppressing correspondence.

The information contained in the notes you enclosed me, I hope is exaggerated as regards to numbers — Grant will get every man he can & 150000 men is the number generally assumed by Northern papers & reports— Unless we can obtain a reasonable approximation to his force I fear a great calamity will befall us. On last Thursday at Burgess' mill we had three brigades to oppose six divisions— On our left two divisions to oppose two corps— The inequality is too great— Our Cav^y at Burgess Mill I think saved the day⁴— I came along our whole line yesterday from Chaffins Bluff to this place.⁵ Today I shall

---

When Law was returned to his command, he was rearrested by Longstreet's orders but was at length restored. As the incident caused much friction, Law was sent to South Carolina (see *From Manassas to Appomattox*, index *Law*; C. M. H., 7, 1, 422 ff.).

⁴ The frank warning here voiced of "a great calamity" unless his army was re-enforced is perhaps the strongest intimation given by General Lee, prior to January, 1865, of his ultimate defeat. The engagement at Burgess' Mill, here commented on, occurred on Oct. 27, 1864, and is known among the Federals as "Boydton Plank Road." Under the latter title numerous Federal reports will be found in O. R., 42, 1. The best Confederate report of the engagement is probably that of Wade Hampton (*loc. cit.*, 949). This engagement is best remembered in the South for its personal loss to the chivalrous Hampton. While the general was himself directing operations, one of his sons was killed in the charge and another was severely wounded. Hampton never flinched.

⁵ Chaffin's Bluff was the northern connection of the system of defences which protected Richmond and Petersburg. From Chaffin's ran the Richmond line. From Drewry's Bluff, across the river, ran a series of works overlooking the

visit the lines here & to-morrow go down to the right. I always find something to correct on the lines, but the great necessity I observed yesterday, was the want of men.

> With great respect
> Your obt servt
> R. E. LEE
> Genl.

His Excy JEFF^N DAVIS
Pres: C. States.

No. 172.

[*Telegram*]

(Copy)
PETERSBURG, Dec. 13/64.

Hon. J. A. SEDDON,
    While Genl. Warren was before Belfield [1] the enemy moved up the Roanoke against Fort Branch and from

---

river, thereby protecting the water route to Richmond, and joining the lines that began on James River opposite Dutch Gap. The latter was the "Howlett line," which ran almost due south across Ashton Creek to the Appomattox River. The line then ran along the river for about three miles, turned gradually, enveloped Petersburg and protected the Weldon railroad for some distance. The line was drawn to protect the Richmond and Petersburg railroad, upon which Richmond was dependent for direct communication with Eastern North Carolina and the States to the South. When this line was cut, Richmond was isolated. The next line of communication with the South was *via* Danville.

    [1] These movements were incidental to what is known in the Federal reports as the "Hicksford raid," the details of which

Newbern against Kinston. Both parties retired before the forces sent against them. All is quiet in that District.

(Signed) R. E. LEE

Resp. submitted for the information of the President.

JAMES A. SEDDON
Secretary of War

Dec. 14/64.

[*Endorsed*]
    Copy
        Telegram
            Genl. LEE to Sec. War.
            Petersburg
                Dec. 13/64.
                    Dec. 14/64.

No. 173.

[*Telegram*]

Telegram in Cipher.

PETERSBURG Dec. 14 1864.

His Excy. The President.

Chief Commissary of this Army received notice yesterday from Richmond that there was no salt meat there to send him, but would forward preserved meat. He thinks he may get enough to last to-

---

will be found in O. R., 42, 1. Lee's loss was "slight" and only "about six miles" of the Weldon railroad track was "broken up" (*see* Lee's telegram of Dec. 13, 1864, O. R., *op. cit.*, 3, 1271).

morrow. Neither meat nor corn are now coming over the Southern Roads, and I have heard there was meat in Wilmington.[1]

(Signed) R. E. LEE

[*Endorsed*]
Telegram from
Genl. R. E. LEE
Petersburg Dec. 14, 1864.
Secty. of War,

Please inform me, what has been or can be done to meet the case as presented within.

J[EFFERSON]. D[AVIS].

14 Dec. 64.

Recd. Dec. 14

---

[1] Little at Wilmington and but 40,000 pounds at Raleigh, N. C. (see telegram of Dec. 22, 1864, *infra*, No. 175). This telegram, unimportant in itself, gives a glimpse of the spectre that was to haunt Lee's army through the winter,—virtual starvation. A commissary which had been poor at best was now weakened still more by the destruction of supplies in the Shenandoah Valley and in Georgia. The speedy closing of the Cape Fear River was to cut off the blockade-runners who had brought "Nassau bacon."

With the correspondence of this date appears a copy of the following telegram:

WYTHEVILLE, Dec. 15/64.
J. W. CROWLEY Supt.

Major J. S. Johnston A. A. G. informs me that there is a very strong probability that the enemy will reach here to-morrow by 12 O'Clock. It is not supposed to be the main force of the enemy, but a select few, with the view to destroy the lead mines, railroad and other property. This is the opinion

No. 174.

[Telegram]

(Copy)

HEAD QUARTERS, Dec. 17/64.

Hon. J. A. SEDDON, Secy. War.

Major J. S. Johnston[1] reports from Dublin that enemy have left Wytheville, retiring by same route they came. Vaughan reported near Wytheville, and lead mines safe.

(Signed) R. E. LEE

Resp. submitted for the information of the President.

JAMES A. SEDDON
Secy. War.

Dec. 18/64.

[Endorsed]
Copy telegram to Sec. War.
R. E. LEE
Dec. 17— 1864.

---

of the A. A. G. to Genl. Breckinridge. We have scouts out, and they will be in at 12 or 1 O'Clock to-night, when I can give you more definite news.

(Signed) C. E. BOWYER
Operator.

[1] Major Johnston was assistant-adjutant-general to General Breckinridge. The raid mentioned was unimportant and was by "a select few" as the operator stated in the telegram quoted in No. 174.

No. 175.

[Telegram]

Telegram in Cypher.

HEAD QRS. ARMY NO. VA.
December 22. 1864.

His Excellency
    JEFFERSON DAVIS.

Genl. Bragg[1] reports his inability to subsist troops and his District exhausted. Expects in one day to consume supply of meat.[2]

Can anything be done in the matter.

R. E. LEE

[Endorsed]

Genl. R. E. LEE HeadQuarters Army No. Va.
    Dec. 22 1864.
        Telegram in cypher
To COM. GENL.

Can you not meet this necessity at once— as Wilmington is being threatened & may be attacked any time. Supplies are of the most importance there.

J. A. S[EDDON],
S[ecretary of War].

23d. Dec./64.
    Recd. Dec. 23 1864.

---

[1] Bragg had been sent to Wilmington, had gone thence to confer with Beauregard and, on December 17, had returned to assume personal charge of the Wilmington defences, relieving Whiting (O. R., 42, 3, 1278).

[2] The necessity for provisioning Bragg's (Whiting's) command was imperative. Fort Fisher was already attacked.

The only meat available is about 40,000 pds. at Raleigh. The want of meat long impending is general.

Respty.

Dec. 23d./64   L. B. NORTHRUP

C[ommissary] G[eneral].

B. of S.

A. G.   V. 151

The quantity at Raleigh had better be ordered at once to Wilmington. 23 Dec./64.

J. A. S[EDDON],

S[ecretary of War].

Ansd. to Genls. LEE and BRAGG. 23 Dec./64.

No. 176.

[Telegram]

Recd. at Richmond Dec. 25/64.

By Tel. from Hd. Qrs. A. N. V. 25.

Hon. J. A. SEDDON

     Secy. of War.

     Col. Leventhorpe reports that on evening of 23rd.

The troops were beleaguered. It is significant that General Lee on October 21, 1864, had urged that ample supplies be furnished Whiting "in case the enemy should succeed in cutting them off from the city" (O. R., 42, 3, 1156). Jones in his diary throws much light on the administration of the commissary one of the weakest branches of the Confederate Government. In the correspondence of this date appears the following dispatch, relative to General A. T. A. Torbert's attempted raid on Gordonsville:

enemy's gunboats passed below Williamston and have probably returned to Plymouth.[1]

(Signed) R. E. LEE

[*Endorsed*]

    Copy telegram from
        Genl. R. E. LEE to Sec. of War.
            Hd Qrs. A. N. V. Dec. 25. 1864.
    Respectfully submitted for the information of the President.

J. A. SEDDON

Secy. War.

Dec. 26/64.

            Recd. Dec. 26.

No. 177.

Hᵈ-QRS: 8 Jany '65.

Mᴿ PRESIDENT

    I have listened with great pleasure to the account given by Genl Ripley[2] of the condition of affairs in

---

                        Rec. at Richmond, Dec. 23/64.
1.35 P.M.—   By Tel. from Gordonsville 23.
    Dr. W. S. MORRIS
    The enemy have been repulsed and punished severely. They are now retreating back towards Sperryville, way they came.   Good many killed laying in field near Gordonsville.

(Signed) H. S. SMITHERS.

    [1] Brig.-Genl Collet Leventhorpe, commanding on the Roanoke River.   The movement here reported was incidental to the siege of Fort Fisher.
    [2] Brig.-Genl R. S. Ripley, at this time commanding the first military district of South Carolina, which included Charleston.   He was, however, soon ordered to join General J. B. Hood.

S. C. & Charleston. It is painful to me to contemplate the evacuation of the city. Its necessity must be determined by the officers on the spot responsible for the act. I do not think it will be abandoned by Genl Beauregard if not imperatively necessary. Its loss would be aggravated if accomp^d by the loss of the army placed there to defend it. I think it safer & perhaps easier to prevent the enemy from reaching Charleston. I hope by concentration of all their forces that Sherman may yet be arrested in his course. If he cannot be, to shut our troops up in the city, without a certainty of supplies & no prospect of a relieving force, might prove their destruction— This question can only be decided by officers on the spot in my opinion. To dictate a line of conduct to them from this distance & in ignorance of the essential elements for a proper judgment might be ruinous.[3]—

I think Genl Beauregard in his dispatch of the 6th from Augusta is mistaken as to the 19th & 23rd corps being with Sherman. The 19th with the exception of one division under Emory at Winchester is with Genl Grant. The 23rd Schofields, was on the 4th just below Alex^a— arrested by ice in the Potomac.

---

[3] General Lee might with some authority have discussed conditions at Charleston, having been in charge of that city's defences in 1862, but here as in every case, where he did not feel that his personal knowledge of a situation was sufficient, he declined to hamper officers on the scene of hostilities. Charleston, it will be recalled, was evacuated on Feb. 18, 1865. Inland communications having been cut off and the city isolated, the garrison withdrew and united with General Johnston's troops in North Carolina.

It is reputed to be on its way to Grant, & prisoners taken Monday stated it had arrived at City P^t on Sunday.[4]   I have informed Genl Beauregard

With great respect

Your obt servt

R. E. Lee

Genl.

His Excy Jefferson Davis
    Pres: C. States.

No. 178.

H^D Q^RS Army N Va.

10th Jany 1865.

His Excy Jefferson Davis
    President Confed States
    Richmond,

Mr. President,

I have received tonight the dispatch from Gen Hardee of the 8th inst: which you have done me the honor to forward.   The dispositions made by Gen Hardee appear to me to be judicious, and as far as I can judge at this distance, the line he proposes to hold is the best.   All he wants is sufficient troops. According to his statement he will have with Connors' brigade, over 20,000 men.   This is exclusive of the 5000 militia promised by Gov Magrath, and also of Gen G. W. Smith's command.   This will swell his

---

[4] Brevet Major-General Wm. H. Emory, commanding the "Middle Military Division," with headquarters at Stephenson's Depot.   The second division of the 19th Corps was ordered to Georgia on Jan'y. 7, 1865.   The 23rd Corps was *en route* to North Carolina, whither Sherman was marching.

force to 27000. Ten thousand additional troops ought to be obtained from Georgia, and I hope no effort will be spared to get them.[1] I do not know what Hood can accomplish, or what he proposes to do, but his force should not be kept idle, and unless he can deal the enemy some important blow, his troops, or at least a portion of them should be brought east. If he adopts a defensive course, no more troops will be required there than enough to hold Thomas in check. The only aid that I can give Hardee in addition to what I have done, is to send down Butler's division of cavalry. Part of it is there now under Young and I will send the balance should you deem it judicious to do so. But in that event I should have to send Gen. Hampton, or it might be merged in Wheeler's cavalry and thus lost.[2] Gen Hardee informs me that he has no command for Gen R. H. Anderson, though he would like to have his assistance.

An expedition has left Grant's army which I think is probably intended to repeat the attack against Wilmington. I have not yet learned its strength, but from the number of transports that have descended James River, I should judge it was not

---

[1] Hardee's dispatch not found. Lieutenant-General W. J. Hardee had been in command of Savannah when General Sherman approached that city at the end of his infamous "march to the sea." With rare skill, Hardee extricated himself and moved into South Carolina where it was hoped he would be able to reorganize and perhaps to meet Sherman. Unfortunately, Charleston had to be evacuated and Columbia was captured. Plans for active operations in the Palmetto State thereupon came to an end.

[2] See No. 179, *infra*.

larger than the former.[3]   Still Gen Bragg may have
to be reinforced, which will further weaken this army.
The 8th corps and a portion of the black troops are
said to form the land troops of the expedition.

I am with great respect

Your obt servt

R. E. LEE

Genl

No. 179.

H[D] QRS: NEAR PETERSBURG 15 Jan '65

M[r] PRESIDENT

I have seen Genl Hampton & concluded under the
discretion given me in your letter of the 11th[1] to
detach Genl Butler's division[2] of Cav[y] to S. C. for
service there this winter, but it is with the understanding that it is to return to me in the spring in time
for the opening of the campaign—Without this condition, I think it would be disadvantageous to send

---

[3] The first expedition against Fort Fisher in the winter of
1864–65 had been under the direction of General B. F. Butler
and had not been successful.   The second, under General
A. H. Terry, supported by a very strong fleet, led to the
reduction of Fort Fisher (Jan. 15, 1865).   The Cape Fear
River, which had the last channel through which the Confederates had been able to run the blockade, was thereafter in the
hands of the Federals.

[1] Not found.

[2] According to the field returns of December 31, 1864 (O. R.,
42, 3, 1369), Major-General M. C. Butler's division was at that
time composed of Butler's brigade (Col. B. H. Rutledge),
Young's brigade and, temporarily, Dearing's brigade.   Rosser's
brigade had been attached to this division (*ibid.*, 1191).
Young was detached.

it. May I ask you to impose this condition & let me know. In the meantime I will get the men ready to start. Genl Hampton thinks he can mount the men in S. C. & will telegraph to the Genl to collect horses, which the men will buy if placed at reasonable prices. The horses here will be placed in camp in N. C. or with Major Paxton at Lancaster, & the men transported by rail If the Genl can give no assurance of their procuring mounts, or if Hampton cannot make arrangements for subsistence of the horses, I will not send them. I think Hampton will be of service in mounting his men & arousing the spirit & strength of the State & otherwise do good. I will therefore send him. He will report the State of affairs on his arrival & then you can determine, whether it will be necessary to take any steps in reference to him.[3] He will take immediate measures to place Butler in the field & I desire Youngs brigade to be ordered to join Butler. I understand Young prefers Comm[g] his brigade to a division under Wheeler.[4]

Genl Bragg telegraphs at 8 P.M. yesterday from Sugar Loaf, that the enemy succeeded on the night

---

[3] See O. R., 46, 2, 1074, Davis to Lee: "The condition that Butler's division should return to you was understood by me to be part of the proposition, and will be distinctly stated. Young's brigade (see note 4) will join the command as soon as it arrives on the field of operations." The order was given on Jan. 19, 1865 (*ibid.*, 1100–01).

[4] Brigadier-General M. B. Young and a detachment of men had been sent to Augusta, Georgia, Nov. 24, 1864 "to procure horses" (O. R., 42, 3, 1228). At the time of this dispatch, he had not returned though Butler had requested that he be ordered back (O. R., 46, 2, 1003).

of the 13th in extending a line across the Peninsula between him & Ft Fisher   That upon close examination he thought it too strong to attack with his inferior force. Fisher has been reinforced with sufficient veterans to make it safe & that the width of the river is such that the enemy cannot controul it even with Art^y of which he has as yet landed none. Bombardment of Fisher on the 14th light-weather continues fine & sea smooth— I have telegraphed in reply to concentrate his forces & endeavour to dislodge him.   That he will land his cannon & besiege Fisher   He gives no estimate of strength of enemy, & makes no call for reinforcements.[5]

      With great respect your obt servt

                      R. E. LEE
                          Genl

His Excy JEFFERSON DAVIS
    Pres: C. States—

No. 180.

H^D Q^{RS} ARMY N VA
            18th Jany 1865

His Excy JEFF^N DAVIS
    Presd^t C States
       Richmond,
MR PRESIDENT

The loss of the port of Wilmington, cutting us off in a great measure, from access to the world by sea,

---

[5] The correspondence relating to the siege and capture of Fort Fisher will be found in O. R., 46, 3. The Confederates were overpowered and overwhelmed by the fire directed against them from the fleet that accompanied Terry's expedition.

renders it important in my judgment to extend and systematize the exchange of our cotton, tobacco and naval stores for articles of necessity. I observe that the enemy is disposed to encourage the importation of cotton &c under the impression that it will weaken us. We on the other hand would do well to exchange these commodities for such things as we need more.

The great difference between the prices of these articles here and in the United States, enables us to offer a strong inducement to traders to exchange with us, an inducement that has already been found sufficient to cause a relaxation in the rigor of the prohibition against traffic, and which if united with such a policy on the part of the Northern Government as is referred to above, may by judicious management on our part, be made to supply the loss we sustained in the fall of Ft Fisher. A great objection to this traffic is its tendency to produce demoralization among our people, who will, if not restrained, engage in it for purposes of profit. This is now the case on those parts of our lines in Va & N C where this tradè is being carried on to some extent to procure subsistence and other supplies. The illicit traffic also interferes seriously with the authorized business of the gov^t agents. Any system that may be adopted must be accompanied with full power to prevent the illegal trade It is impossible to do this by guards, as the frontier is too extensive for us to watch. And as the law now stands, the penalty for its violation, being only the confiscation of the property seized, by a slow process, is entirely inadequate, and has no application to those who elude the guards & escape seizure There must be added a personal penalty of fine and imprisonment, and as it is an offence against the safety of the country, it should be punished with great promptness and severity. Another requisite will be to empower the Gov^t to impress cotton tobacco & naval stores, especially where they are found in localities exposed to the enemy, or from which they can be easily taken across the lines. This has been recommended by intelligent officers in N C as the only certain means of putting a stop to the illicit traffic there, and is recommended by other obvious considerations. I would suggest that the power of immediate impressment for Gov^t use be extended to all contraband articles taken in transit to or across our lines without authority. This would be more effectual than the slow process of forfeiture now provided for to prevent this traffic. With these restrictions, and the organization of a regular system of barter under the direction of a practical and experienced man of business, much good can be accomplished. The best system would be to give contracts for supplies to the lowest responsible bidder, who should be paid in cotton with the privilege of removing it from the country. This is preferable to employing govt agents directly in making exchanges, as is now done. It will enlist private enterprise & cupidity in the service of the government, instead of putting it in competition with it as is now the case. It will also induce great numbers of persons to engage in it, and the aggregate of the supplies received from all will be greater than one agent can possibly get. It will also prevent the immediate appearance of the gov^t in the business of bringing supplies over the lines, and thus arousing the suspicions of the enemy. The business will easily be made to assume the character of private trade, such as furnishing supplies to devastated sections of the country, or pretexts of that nature, which with the large margin of profit, can readily be made satisfactory to the Federal agents, by the parties engaged. The interest and cupidity of individuals will be found far more effectual in overcoming the difficulties that beset the traffic, than the most energetic efforts of regular government agents stimulated only by the desire to do their official duty.

The trade should be extended to all parts of the country that offer facilities for bringing in supplies, and should embrace all kinds of articles required by the army. Clothing, shoes, and food I believe could be obtained in great quantities by intelligent and judicious management. At the same time, it seems to me that the Govt should extend every encouragement to the production of articles of necessity in our own country, by liberal contracts with manufacturers. I believe that we should now be more independent had this policy been pursued from the beginning. Much capital has been employed in trustful speculation, which would now be engaged in useful manufactures had not the capitalists been apprehensive that the return of peace would leave them with their means invested in an unprofitable business. If it be practicable to give encouragement to home production now, I think it a much better policy than for the government to engage in the business itself. I respectfully submit these considerations to your better judgment, and trust that you will be able to devise some means to make our large resources valuable and available to the army.[1]

With great respect
Your obt servt
R. E. LEE
Genl

No. 181.

H^D–QRS: ARMY N. VA: 19 Jany '65.

Mr PRESIDENT

I rec^d tonight your letter of the 18^h Inst: stating that it had been reported to you that I had changed my opinion in regard to the extension of my duties, while retaining command of the army of N. Va— I do not know how such a report originated, nor am I aware of having said anything to have authorized it. I do not think that while charged with my present command embracing Virginia & N. C. & the immedi-

---

[1] *Cf.* Lee to the Secretary of War, Jan. 16, 1865, O. R., 46, 2, 1075. An interesting monograph in economic history might be written on Cotton Trading during the War between the States. A large element in the South, led by the far-seeing Alexander H. Stephens, believed that the South had only to put its cotton in bond to establish credit sufficient to finance the war. The dominant party contended that English intervention would come only by cutting off the cotton crop and thereby closing the mills. With this conflict in policy, the enactments of the Confederate Congress were not heeded by the people. Cotton was sent out whenever possible by blockade-runners and formed a staple for unlawful trading, especially in those parts of the Confederacy where the country was over-

ate controul of this army I could direct the operations of the armies in the S. Atlantic States. If I had the ability I would not have the time. The arrangement of the details of this army extended as it is, providing for its necessities & directing its operations engrosses all my time & still I am unable to accomplish what I desire & see to be necessary. I could not therefore propose to undertake more. I am greatly gratified by the expression of your confidence in offering me the extensive command proposed in your letter, but I must state that with the addition of the immediate command of this army I do not think I could accomplish any good. I am willing to undertake any service to which you think proper to assign me, but I do not wish you to be misled as to the extent of my capacity.[1]

I am with great respect

Your obt servt

R. E. LEE

Genl.

His Exc[y] JEFFERSON DAVIS
    Pres: C. States—

run by Federals. An interesting sidelight on the value of cotton at this time and the demand for it in the North will be found in the correspondence of Brigadier-General W. N. R. Beall, P.A.C.S. (Freeman, *Calendar Confederate Papers*, 73 ff.). Beall, at the time a prisoner of war, was paroled by agreement between the Confederate States and the United States to act as agent for the sale of cotton passed through the blockade by consent for the relief of Confederate prisoners in the North. The middling was sold at 93 cents the pound, the pickings 42 cents and 47 cents the pound. During 1864, cotton reached $1.90 in New York.

[1] The "extension of my duties" to which General Lee refers was the position of commander of all the armies of the Con-

No. 182.

H^D-QRS: PETERSBURG 20 Jan^y '65

His Excy JEFFERSON DAVIS
    Pres: C. States— Richmond
MR PRESIDENT

I am aware that it will take some time to regulate
& perfect the Piedmont R. R. & that the whole

---

federacy to which President Davis proposed to appoint him.
The exact date of the proposal and the events leading to it are
somewhat in doubt. On January 17, 1865, the General Assembly of Virginia unanimously passed a secret resolution
stating their belief that Lee's appointment "to the command
of all the armies of the Confederate States would promote their
efficiency and operate powerfully to reanimate the spirit of the
armies, as well as of the people of the several States, and to
inspire increased confidence in the final success of our cause"
(O. R., 46, 2, 1084). The President must, however, have talked
with General Lee on the subject before the date of the above
resolution, because in the letter Lee here acknowledges, the
President speaks of the plan as though it were well understood.
He writes: "It has been reported to me that you have changed
your opinion in regard to the extension of your command while
retaining command of the Army of Northern Virginia. I
therefore renew to you the proposal that you should exercise
command over the South Atlantic States, together with
Virginia and North Carolina, and now offer the larger sphere
of all the forces east of the Mississippi River; or, if you think
it practicable, that you should resume your former position of
commander of all the armies of the Confederate States, with
the addition of the immediate command of the Army of
Northern Virginia" (O. R., *loc. cit.*, 1091). General Lee,
it might be well to remark, had occupied in 1862 the extra-
legal position held by General Bragg during the summer of
1864, "commander of the Confederate armies,"—a position

difficulty cannot at once be overcome by the Governments taking it in charge— Its condition is so important to our military operations as well as to the welfare of the community that I venture to enclose a letter lately rec^d from Genl Martin. I do not see how

largely advisory in character and subordinate to the President. In reply to the resolution of the General Assembly, Mr. Davis wrote a very warm encomium on Lee (*ibid.*, 1091–92). On January 23, 1865, the Confederate Congress passed an act for the appointment by the President of "an officer, who shall be known and designated as General-in-Chief, who shall be ranking officer of the Army, and as such shall have command of the military forces of the Confederate States." To this office President Davis appointed General Lee, February 6, 1865 (O. R., *loc. cit.*, 1205). Lee accepted and took command on February 9. In reply to a dispatch which has not been found, Davis wrote on February 10 a letter to General Lee which is most creditable to the President. He said: " . . . I have not failed to appreciate the burden already imposed on you as too heavy to enable an ordinary man to bear an additional weight. Your patriotic devotion I knew would prompt you to accept anything which was possible, if it promised to be beneficial to the country. The honor designed to be bestowed has been so fully won that the fact of conferring it can add nothing to your fame. . . . " (*Ibid.*, 1127). During the brief remainder of the war, General Lee acted in an advisory capacity over the operations in the far South, to which numerous references will be found in this correspondence. He was careful, however, as has already been pointed out, not to restrict the movements of competent officers who were familiar with conditions unknown to him. He always allowed the commanders in the South the widest discretion and in reality discharged with authority the duties he had informally assumed during the campaign of 1864 at the President's request. Though his appointment to this post came too late to accomplish good, it had a salutary effect upon the spirit of the South.

a road can be worked advantageously & to its full extent without a regular schedule for running the trains— Under a temporary pressure it might be operated by special instructions by telegraph— I understood that the road was so operated while under charge of the Danville Compy, & I presume there is some reason for continuing it, but as soon as a fixed schedule can be established & regular connections made with the roads north & south the better. I would also suggest that a competent Engineer with four or five hundred labourers be sent to ditch drain & repair the road along its whole extent. From the character of the present Supt I trust the road if once put in good order, will be efficiently managed.[1]

I have the honour to be
Your obt servt
R. E. LEE
Genl

---

[1] The Piedmont Railroad, frequently mentioned in these dispatches, was a necessary link in the communications with the South after Lee abandoned his efforts to keep the Weldon Railroad open. The road in question was from Danville to Greensboro and gave much concern to the Government. In December, when Hoke attempted to proceed by it to North Carolina, he had great difficulty and lost three days in transporting a single brigade forty-eight miles. He urged upon General Lee the wisdom of seizing the railroad, repairing it and operating it directly (O. R., 46, 2, 1026-27). In January bad conditions were made worse by a disastrous flood which damaged the road-bed for twenty miles and made it impassable. This mishap led to virtual starvation in Lee's army (*ibid.*, 1034). The "Genl Martin" to whom reference is made in this letter was Brig.-Genl James G. Martin of North Carolina, at this time commanding the reserves in the Western District

No. 183.

PETERSBURG 21 Jan^y '65

Mr PRESIDENT

I have just rec^d the copy of the dispatch of the 20th from Genl Hardee, which you did me the honour to send to me, in reference to his holding the city of Charleston. It would certainly be of great import-ance to hold the City in every point of view, but if it cannot be held successfully, it had better be evacu-ated. As to the requisite means Genl Hardee must judge. By contesting the advance of the enemy, col-lecting all the men in Georgia & S. C. his approach may be retarded, till the arrival of Genl Beauregard with forces from Hoods army.[1]

Very respy your obt servt
R. E. LEE
Genl.

His Exc^y JEFFERSON DAVIS
Pres: C. States

---

of North Carolina under Lieut.-Genl T. H. Holmes. He had seen service in Virginia during the campaign of 1864 (see C. M. H., 4, 332 ff.).

[1] With the Trans-Mississippi Department cut off, with no effective opposition to the Federals in Alabama and Mississippi, with Georgia overrun and with Hood impotent in Tennessee, the only hope of the Confederates was to draw in their forces before the northern advance of Sherman and to consolidate all of them in one compact fighting force. When Lee was forced to evacuate the Petersburg–Richmond lines in April, his plan was to carry his troops to meet Johnston in North Carolina. Charleston, the defence of which is discussed in this dispatch, had to be evacuated on February 18 after it had been completely isolated.

No. 184.

H^DQ^{RS} AN V_A

28th Jany 1865

His Exc^y J_{EFF}^N D_{AVIS}

    Presd^t C States,

      Richmond,

M_R P_{RESIDENT}

I beg leave to repeat the suggestion I made to you in Richmond with reference to the publication of a stringent order requiring all cotton, tobacco & naval stores to be burned to prevent them from falling into the hands of the enemy.[1] I think the acquisition of these commodities, especially cotton, is greatly desired by the enemy for many reasons, as is shown by the seizure of all they can get access to, and by the intimation of their willingness to encourage the trade in it. I think if an order were issued, and published in all the papers, directing that all cotton &c in places exposed to the enemy, be stored in such a way that it can be fired on his approach without endangering other property, and that when this cannot be done for want of time, that it be burned in the streets and roads, at the same time holding military commanders responsible for the faithful execution of the order, it would have a very good effect in enabling us to make arrangements to render our cotton &c available as it is desired to do. The enemy would see that they can only get the cotton on the terms we propose, and besides, I think

---

[1] *Cf. supra*, No. 180 and note 1. At Savannah alone, Sherman had captured approximately 25,000 bales of cotton.

it very desirable to prevent him from getting it on any other.[2]

With great respect,

Your obt servt

R. E. LEE

Genl

No. 185.

H^D-QRS: PETERSBURG 29 Jany '65

MR PRESIDENT

In a dispatch rec^d from Genl Early to-day, he states that Major McDonald comm^g the picket line on Lost river, reports from information rec^d from his Scouts, "that a large portion of Thomas Army is passing over the Bal: & Ohio R.R. to Grant." I have directed him to ascertain the truth of the report. A grand movement was announced in a N. Y. paper sometime since on the part of Thomas, (about the time that Hood was reported to have crossed the Tennessee,) which indicated his appearance in another quarter. Since that the Northern papers asserted that he was going into Winter qrs: & further operations need not be expected from him for some time. The latter report may have been intended to call attention from the former. I think it probable that in the present condition of the army of Tennessee Grant may determine to strengthen his

---

[2] This policy was pursued at Columbia and at Petersburg, where much cotton and tobacco respectively were stored. On the evacuation of Richmond, the destruction of tobacco probably led to the memorable fire that laid in ashes the business section of the city.

own with a portion of Thomas, to enable him to operate against Richmond. His present force is so superior to ours, that if he is reinforced to any extent, I do not see how in our present position he can be prevented from enveloping Richmond. Such a combination is his true policy & therefore I fear it is true. It is possible however that these troops may be a part of Shermans on the way to him. I saw it stated, that parts of two corps were in Nashville preparing to join him. Reinforcements to Sherman would be almost as bad in its consequences as to Grant— A few days I presume will discover the movement[1]

With great respect
Your obt servt
R. E. LEE
Genl

His Exc^y JEFFERSON DAVIS
Pres: C. States

No. 186.

H^D-QRS: 30 Jany '65

MR PRESIDENT

In my letter of the 29^h Inst: I informed you of the report of the Scouts west of the Valley, relative to the passage of troops over the Bal: & Ohio R.R. from Genl Thomas to Genl Grant. This report is confirmed by Fitz Lees Scouts in the vicinity of Winchester, who state that 15000 troops have passed over

---

[1] These troops were Schofield's (Twenty-Third) corps. For further references to them, see O. R., 46, 2, 1164, 1165, 1241, 1299 and 1301.

said road going to Grant. A second dispatch from Genl Early states that Major Gilmer reports from Hardy Co that large bodies of troops from Thomas army are passing over the Bal: & Ohio R. R. & Northern Central, Eastward, estimated between twenty & forty thousand. The Wheeling Intelligencer of the 23rd says ten or fifteen thousand of Thomas troops were in Bellaire awaiting transportation on B & O R.R. I presume there is no doubt of the fact, & probably the delay in rec^g Messrs Stephens, Hunter & Campbell, is occasioned by the arrival of some of these troops in James river, which they do not wish disclosed.[1] Grant seems to be taking advantage of the condition of things with the West to bring all his troops East, & will probably move against Richmond the first opportune moment. Hoods army & the troops West of the Mississippi will have little to oppose them, & as they cannot operate there, they should be moved East as rapidly as possible— As stated in my former letter I fear with our present force here, Grant will be enabled to envelope Richmond, or turn both of our flanks & I see no way of increasing our strength.[2]

Very resp^y your obt servt

R. E. Lee

Genl.

His Excy Jefferson Davis
Pres: C States—Richmond.

---

[1] Alexander H. Stephens, R. M. T. Hunter and James A. Campbell, then *en route* to the so-called "Hampton Roads Conference," for which see Nos. 187 and 188 and notes thereto.

[2] This is frank warning of what Lee believed to be the inevi-

No. 187.

H^D-QRS: 30 Jany '65

MR PRESIDENT

I rec^d tonight the accomp^g letter from Judge
Campbell, with the request that I would forward it
to you by telegraph in cypher.   As I could not get it

---

table outcome of the operations against his army and in other
parts of the South.   After the battle of the Crater, July 30,
the feint on Richmond, August 13, and the movement on the
Weldon railroad, August 18, Grant settled down in front of
Lee to await developments in the South which would subdue
the army he felt himself unable to beat in the field.   While
Sheridan was harrying the Valley of Virginia and Sherman was
preparing for his march to the sea, Grant remained in his
works.   On September 29, however, he captured Fort Harrison on the north side of the James at the cost of 2,300 men
and held it in spite of Lee's effort to dislodge him.   The engagement at Poplar Spring Church on September 30 and Lee's attack on Kautz' cavalry on October 7 were preliminaries to the
battle of the Boydton Plank Road, mentioned above.   "From
this time on," writes Grant, "the operations in front of Petersburg and Richmond, until the spring campaign of 1865, were
confined to the defence and extension of our lines and to offensive movements for crippling the enemy's lines of communication and to prevent his detaching any considerable force to
send South."   But the end was in sight at the time of this
dispatch.   Grant was extending his line to Hatcher's Run,
Early was on the defensive in the Valley of Virginia, opposition
in Tennessee was almost crushed out and Sherman, having
reached Savannah in December, was turning north to oppose
Hardee in South Carolina and Johnston beyond him.   With
supplies cut off by the devastation of the Valley of Virginia
and by the capture of the Weldon railroad, General Lee was
forced to rely on the feeble communication south of Danville.
This did not suffice to keep his men from starvation.

to you in time for your action to-night, I have determined to send it by a special messenger on the early
train tomorrow, when I hope it will reach you as
soon as it could be decyphered & placed before you if
sent by telegraph.[1]

With great respect
Your obt servt
R. E. LEE
Genl.

His Excy JEFFERSON DAVIS
Pres: C. States

---

[1] Judge Campbell was one of the Confederate commissioners
designated to discuss possible terms of peace.   His dispatch
has not been found but it was probably a report of the conference with the Federals at which request for a safe conduct to
Washington was made in writing.   The Federal correspondence regarding the famous Hampton Roads Conference will be
found in O. R., 46, 2, 505-513.   Mr. Stephens' statement, in
his *Constitutional View of the Late War* states the Confederate
position fully.   To all projects for peace during the early
stages of hostilities, there had been the insurmountable
obstacle of Lincoln's positive and repeated refusal to recognize
the Confederate States or to treat with their representatives
except as rebels.   His first and unyielding demand was that
the Confederates lay down their arms before talking of peace.
President Davis was of all men the one who would least accept
such terms, and he met the various advocates of peace with the
insistent requirement that decent recognition, at least as
belligerents, had to be accredited the Confederate States before
he could discuss peace.   The Hampton Roads Conference was
brought about through the efforts of Francis P. Blair, Sr.,
of Missouri.   Acting with Lincoln's knowledge and tacit
approval, and proceeding under a Federal pass, Blair came to
Richmond, had conferences with President Davis and proposed

No. 188.

H^D-QRS: 31 Jany '65

His Excy JEFFERSON DAVIS
    Pres: C. States—Richmond
MR PRESIDENT

I rec^d from Mr Stephens this ev^g the following dispatch which he desired might be sent to you.

"By note of invitation from Genl Grant Messrs Stephens, Hunter & Campbell left for City Point at 5 o'clock this ev^g, to meet at that point gentlemen expected there from Mr Lincoln. Should these gentlemen not arrive, Genl Grant promises to return Mr Stephens & party to our lines"¹

---

a plan by which he hoped it might be possible to unite the North and the South for a campaign against Mexico. Mr. Davis listened, considered carefully and sent Mr. Blair away with the assurance that the South would listen to any reasonable terms if respectfully presented. The negotiations to which these dispatches refer then followed. The Conference was held on February 3 but failed through Lincoln's refusal to consent to any peace the first terms of which were not an absolute and complete restoration of the Federal authority. See note to No. 188, *infra*.

¹ The correspondence between General Grant and the Confederate commissioners, dated January 30, 1865, is printed in O. R., 46, 2, 297 and 312 as follows:

PETERSBURG, V..., January 30, 1865.
Lieut. Gen. U. S. GRANT:

SIR: We desire to pass through your lines under safe conduct and to proceed to Washington to hold a conference with President Lincoln upon the subject of the existing war, and

I have thought it better to send this by courier on the early train in the mor^g rather than by telegraph

Very resp^y your obt servt
R E LEE
Genl

---

with a view of ascertaining upon what terms it may be terminated, in pursuance of the course indicated in his letter to Mr. F. P. Blair of January 18, 1865, of which we presume you have a copy; and if not, we wish to see you in person, if convenient, and to confer with you upon the subject.

Yours, very respectfully,

ALEXANDER H. STEPHENS.
J. A. CAMPBELL.
R. M. T. HUNTER.

January 31, 1865.

Hon. ALEX. H. STEPHENS,
Hon. J. A. CAMPBELL,
Hon. R. M. T. HUNTER:

GENTLEMEN: Your communication of yesterday, requesting an interview with myself and a safe conduct to Washington and return, is received. I will instruct the commanding officer of the forces near Petersburg to receive you, notifying you at what part of the line and the time when and where conveyance will be ready for you.

Your letter to me has been telegraphed to Washington for instructions. I have no doubt but that before you arrive at my headquarters an answer will be received directing me to comply with your request. Should a different reply be received, I promise you a safe and immediate return within your own lines.

U. S. GRANT,
Lieutenant-General.

President Lincoln, it will be remembered, had dispatched an aide-de-camp, Major T. T. Eckert, to confer with the commissioners and to state the conditions upon which they would

No. 189.

H^D-QRS: PETERSBURG 9 Feby '65

Mr PRESIDENT

A dispatch rec^d from Genl Bragg today says he will leave Wilmington tomorrow to wait on you¹

Very resp^y your obt servt

R E LEE

Genl

His Exc^y JEFFERSON DAVIS
Pres: C. States

No. 190.

[Telegram]

Dated Hd. Qrs. Armies C. S. Feb. 24th. 1865.
Recd. at Richmond 5 O'Clock P.M.

To His Excellency JEFFERSON DAVIS
President.

Hampton reports from Chesterville yesterday evening no enemy nearer than White Oak. A large

---

be received. Although these conditions were not in accordance with the instructions of the Confederate commissioners, they waived the point and reported themselves ready for conference. But this was not accepted, and it was only at the insistence of General Grant, who showed an excellent spirit throughout, that the commissioners were eventually given a hearing.

¹ Bragg had been ordered to Richmond for conference. He was returned to his command beyond Wilmington, with instructions to co-operate with General Joseph E. Johnston in opposing the northward advance of General W. T. Sherman.

force of Cavalry moved from Hopewell Church towards Rocky-mount ferry on Wateree. Butler is across river and Hampton will place himself in front of enemy, leaving a brigade to press his rear. Cheatam on 22nd. was reported at Jones ferry on Ennonee. He and Stewart are marching via Unionville and Chesterville. Hardee is ordered to hasten his march from Cheraw. Genl. Beauregard thinks enemy's movements indicate march on Cheraw and Fayetteville.[1] Have suggested to Genl. Johnston that he may be endeavoring to reach Pedee Valley for subsistance. Hardee would then be in position, and that all provisions, stores, cattle &c. should be removed. Genl. Taylor reports from Meridian on 15th. that twenty five (25) transports reached Vicksburg on 13th loaded with troops under General Thomas[2]

R E LEE

140W/Free
H. T.

---

[1] Reported in Beauregard to Lee, February 24, 1865 (O. R., 47, 2, 1267). Several mistakes in names are made in the dispatch as forwarded by General Lee   "Chesterville" should be "Chesterfield," "Ennonee" should be "Ennoree," and "Cheatam" should be "Cheatham."

[2] Sent without comment, these items of news confirmed the gloomy forecast which General Lee made in a dispatch of February 22, 1865, to the Secretary of War (O. R., 46, 2, 1247) when he declared that the advance of Sherman must be stopped. Nothing could be done to strengthen the outlying, unprotected sections of the country, he stated "until I abandon James River." He concluded: "You will see to what straits we are reduced; but I trust to work out "

No. 191.

[Telegram]

(Copy)

HEAD QRS. Mar 21/65.

Hon. J. C. BRECKENRIDGE,
　　　Secy. of War. [1]

Genl. Vaughan reports this morning "that Thomas is at Knoxville, that three regiments and some negro troops are repairing the East Tennessee Railroad, and that enemy have commenced their advance."

Genl. J. E. Johnston, at 9.20 A.M., at Bentonville, reports: "that he is removing his wounded to Smithfield;—the enemy's entrenched position and greatly superior numbers, Sherman's army being in our front, make further offensive movements impracticable." [2]

R. E. LEE

Respectfully submitted for the information of the President

By order
J. A. CAMPBELL
Asst. Secy. of War.

Mar 22/65.

---

[1] Succeeded James A. Seddon of Virginia on February 6, 1865. The name is properly Breckinridge, but is frequently spelled Breckenridge in official correspondence.

[2] This information was repeated in a dispatch from General Lee bearing date of March 22. *Cf.* O. R., 49, 2, 1141.

No. 192.

[Telegram]

HD. QRS. March 23. 1865.

His Excellency
   JEFFERSON DAVIS
President.

Genl. Johnston at 1.30 P.M. today telegraphs from Smithfield "Sherman's whole army being entrenched in my front morning of 20th. we did not attack, but held our position to cover removal of wounded and occupy enemy. There was heavy skirmishing 20th. & 21st., and several partial attacks by him handsomely repulsed. Troops of Tennessee Army have fully disproved slanders that have been published against them   Evening and night of 21st. enemy moved towards Goldsboro where Schofield joined him, and yesterday we came here.

Sherman's course cannot be hindered by the small force I have. I can do no more than annoy him. I respectfully suggest that it is no longer a question whether you leave present position. You have only to decide where to meet Sherman."[1]

Please give me your counsel.

(Signed) R. E LEE

[Endorsed]
   Genl. R. E. LEE
      Hd. Qrs. March 23. 65.
         Telegram in cypher.
            Recd. March 23. 65.

---

[1] Printed in O. R., 47, 2, 1453, with these words added after "Sherman" in the concluding paragraph: "*I will be near him.*"

No. 193.

[*Telegram*]

(Copy)

HEAD QRS. March 24/65

Hon. J. C. BRECKENRIDGE,
    Secy. of War.

A scout just escaped from the prison barge off City Point reports fifteen monitors and forty-five gunboats above Bermuda Hundred.[1]   He is a very bold man, but I think there must be some error in his report.[2]

R. E. LEE

Respectfully submitted for the information of the President.

JOHN C. BRECKENRIDGE
Secy. of War.

Mar. 25/65.

[*Endorsed*]
    Genl. R. E. LEE
        Hd. Qrs. March 24 1865.
            Copy telegram to Secy. War.

A scout reports fifteen Monitors and forty-five Gun-boats above Bermuda Hundred.—There must be some error in his report.

Recd. March 25. 1865.

---

[1] Located on the James River just above City Point, the headquarters of General Grant.   General Lee doubts that the enemy has as many vessels in the channel.

[2] With the correspondence of this date are two dispatches from F. G. De Fontaine, Charlotte, N. C., to the (Southern) Associated Press, as follows:

No. 194.

H^DQ^RS C S ARMIES
26th March 1865

His Exc^y JEFFERSON DAVIS
President C States
Richmond,

MR PRESIDENT,

My dispatch of yesterday to the Secretary of War will have informed you of the attack made upon

---

CHARLOTTE 24th. 1865.

Charlotte friday 24th. indebted to enterprise Southern Express Courier Augusta papers to 20th. no important Military movements reported. Capt. Dickinson Florida made Captures several officers men during late raid— Forrest placed Command all Cavalry. district Mississippi East La. West Tennessee his first General Order promises reorganization discipline and threatens extermination Confederate Stragglers Robbers deserters. Thomas's Troops being mounted for supposed march through Alabama—raids being made from Hernando Mississippi towards Senatobia— Many Compliments of Kirby Smith in west. Wafford in command at Atlanta— reorganization in Georgia already commenced—reinforcements from Northern Mississippi sent to Grant. Large bodies of troops moving in west and important movements reported. Legislature of Mississippi about to convene in extra session said for purpose calling state convention. Message Governor Brown of Georgia commences by defence state against attacks of the Press for permitting Sherman march unmolested through state says she was abandoned to her fate neglected by Confederate Authorities and while her Army of able bodied Sons were held for defence of other States were denied privilege strike next blow for protection of homes. Georgia was compelled to rely upon few old men and boys claims golden opportunity lost for over-throwing Sherman, had he been resisted from start

a portion of the enemy's lines around Petersburg, and the result which attended it. I have been unwilling to hazard any portion of the troops in an assault upon fortified positions, preferring to reserve their strength for the struggle which must soon commence, but I was induced to assume the offensive from the belief that the point assailed could be carried without much loss, and the hope that by the seizure of the redoubts in the rear of the enemy's main line, I

---

forced to fight and exhaust ammunition surrender would have been certain—recommends establishment of Militia System to be in no case turned over to Confederate Govt. but retain for home defence says only fourteen hundred and fifty exempts in state and mostly over age recommends passage law authorizing impressment provisions in hands of persons under bond to Confederate Government who refuse to sell surplus to indigent families Soldiers complains that Confederate Agents can lock corn cribs & smoke house against State purchasing officer—referring to penitentiary says more than half convicts released to fight—since deserted—recommends death punishment for robbery, horse stealing, burglary, oppose arming slaves believes them more valuable in agricultural labors they dont wish to go in army and principal restraint now upon them is fear that if they leave enemy may make them fight. Compel them to take up arms and they desert by thousands whatever may be our opinion of their normal condition or interests we cannot expect them to perform deeds of heroism when fighting to continue enslavement of wives and children. Not reasonable to demand it of them whenever we establish fact they are Military people we destroy our theory that they unfit to be free when we arm slaves we abandon slavery. Complains of usurpations of Confederate Congress in disproportion of Taxation and says much most objectionable legislation imposed upon by votes of men who act without responsibility to constituency . . . Army takes Government to task for

could sweep along his entrenchments to the south, so
that if I could not cause their abandonment, Genl
Grant would at least be obliged so to curtail his lines,
that upon the approach of Gen Sherman, I might be
able to hold our position with a portion of the troops,
and with a select body unite with Gen Johnston and
give him battle.   If successful, I would then be able
to return to my position, and if unsuccessful I should
be in no worse condition, as I should be compelled

---

great Vanity alleged abuses such as illegal imprisonment arrest
of Citizens without authority by provost guards the passport
system and partiality of Government to men of wealth who are
given nominal positions which keep them out of army while
poor men boys forced into ranks— Animadverts severely
upon Generalship of President and traces his Military career
during war.   Claims our Govt. now Military despotism drift-
ing into Anarchy and that if present policy persisted in must
terminate reconstruction with or without subjugation.   Brown
states utterly opposed to both but if he favored either he
would give earnest support to President's policy as surest
mode of diminishing our armies exhausting resources breaking
spirits of our people and driving them in despair to seek refuge
from worse tyranny by placing themselves under Government
they loath and detest in case existing evils recommends repeal Conscription act return to Constitutional mode of raising
troops by States—observance good faith with Soldiers
prompt pay abandonment of impressments and Secret Sessions
and no more representation without Constituency and finally
taken from President his power Commander in Chief Calls
for Convention of States to amend Constitution and closes in
following language— My destiny linked with my country if
we succeed I am free man if by obstinacy weakness rules we
fail common ruin awaits us all.   The night is dark the tempest
howls the ship is lashed with turbulent waves the helmsman
is steering to the whirl pool—our remonstrances are unheeded

to withdraw from James River if I quietly awaited his approach. But although the assault upon the fortified works at Hair's Hill was bravely accomplished, the redoubts commanding the line of entrenchments were found enclosed and strongly manned, so that an attempt to carry them must have been attended with great hazard, and even if accomplished, would have caused a great sacrifice of life in

---

and we must restrain them or the Crew must sink together buried in irretrievable ruin."

No Alarm in Charlotte enemy reported moving in direction Camden Cheraw Fayetteville thought that raiders and not main column visit city—during retreat from Columbia train cars filled with ladies broke down enemy threatened Capture. Hampton with cavalry threw himself in position to defend them with the life of every man in his command. Hampton Butler Wheeler done most fighting on retreat main force not being generally engaged from best information western portion of Columbia burned supposed by Cotton ignited in streets reported extent of fire from Main Street to Charlotte Depot nearly three fourths of mile doubtful as to magnitude but positive as to some fire-persons preparing to return.

F. G. De Fontaine

Charlotte 25th. 1865.

To the Associated Press:

No additional News from front Still supposed Enemy making way North by Cheraw on Fayetteville. News from Columbia corroborated kind treatment inhabitants. Ursuline Convent protected by guard. No public property allowed burned in city private residences. Sherman's Hd. Qrs. Monday Nickerson's Hotel. Large force reported western portion city. Alarm Charlotte partially subsided. Weather bad roads heavy interfering with rapid military movements.

F. G. DeFontaine

the presence of the large reserves which the enemy was hurrying into position I therefore determined to withdraw the troops, and it was in retiring that they suffered the greatest loss the extent of which has not yet been reported. I fear now it will be impossible to prevent a junction between Grant and Sherman, nor do I deem it prudent that this army should maintain its position until the latter shall approach too near. Gen. Johnston reports that the returns of his force of the 24th inst; gave his effective infantry thirteen thousand five hundred. He must therefore have lost, after his concentration at Smithfield about eight thousand men. This could hardly have resulted from the casualties of battle, and I fear must be the effect of desertion. Should this prove to be the case, I can not reasonably expect him to bring across the Roanoke more than ten thousand infantry, a force that would add so little strength to this army as not to make it more than a match for Sherman, with whom to risk a battle in the presence of Grant's army, would hardly seem justifiable. Gen Johnston estimates Gen Sherman's army, since its union with Schofield and the troops that were previously in N Carolina, at sixty thousand. I have no correct data upon which to form an estimate of the strength of Gen Grant's army. Taking their own account, it would exceed a hundred thousand, and I fear it is not under eighty thousand. Their two armies united would therefore exceed ours by nearly a hundred thousand. If Gen Grant wishes to unite Sherman with him without a battle, the latter after crossing the Roanoke has only to take an easterly direction towards Sussex, while the former moving two days march towards Weldon, provided I moved out to intercept Sherman, would render it impossible for me to strike him without fighting both armies.

I have thought it proper to make the above statement to your Excellency of the condition of affairs, knowing that you will do whatever may be in your power to give relief.[1]

I am with great respect
Your obt servt
R E Lee
Genl

---

[1] This important letter supplements the meagre information given in the *Official Records* regarding the effect upon General Lee's plan of the attempt on Fort Stedman. On the morning of the 25th General Gordon made the attack, the details of which are given in General Lee's report of the same date to the Secretary of War, as follows (O. R., 46, 1, 382–83):

HEADQUARTERS,
March 25, 1865.

At daylight this morning, General Gordon assaulted and carried enemy's works at Hare's Hill, captured 9 pieces of artillery, 8 mortars, between 500 and 600 prisoners, among them one brigadier-general and number of officers of lower grade. Enemy's lines were swept away for distance of 400 or 500 yards to right and left, and two efforts made to recover captured works were handsomely repulsed; but it was found that the inclosed works in rear, commanding enemy's main line, could only be taken at great sacrifice, and troops were withdrawn to original position. It being impracticable to bring off captured guns, owing to nature of ground, they were disabled and left. Our loss reported is not heavy. Among wounded is Brigadier-General Terry, flesh wound, and Brig. Gen. Phil Cook, in arm. All the troops engaged, including two brigades

No. 195.

H$^\text{D}$-Q$^\text{RS}$: Petersburg 29 Mar '65

M$^\text{R}$ President

I have rec$^\text{d}$ the telegrams of Genl Kirby Smith of the 24th Feby & 8$^\text{th}$ March, which you did me the honour to cause to be transmitted to me— As regards the first, I fear the physical difficulties mentioned by Genl Smith, of crossing the Mississippi at this time are real, & if so they cannot be overcome. When Genl Smith does cross the Mississippi, I see no necessity of his turning over the command of the Trans-Miss$^\text{pi}$ Dept to any one, & I did not understand it

---

under Brigadier-General Ransom behaved most handsomely. The conduct of the sharpshooters of Gordon's corps, who led assault, deserves the highest commendation. This afternoon there was skirmishing on the right between the picket-lines with varied success. At dark enemy held considerable portion of the line farthest in advance of our main works.

R. E. Lee.

Hon. J. C. Breckinridge,
        Secretary of War.

It is not too much to say that this attack on Fort Stedman determined General Lee's line of retreat from in front of Petersburg. Had he been able to shake Grant off, as he hoped, by this daring assault, Lee might possibly have withdrawn the greater part of his troops and joined Johnston. Whether or not such a movement would have even delayed the outcome may be questioned. At any event, the additions to Sherman's army and the reported weakness of Johnston rendered such a move neither desirable nor practicable after the failure to take Fort Stedman. The letter here printed deserves careful reading as a genuine contribution to the strategy of these dark days. As Grant continued steadily to extend his flank, threatening Lee's line of retreat, nothing remained but a withdrawal.

was your intention for him to do so, but that his jurisdiction should embrace the Eastern bank of the river. If Genl Buckner can command the Dept: while Genl Smith visits Richmond, I think he could be entrusted with its direction, under the general controul of Genl Smith, while necessary for him to be on the East bank— Although the dispatch is obscure I infer that Genl Smith is contemplating a movement into Missouri, with which his crossing the Mississippi will interfere— If he has any prospect of maintaining himself in Missouri, so as to call off the troops operating to the East of the Mississippi it will have the same effect as to bring his army here to oppose them. That would produce a beneficial result— A mere expedition into Mo: similar to those previously undertaken, will give no material benefit— I put little credence in the report from New Orleans of the expedition against Texas. It was doubtless circulated to cover the real movement against Mobile. It is the usual practice of the enemy— He could not raise as large a force as that represented & has only sufficient for one expedition.[1]

With great respect

Your obt servt

R E LEE

Genl

His Exc^y JEFFERSON DAVIS
    Pres: C States—Richmond

---

[1] General E. Kirby Smith, who was in command of the Trans-Mississippi Department, had for some time been isolated from the rest of the Confederacy and had been unable to give any co-operation. With good judgment the Federals had

No. 196.

[*Telegram*]

(Copy)

HEAD QRS. March 29/65.

Hon. J. C. BRECKENRIDGE,
      Secy. of War.

Genl. R. Taylor telegraphs from Meridian, on the 28th., that the enemy has thrown a large force ashore on Eastern side of Mobile Bay, leaving nothing on West side. That he is ready to receive any attack he may make at Mobile. Enemy's Cavalry from Florida coast has struck Montgomery Railroad at Evergreen. Raiding expeditions are advancing from North and Northeast Alabama towards Selma and Montgomery, and another threatening prairie region from Memphis. Genl. Taylor will endeavor to destroy these detached columns before they advance far into the county or unite. He will use his force in keeping open communications with Mobile, or in reopening them, if interrupted.[1]

(Signed) R. E. LEE

---

maintained sufficient troops in the territory he occupied to keep Smith on the alert without giving him opportunity of demolishing the enemy and of taking the offensive in co-operation with the Confederates east of the river. His 40,000 men were thus unable to assist in the final crisis. They were, however, the last to surrender.

[1] The Confederate forces in Alabama and Mississippi were badly scattered and at a disadvantage for all operations.

Genl. R. E. LEE
Hd. Qrs. March 29. 1865.
Copy telegram to Sec. of War.

Reporting movements of Enemy about Mobile, and No. Alabama; and Genl. R. Taylor's preparations to counteract them &c.

Recd. Mar' 29. 1865.

Richard Taylor, commanding the Department of Alabama and Mississippi, had been ordered to send all the troops he could spare to join the army it was hoped could be organized in the Carolinas to contest Sherman's advance. Nathan B. Forrest, commissioned as lieutenant-general, was given the arduous task of defending with his cavalry the few positions left to the Confederates. He was also expected to protect civilians from the ravages of deserters and bush-whackers who infested the country. Before the end of the war, Taylor, Maury and Forrest were able to unite their forces but were forced to surrender after Lee and Johnston had been compelled to lay down their arms. In the De Renne correspondence of this date appears the following:

AUGUSTA, March 29/65.
DR. W. S. MORRIS,

Merriwether reports enemy three thousand strong advancing on Montevallo, a station on the Blue Mountain line, fifty miles North of Selma. The officers on that line have been instructed what to do. Nettles is put in charge of the line and its repairs for the occasion. It is thought Genl. Forrest has sufficient force in the vicinity of Montevallo to stop them. Still fighting at Spanish Fort, without any result as yet.

(Signed) J. B. TREE
Genl. Supt.

No. 197.

[*Telegram*]

(Copy)

HEAD QRS. March 29/65.

HON. SECRETARY OF WAR.

Vaughan's Scouts report that Stoneman with about four thousand Cavalry passed Elizabethtown on the Watauga and is going up the Watauga. He may intend to cross by Lenoir to the Yadkin, or turn down New River into Grayson and the lead mines. The Chiefs of Bureaux should give orders for safety of their property.[1]

(Signed) R. E. LEE

Respectfully submitted for the information of the President.

By order

J. A. CAMPBELL

Asst. Secy. War.

March 29/65.

[*Endorsed*]

Telegram

R. E. LEE

29 March 65.

---

[1] General George Stoneman had originally been ordered to go into South Carolina and to return to East Tennessee by way of Salisbury, but owing to a delay in his start, was instructed by General Grant to move down the Virginia and Tennessee railroad toward Lynchburg, destroying the line as he went (O. R., 46, 1, 46–47). He was driven back near Liberty and moved thence into North Carolina (*ibid*, 58–59).

No. 198.

[Telegram]

(Copy)

HEAD QRS. Mar. 30/65.

HON. SECY. WAR,

Genl. Gordon reports that the enemy, at 11 P.M. yesterday, advanced against a part of his line defended by Brig. Genl. Lewis, but was repulsed. The line of Artillery and Mortars continued for several hours with considerable activity. No damage on our lines reported.

The enemy still maintains his position West of Hatcher's Run, occupying Dinwiddie C. H. with Sheridan's Cavalry. Skirmishing was frequent along the lines to-day, but no serious attack. Part of Merritt's Division, under Genl. Gibbs, attacked Genl. Fitz Lee twice this morning at Five Forks, but was repulsed. About 3 P.M., Fitz Lee attacked him and drove him from his position, capturing a few prisoners. The force of the enemy West of Hatcher's Run consists of the fifth Corps, part of the second and part of the sixth, with Gregg's and Sheridan's Cavalry.[1]

(Signed) R. E. LEE

---

[1] While Lee was making a last effort against the Federals at Fort Stedman, Grant was being strongly reinforced by Sheridan's cavalry, back from its house-burning expedition into the Valley of Virginia. Grant's first idea was to dispatch Sheridan to join Sherman but he had to abandon this plan because of the condition of the roads and streams. He thereupon determined to use Sheridan in the extension of his

Resp. Submitted for the information of the President.

By order
J. A. CAMPBELL
Asst. Secy. War.

Mar 30/65.

[*Endorsed*]
Genl. R. E. LEE
30 March 65.

No. 199.

[*Telegram*]

(Copy)

HEAD QRS. Mar 31/65.

HON. SECRETARY OF WAR,

Genl. Taylor reports enemy has commenced the siege of the Eastern defences of Mobile.   Our fire,

---

lines to Dinwiddie Court-house, confident that Lee's weakened army could not meet him.   On March 27, he sent three divisions of the 24th and 25th Corps to Hatcher's Run and had the 2nd and 5th Corps follow them.   Sheridan's cavalry moved quickly to Dinwiddie Court-house.   The movement here reported was a brilliant repulse of the Federal advance.   On April 1, however, Sheridan's cavalry and Warren's corps overwhelmed Pickett's division at Five Forks.   The next day, the Federals broke through the line southwest of Petersburg and necessitated the evacuation upon which General Lee had decided.   The retreat to Appomattox followed.   For the effect of the battles of March 31–April 1 on Lee's plans, see *infra* No. 204.   Major-General Fitzhugh Lee's report is perhaps the fullest for these final movements (O. R., 46, 1, 1263–64, 1298 ff.).

so far, is superior. Our casualties few and slight. On the 28th. the Federal fleet attempted to co-operate in the attack, but was driven off. One Monitor was sunk on the Western shore and gunboat disabled approaching the batteries.[1]

(Signed) R. E. LEE

No. 200

[Telegram]

(Copy)

HEAD QRS. Mar 31/65.

HON. SECRETARY WAR,

Genl. Taylor, on the 30th., reports that the enemy's column from the Tennessee River is seventy miles from Selma.[2]

(Signed) R. E. LEE

---

[1] Mobile Bay had fallen into the hands of the Federals after the naval engagement of August 5, 1864; Fort Morgan, the main defence of the Bay, surrendered on August 23, 1864. Not until January, 1865, however, were operations begun against the land fortifications, by a force that outnumbered the defenders at least four to one. On March 17, the formal advance on the land side began and on March 27 the Spanish Fort was besieged. The city made a gallant defence and did not surrender until after the Spanish fort was taken on April 8. Major-General Dabney H. Maury of Virginia, the commander, was able to bring away most of his troops and later joined Richard Taylor and N. B. Forrest. His command surrendered with theirs to Canby on May 4, 1865.

[2] This was a part of Wilson's raid on Selma, Alabama, undertaken while Maury was defending Mobile. Wilson moved in three columns, united his forces at the ford on the Black

Respectfully submitted for the information of the President.

By order

J. A. CAMPBELL
Asst. Secy. War.

April 1/65.
[*Endorsed*]
Copy Tel.
Gen. R. E. LEE to Sec. of War.
Hd. Qrs. Mar 31. 1865.
Genl. Taylor reports movements of enemy against Mobile.

Recd. April 1. 1865.

No. 201.

[*Telegram*]

(Copy)

HEAD QRS. Mar. 31/65.

HON. SECRETARY WAR,

Finding this morning that the enemy was extending his left to embrace the White Oak Road, Genl. Anderson placed three Brigades in position to repel him. Before the disposition was completed, the enemy advanced and was finally met by our troops and driven back with loss to his position near the Boydton Plank Road. Our troops were then withdrawn, and were followed by the enemy, who in turn

---

Warrior and was able to hold his own against Forrest. He besieged and captured Selma and destroyed the important arsenal and foundry located there.

drove us back to our lines.   Our loss was not large, and we captured over four hundred prisoners.[1]

(Signed) R. E. LEE

Respectfully submitted for the information of the President.

By order
J. A. CAMPBELL
Asst. Secy. War.

April 1/65.

[*Endorsed*]

Genl. R. E. LEE
Copy Tel. to Sec. War.
Hd. Qrs. Mar 31. 1865.
Operations of enemy on our right.
Recd. April 1. 1865.

---

[1] This engagement was simultaneous with the fighting around Five Forks.   While Anderson was thus engaged, Lee, with three brigades from the right, was driving Warren across Gravelly Run.   The advantage, however, was lost by the disaster at Five Forks.   See No. 198, *supra*.

With the correspondence of this date is the following, marked:

"Copy of telegram dated Petersburg 2 P.M. March 31 to Dr. Morris, from the operator there."

Operator at Anderson's Hd. Qrs. states we are driving the enemy rapidly.   Genl. Picket who is on their flank or rear, has not yet been heard from, he promises us particulars this P.M. Will telegraph you again.

(Signed) Taylor

For his Excellency
The President.
R. G. H. KEAN
Chf. of Bu. of War.

The correspondence also contains another private telegram, marked:

No. 202.

[Telegram]

Dated Hd. Qrs. March 31 1865.   10 O'Clock P.M.
To His Exc. Presdt. Davis,
   Will enquire whether Genl. Morgan¹ can be spared. Have notified Gov. Watts² & requested him to name another suitable person if Genl. Morgan cant go.

R. E. LEE

[Endorsed]
   Genl. R. E. LEE
   31 March/65.

"Copy of telegram from operator at Petersburg to Dr. Morris dated March 31. Recd. 2 P.M." as follows:
   Heavy firing heard this morning in the direction of yesterday's battle. Cannonading not more audible owing to high wind blowing contrary direction. Genl. Pryor informed me about 10 o'clock that he left vicinity of Genl. Lee's Qrs. at dark last night, that he had then captured enemy's picket lines for purpose of making general disposition of his forces preparatory to general engagement this morning, that there was no doubt a severe battle would be fought to-day. If anything comes to hand deemed reliable, will send it immediately.

A. F. CRUTCHFIELD.

For his Excellency
   The President.
      R. G. H. KEAN
         Chf. of Bu. of War.

¹ Brig.-Genl. John T. Morgan of Alabama.
² Thos. H. Watts, former Attorney-General, C. S. A., and from December 1863, Governor of Alabama. See No. 203, *infra*.

No. 203.

[Telegram]

Dated at Hd. Qrs April 1, 1865.
Rec'd at Richmond 11 o'clock P.M.
To His Excellency
PRESIDENT DAVIS
Brig Genl John E. Morgan can be spared for the purpose indicated by Gov. Watts He is not with his Brigade but Gov Watts knows where he is[1]
D. H.   R. E. LEE.

No. 204.

H⁰ Q^RS C S ARMIES
1st April 1865

His Excy JEFF^N DAVIS
Presd^t C States
Richmond
MR PRESIDENT,
The movement of Gen Grant to Dinwiddie C. H. seriously threatens our position, and diminishes our ability to maintain our present lines in front of Richmond and Petersburg In the first place, it cuts us off from our depot at Stony Creek at which point, forage for the cavalry was delivered by the

---

[1] General John T. (not E.) Morgan had been "left with his command South of Atlanta to watch and harass General Sherman." He was probably wanted by Governor Watts "to raise regiments for the depleted ranks of the army" (C. M. H., 7, Ala., 429).

Weldon R.R., and upon which we relied to maintain it. It also renders it more difficult to withdraw from our position, cuts us off from the White Oak road, and gives the enemy an advantageous point on our right and rear. From this point, I fear he can readily cut both the south side & the Danville Railroads being far superior to us in cavalry. This in my opinion obliged us to prepare for the necessity of evacuating our position on James River at once, and also to consider the best means of accomplishing it, and our future course.[1] I should like very much

---

[1] It is a tribute to Southern confidence in General Lee's ability that although he had suggested the possibility of the evacuation of Richmond in 1864 and had urged preparations to that end certainly from as early as February 25, 1865 (O. R., 46, 2, 1257), the authorities did not take him at his word. The Secretary of War pleaded for more time; the President notified General Lee that removal on the evening of April 2, 1865, would mean "the loss of many valuables, both for the want of time to pack and of transportation." (See O. R., 46, 3, 1378, 1379). The Southern people could not believe that Lee would be forced to abandon the capital from which he had struck back every assault since the day he took command. Soldiers and civilians alike could not understand that any odds were too great for him or any obstacle insurmountable. But as he explained in his dispatch regarding the attack on Fort Stedman, failure on that day removed his last hope of any other course than a retreat. The action at Five Forks and the pressure on his flanks rendered the necessity for retreat immediately pressing. When the Federals broke through his weak lines on April 2, he had to notify the President that he would evacuate them the same night. A week later, April 9, his army was surrounded and his brilliant days of warfare were at an end.

to have the views of your Excellency upon this matter as well as counsel, and would repair to Richmond for the purpose, did I not feel that my presence here is necessary. Should I find it practicable I will do so, but should it be convenient for your Excellency or the Secretary of War to visit H^d Q^{rs}, I should be glad to see you. The reported advance of Stoneman from the West, and the movement of the enemy upon the Roanoke, add to our difficulties.

Very respectfully

Your obt serv't

R. E. LEE

Genl.

APPENDIX

No. 205

[MS in Robert Edward Lee Papers, Duke University Library]

H^d Qrs: 4 Aug 1862

The Communication of Govr [Francis W.] Pickens [of South Carolina] of the 19th ulto:[1] to his Excl the President has been read with much attention. I agree with him as to the importance of the preservation of the R. R. to Charleston, Savannah & Country[?].[2] I also Concur in his opinion that the Cavl under Col: [William S.] Walker & such Infy force as is available ought to be able to protect it against the present force of the enemy. It is hoped the troops retained in & near Charleston will be Sufficient to hold the harbor & the portion of the road near it. Our experience & the result of our operations against the enemy does not prove that troops extended along a line of R. R. are able to protect it. It is better they be massed at Salient & Commanding points, to repress the attack of the enemy & strike him if he advances. The regulars under Col: [John] Dunovant were retained in S. C. as their Services were supposed important for its

---

[1] Not found.
[2] Charleston and Savannah Railroad.

defence, not their value was overlooked in the operations here.[3]

respy Submitted to the President

R E LEE
Genl

No. 206

[MS in Robert Edward Lee Papers,
Duke University Library]

CAMP NEAR WINCHESTER
1. Octo: 1862.

His Excy JEFF^N DAVIS
President C. S. A.

MR PRESIDENT

I have the honor to send herewith a copy of the "Balt^o American" of the 29th ult^o which besides containing the latest news from the Northern States, gives an account of the plundering of Genl. Taylor's plantation, which though painful to read, I have thought might be of interest to you.[4]

I am with high esteem
Very truly yours
R. E. LEE
Genl.

By W. H. TAYLOR
Maj & A D C

---

[3] On May 23, 1862, Governor Pickens wrote Lee (O. R., 14, 515) suggesting that Dunovant's "fine regiment of regulars" be kept in South Carolina. See also Davis to Governor Pickens, August 5, 1862, O. R., 14, 593-594.

[4] Probably Richard Taylor's "Fashion Plantation"—over a thousand sugar-producing acres in St. Charles Parish, Louisiana. Davis' first wife was Richard Taylor's sister.

P. S. I also send you a copy of the [Baltimore] "Sun" of the 22d ulto containing an account of the battle at Sharpsburg: from which it will be seen how little ground they have to claim a victory, even from their own version of the engagement.

Yours respy

R. E. L.

No. 207

[MS in Robert Edward Lee Papers,
Duke University Library]

Head Quarters A N Va
April 25th 1864
Res. returned to his Excellency the President. The best way for the citizens of the Northern Neck [of Virginia] to save their cattle[,] grain[,] bacon &c from these marauding parties is to send them across the Rapp[ahannoc]k and sell them to the Confederate government. To keep their produce stored in large quantities is but to invite the enemy. A proper combination & energy on the part of the citizens with what aid government agents can give would in this way save a great deal for the army & the people. Much has been accomplished by this means in the past winter. There are no companies which I can well detach for duty in this region. If the members of the two companies spoken of by Mr Newton are liable to conscription they should be in

the army. If not then they form very good material for protection against raiding parties being thoroughly acquainted with the country.   If they act with the boldness & spirit which should characterise men who are protecting their families from insult & their homes from desolation they would give the enemy a wholesome fear of coming into the country.[5]

R E Lee
Genl

No. 208

[MS in Robert Edward Lee Papers,
Duke University Library]

Hᴰ Qᴿˢ A N Vᴀ
3½ P M 31ˢᵗ May 1864

His Exᶜʸ Jᴇꜰꜰᴺ Dᴀᴠɪs
Presdᵗ C States
Mʀ Pʀᴇsɪᴅᴇɴᴛ,

I have just received your note of today informing me that the bill has passed permitting assignment to temporary rank.[6]   I regret that Col [James B.]

---

[5] The problems of Northern Neck farmers are also discussed in Dispatch No. 142 (pp. 259-260).   After seeking advice from the famous raider John S. Mosby, Lee recommended that a local defense unit be established in the Northern Neck but that it not include "any absentees from the army or persons liable to enrollment in the general service." Lee to Secretary of War James A. Seddon, August 9, 1864, O. R., 43, 1, 990-991.

[6] See Davis to Lee, May 31, 1864, O. R., 51, 2, 973-974.

Terrill cannot be nominated to the command of Pegram's brigade. In the attack last night, he was either killed or left wounded in the hands of the enemy. Col E[dward] Willis of Ga whom I had assigned yesterday to the command of the brigade, was mortally wounded, and I understand has since died. At present I can name no one to you to fill the vacancy in this brigade, but hope to do so tomorrow.

I request that [Stephen D.] Ramseur be promoted temporarily to the command of Early's division. I will send in the name of an officer tomorrow to command Ramseur's brigade.

Before leaving Orange C. H[ouse] I recommended that Gen [Joseph B.] Kershaw should be promoted to the permanent command of McLaws' division. I consider him a better commander & wish to retain him. He has done well in every fight, is prompt, quick and bold. If this request cannot be complied with, I desire that he be advanced to the temporary command.

Col [Lawrence M.] Keitt's reg^t having been assigned to Kershaw's brigade, he will be the ranking officer. I think he had better exercise the command some time before any appointment is made for the brigade.[7]

I am now separated from the papers connected with this subject, and can only refer you to such recommendations as I have already made, and must defer making others until tomorrow.

---

[7] Keitt was mortally wounded the next day.

The firing along the lines today has been un-important.

Very resp^y

Your ob^t serv^t

R E LEE

Genl

P. S. I did not include Gen [Jubal A.] Early among those to be promoted, as you stated that you had directed him to be nominated.

R E L

No. 209

[MS in Robert Edward Lee Papers, Duke University Library]

H^D Q^{RS} A N VA

4½ P M 31st May 1864

His Exc^y JEFF^N DAVIS

Presdt C States,

MR PRESIDENT,

In my letter of this P M recommending certain promotions, I entirely omitted the names of Maj Gen R[ichard] H Anderson & Brig Gen [William] Mahone.[8] The former has been command^g Long-street's Corps, and the latter Anderson's div^n since

---

[8] On Anderson see page 10. Mahone had emerged as a fierce fighter in 1864, becoming famous during the Petersburg Campaign. "Have ordered the promotion of General Mahone to date from the day of his memorable service [at the Battle of the Crater], 30th of July," Davis wrote Lee on August 2, 1864 (O. R., 42, 2, 1156).

Gen Longstreet was disabled.[9] They have discharged their duties to my entire satisfaction, and deserved the promotion to which I now recommend them, Gen Anderson to the temporary command of Longstreet's Corps, and Gen Mahone to that of Anderson's div^n.

I am with great respect

> Your ob^t serv^t
> R E LEE
> Genl

No. 210

[Typescript in Robert Edward Lee Papers, Duke University Library]

CAMP PETERSBURG, 6 July '64

MR. PRESIDENT:

I am very much obliged to you for the perusal of the letters from Mr. Mason [10] & Genl. Williams.[11] I hope that the favourable anticipations of the former may be realized. As far as I have been able to

---

[9] Longstreet was wounded in the Battle of the Wilderness and was not again fit for field service until the fall of 1864. An interesting account of how Anderson was selected to replace Longstreet is given in Douglas Southall Freeman's *Lee's Lieutenants: A Study in Command* (3 vols., New York: Charles Scribner's Sons, 1944), III, 373-375.

[10] James Murray Mason, Confederate Commissioner to Great Britain. See Mason's letter to Secretary of State Judah P. Benjamin, June 1, 1864, in James D. Richardson (ed.), *A Compilation of the Messages and Papers of the Confederacy, Including the Diplomatic Correspondence, 1861-1865* (2 vols., Nashville: United States Publishing Company, 1905), II, 645-648.

[11] Possibly James Williams, who "from time to time . . . addressed communications to the President touching Mexican affairs." On March 16, 1864, Williams asked James M. Mason to forward another "note" to Davis. See Dunbar Rowland (ed.), *Jefferson Davis Constitutionalist: His Letters, Papers and Speeches* (10 vols., Jackson: Mississippi Department of Archives and History, 1923), VI, 206-208.

judge, this war presents to the European World but two aspects. A Contest in which one party is contending for abstract slavery & the other against it. The existence of vital rights involved does not seem to be understood or appreciated. As long as this lasts, we can expect neither sympathy or aid. Nor can we expect the policy of any Government towards us to be governed by any other consideration than that of self interest. Our safety depends upon ourselves alone. If we can defeat or drive the armies of the enemy from the field, we shall have peace. All our efforts & energies should be devoted to that object. I return the letters you did me the honour to enclose & am

With great respect,
Your obt. Servt.
R. E. LEE
Genl.

His Excl. JEFFN. DAVIS
  Pres. C. States.

No. 211

[MS in Robert Edward Lee Archives,
Washington and Lee University]

HᴰQʀꜱ: 13 Aug '64

MR PRESIDENT

I have had the honour to receive your despatch of today.[12] Unless [Matthew C.] Butler is promoted no one can be promoted to his Brigade— I believe [John] Dunovant gives the fairest promise

---

[12] See Davis to Lee, August 13, 1864, in Rowland (ed.), *Jefferson Davis*, VI, 315.

among the S. C. Colonels & [Wade] Hampton recommends him— I think too he is the Senior Col: in
the Brigade— I have not heard of his return to duty
& it is not my habit to recommend officers for
promotion when absent from their Commands—[13]
What our officers most lack is the pains & labour
of incubating discipline. It is a painful tedious
process, & is not apt to win popular favour. Many
officers have too many selfish views to promote to
induce them to undertake the task of instructing &
disciplining their Commands. To succeed it is necessary to set the example, & this necessarily con-
fines them to their duties, their camp & mess, which
is disagre[e]able & deprives them of pleasant visits,
dinners &c. If I had have known Genl George [H.]
Steuart would have been so soon available I would
have proposed him for the Command of the Cavalry
in Western Virg^a.[14] I believe it would be a good
plan now to give him Command of two of the brigades— He did remarkably well in the Infy. Had
the best Camp, more order among his trains &c
than any brigade in the army unless it might have
been Mahone[']s— He is brave too & always obeys
orders— How he would administer when alone is
the only question— I have to get a Brig^r for [name
illegible] brigade & I do not know where to find
one— I was at Howlett[']s [house] today & witnessed the firing at the enemy[']s camp at Dutch

---

[13] Dunovant was promoted but on October 1 he was killed "at the head
of his brigade."

[14] Steuart had been captured in the Battle of Spottsylvania. Exchanged
in August, 1864, he was assigned to the command of a brigade in Longstreet's Corps.

Gap. The enemy was kept very close & under cover, but did not move his camp— The practice on our side was very good. The battery at Howlett[']s kept the two upper batteries of the enemy engaged— The lowest battery was too distant to reach, but it divided its attention between our gunboats & Howlett[']s— Our gunboats planted some excellent shots in the enemy[']s camp— I could discover no canal. I saw their customary lines of entrenchments in front & rear of their camp, entering across the neck, with rifle pits in advance of each line for their pickets— But I saw nothing approaching a canal. Still deserters & prisoners so report—[15] With great respect your obt sevt

R E LEE
Genl

His Excl JEFF^N DAVIS
Pres: C. States

No. 212

[MS in Robert Edward Lee Papers,
Duke University Library]

H^DQRS: PETERSBURG 4 Feb^y '65

MR PRESIDENT

I rec^d to night your letter of the 3rd Inst: giving Copies of three telegrams from Genl Beauregard at

---

15 A canal was being dug. General Benjamin F. Butler had persuaded Grant that war vessels could by-pass the strong Confederate battery commanding Trent Reach—a shallow part of the James River—and attack Richmond if a canal was cut through a narrow neck of land known as Dutch Gap. Work on the canal began on August 10, 1864, using Negro troops. Impeded by Confederate artillery, construction was difficult and when ultimately completed the canal was of no military value.

Augusta & your reply.[16] I do not think it possible
to send more reinforcements from here under present circumstances, nor do I believe they can be furnished from N. C. As Genl Beauregard can only
rely upon the forces in his Dept: unless Columbia
offers better ground, than any other spot, I see no
advantage in concentrating his troops there than at
Branchville, or some more advanced point to Con-
front the enemy. Everything should be brought
from Charleston & elsewhere & every effort made
to defeat Sherman whenever he can be struck to
most advantage—

I am with great respect

Your Obt Sevt

R E LEE

Genl

His Excl JEFFERSON DAVIS
Pres: C. States— Richmond

No. 213

[MS in Robert Edward Lee Papers,
Duke University Library]

Confidential

NEAR PETERSB^G 2 Mar '65

MR PRESIDENT

I rec[d] today the letter from Genl Longstreet to
which you referred in your note of the 28th Ulto—[17]

---

[16] See O. R., 47, 2, 1090. Unhappy serving under Lee at Petersburg,
Beauregard had been given command of the Military Division of the West
in October, 1864.

[17] See O. R., 46, 2, 1264, 1275-1276.

I have proposed to Genl Grant an interview, in the hope that some good may result, but I must Confess that I am not sanguine. My belief is that he will Consent to no terms, unless Coupled with the Condition of our return to the Union. Whether this will be acceptable to our people yet awhile I Can not say— I shall go to Richmond tomorrow or next day to see you, & hope you will grant me an hours Conversation on the Subject— Genl Longstreet proposed that I should meet Genl Grant at the point where he met Genl [Edward O. C.] Ord, & desired to have two or three days notice. I have therefore appointed Monday next for the interview with Genl Grant [18]

With great respect your Obt Sevt

R E LEE
Genl

His Excl JEFFERSON DAVIS
    Pres: C. States. Richmond

---

[18] "Sincerely desiring to leave nothing untried which may put an end to the calamities of war," Lee wrote Grant, "I propose to meet you . . . with the hope that upon an interchange of views it may be found practicable to submit the subjects of controversy between the belligerents to a [military] convention" for settlement. Grant replied that he had no authority to meet Lee "for a conference on the subject proposed. Such authority is vested in the President of the United States alone." O. R., 46, 2, 824-825.

No. 214

[MS in Robert Edward Lee Papers,
Duke University Library]

H^D Q^{RS} ARMIES C S
10th March 1865

His Exc^y JEFF^n DAVIS
    Presd^t C States
    Richmond
        MR PRESIDENT,

I do not know whether the law authorising the use of negro troops has received your sanction, but if it has, I respectfully recommend that measures be taken to carry it into effect as soon as practicable.[19]

It will probably be impossible to get a large force of this kind in condition to be of service during the present campaign, but I think no time should be lost in trying to collect all we can. I attach great importance to the result of the first experiment with these troops, and think that if it prove successful, it will greatly lessen the difficulty of putting the law into operation.

I understand that the Governor of Virginia is

---

[19] Three days later Davis replied (O. R., 46, 2, 1308) : "I am in receipt of your favor in regard to the bill for putting negroes in the army. The bill was received from the Congress to-day and was immediately signed. I shall be pleased to receive such suggestions from you as will aid me in carrying out the law, and I trust you will endeavor in every available mode to give promptitude to the requisite action." The law allowed Davis to requisition as many slaves as were needed to defend the country (with the reservation that not more than one fourth of the slaves of any state would be called). Although the bill made no promises of freedom, it was generally understood that slaves who served in the army would be manumitted by the states. Some Negro troops were raised, but the law came too late to be of any value.

prepared to do all that may be required of him under the authority he possesses.[20] I hope it will be found practicable to raise some negro companies in Richmond, and have written to Gen Ewell to do all in his power to get them, as soon as he shall be informed in what manner to proceed.[21] In the beginning it would be well to do everything to make the enlistment entirely voluntary on the part of the negroes, and those owners who are willing to furnish some of their slaves for the purpose, can do a great deal to inspire them with the right feeling to prepare them to become soldiers, and to be satisfied with their new condition. I have received letters from persons offering to select the most suitable among their slaves, as soon as Congress should give the authority, and think that a considerable number would be forthcoming for the purpose if called for.

I hope that if you have approved the law, you will cause the necessary steps to carry it into effect to be taken as soon as possible.[22]

With great respect
Your ob^t serv^t
R E LEE
Genl

---

[20] "The governor of Virginia calls my attention to the fact that he has not received a requisition for slaves, as provided for in the act of the General Assembly," Davis informed Lee on March 24. Lee immediately asked Davis to "call upon the governor . . . for the whole number of negroes, slave and free, between the ages of eighteen and forty-five, for service as soldiers. . . . The services of these men are now necessary to enable us to oppose the enemy." O. R., 46, 3, 1339.

[21] Unfit for further field service, Ewell was in command of the Richmond defenses. See page 256n.

[22] On April 1, Davis unhappily informed Lee (O. R., 46, 3, 1370): "I have been laboring, without much progress, to advance the raising of negro troops."

No. 215

[MS in Robert Edward Lee Papers,
Duke University Library]

[Telegram]

Petersburg April 2ᵈ 1865 3.K 30 P. M.

His Excly Jeffn Davis

Your telegram recd.[23] I think it will be necessary to retire[?] tonight. I shall Camp the troops here north of the Appomattox. The Enemy is so strong that they will cross above us to Close us in between the James & Appomattox Rivers— If we remain—

R E LEE

---

[23] See O. R., 46, 3, 1378.

INDEX

A

Ajax, one of Lee's horses, 5 n.

Alabama, Davis' tour through, 68 n.; 170 n., 283

Alexander, Brigadier-General E. P., *Military Memoirs* by, xxxiv; blames Jackson for miscarriage of Lee's plans, 33 n.; estimates Pope's forces, 50 n.; gives valuable account of Gettysburg, 111 n.; quoted, 20 n.; cited, 10 n., 58 n.; iii, 74 n.

Alexandria, number of men reported at, July 25, '62, 37; commonwealth seat at, 163 n.; 231, 232

Allred, Private S. C., pardon asked for, 150

Ambler, C. M., Ritchie's biography by, 241 n.

Amissville, General Ripley at, August 29, '62, 59

Ammunition, Federal, captured at Harpers Ferry, 63 n.

Amnesty, recommended by Lee presumed on by men, 123; quoted, 123 n.

Anderson, General Richard Henry, Lee writes of, 10; biography of, in C. M. H., 10 n.; appointed Brigadier-General, 33 n.; given a division under Longstreet, 33 n.; division of, 35 n.; Colonel Smith attached to division of, 41 n.; division to Gordonsville, 47; division of, 51 n.; division Longstreet's Corps, 58 n.; and division join Lee August 30, '62, 58; and division return to Chancellorsville, 90; commendation of, 92 n.; division of, 181 n.; repulses Federal assaults, 213 n.; ordered to Bermuda, 244; ordered to

Petersburg, 251; Georgia cavalry under, 274; drives back Federals, 355; 33, 34 n., 192 n., 315

Anderson's Corps, itinerary of, 172 n.

Anderson's Ford, 200

Andrews' battery of artillery joins Holmes, 24 n.

Anna, North, the, Lee's army, south of, 194; Lee withdraws from, 200; 193 n., 213 n.

Anna, South, the, 193 n.

Annapolis, Lee at, 159; Burnside at, 159; 145 n.

Annas, the (rivers), 192

Antietam, campaign of, xxiv; formal beginning of campaign, 61 n.; Lee falls back on, 63 n.; battle of, referred to, 65 n., 66 n.; General Rodes serves at, 89 n.

Appomattox River, Lee's ride to, xxxii; General Rains on the, 9 n.; Butler "bottled up" at, 203 n.; hostilities carried to the, 227 n.; "Howlett line" to, 306 n.; Lee's retreat to, 353 n.; xvi, xvii, 252

Aquia Creek, General Burnside reaches, August 3, '62, 49 n.; troops required from, 54; railroad building at, 193; 47, 180

Archer's brigade, 97 n.

Arcola, reference to, xviii

Armistead's brigade in Anderson's division, 33 n., 58 n.

Army organization, 81 *et seq.*

Army of the Potomac, advance guards of, 228 n.

"Army of Virginia," Major-General Pope in command of, 37 n.

Arnold, Private James, pardon asked for, 149

Artillery, organization of, 73 *et seq.*; service, promotions in, 76 n.; comparison of Grant's and Lee's, 184 and note

Index

385

385

Index

Index